# NITTY GRITTY
# GRAMMAR

## Sentence Essentials
## for Writers

# NITTY GRITTY GRAMMAR

## Sentence Essentials for Writers

**A. Robert Young**

El Camino College

**Ann O. Strauch**

El Camino College

CAMBRIDGE
UNIVERSITY PRESS

*To Damien, Colin, and Adrian*


*To Walt, Mark, Reynalda, and Teresa*

PUBLISHED BY THE PRESS SYNDICATE OF THE UNIVERSITY OF CAMBRIDGE
The Pitt Building, Trumpington Street, Cambridge, United Kingdom

CAMBRIDGE UNIVERSITY PRESS
The Edinburgh Building, Cambridge CB2 2RU, UK    http://www.cup.cam.ac.uk
40 West 20th Street, New York, NY 10011–4211, USA    http://www.cup.org
10 Stamford Road, Oakleigh, Melbourne 3166, Australia

First published by St. Martin's Press, Inc. 1994

Reprinted 1998
Second Printing 1999

Printed in the United States of America

Library of Congress Cataloging-in-Publication Data Available

ISBN 0 521 65783 0 Instructor's Manual
ISBN 0 521 65784 9 Student's Book

*Acknowledgements*

Joseph Krumgold, text excerpt from . . . *and now Miguel*, Copyright © 1953 by Joseph Krumgold. Reprinted with permission of HarperCollins Publishers.

Excepts from "Love," by Jesse Stuart. Copyright Jesse Stuart and the Jesse Stuart Foundation. Reprinted by permission of the Jesse Stuart Foundation, P.O. Box 391, Ashland, KY 41114.

Excerpt from *Danny: The Champion of the World* by Roald Dahl. Text copyright © 1975 by Roald Dahl. Reprinted by permission of Alfred A. Knopf, Inc.

Text excerpts from pp. 16, 22, 31 from *So Far from the Bamboo Grove* by Yoko Kawashima Watkins. Text: Copyright © 1986 by Yoko Kawashima Watkins. By permission of Lothrop, Lee & Shepard Books, a division of William Morrow & Company, Inc.

James Thurber, "The Unicorn in The Garden." Copyright © 1940 James Thurber. Copyright © 1968 by Helen Thurber. From *Fables for Our Time*, published by HarperCollins.

Alice Taylor, *To School through the Fields*. Copyright © 1990 by Alice Taylor. From the book *To School through the Fields* by Alice Taylor and reprinted with permission from St. Martin's Press, Inc., New York, NY.

Acknowledgments are continued on page 260

# PREFACE

## Student Audience

Our intention in writing *Nitty Gritty Grammar: Sentence Essentials for Writers* is to provide a grammar for high-beginning to low-intermediate ESL *writing* students. Many of these students already have some fluency and can read at a more advanced level than general high-beginning to low-intermediate students, but for one reason or another have not developed their writing skills.

## Philosophy/Approach

One of the proverbs that appear in the text is "If you wish to be a writer, write." This adage reflects our overriding philosophy for composition instruction. We firmly believe that the major emphasis in any writing course should be on composition (prewriting, writing, revising, editing, and rewriting) rather than on grammar rules. The study of sentence structure, then, should be secondary and based on the specific weaknesses demonstrated by the students in each individual class.

We also believe that the study of grammar should be contextualized within lively, engaging, and reasonably challenging models. Thus, we have tried to select materials that will hold the students' interest as well as present the concepts within realistic contexts.

The readings and examples come from a variety of sources. They also vary in their level of challenge, with some being clearly easier than others. This reflects our belief that a variety in content and level of difficulty will best meet the needs of students who possess a variety of interests as well as proficiency levels.

Wherever possible, we have used excerpts from literature as examples. Our rationale is that literary passages not only provide engaging contexts, but also prepare students for more advanced English courses in which they will be required to read and analyze literary pieces. Troublesome vocabulary is defined in the margins of the text.

We believe that students learn best when they are engaged as actively as possible in the learning process. Thus, we favor the inductive approach. Wherever appropriate, we also incorporate group activities in order to maximize student interest and involvement.

Learning to compose is a lifelong process for both first- and second-language learners, and certainly the assimilation of sentence structure rules must be an especially daunting challenge for the second-language learner. Furthermore, experienced instructors agree that learning structure rules alone does not translate into proficient composition skills. With these points in mind, we strongly oppose the notion that the students' primary goal must be to "learn" as many rules regarding sentence structure as possible. Instead, we hope that students will be encouraged to focus on progress rather than perfection and to continue to write, write, write!

## Scope of the Material

*Nitty Gritty Grammar: Sentence Essentials for Writers* developed out of a penciled list (written on the inside of a manila file folder) that recorded the types of sentence structure problems that low-level composition students demonstrated again and again throughout our combined thirty years of community college teaching. The grammar points covered in this text, then, are intended to get students on the road to solving the specific problems that appear in real student writing at this level.

Since this text is designed for low-level ESL writers, its aim is to help solve the kinds of problems that developing ESL writers tend to display, such as run-ons, fragments, and verb problems. A comprehensive general grammar is not appropriate. Thus, several of the grammar points that are traditionally covered in a general grammar do not appear in this text. For example, the following points are either not covered at all or are mentioned only briefly: negation, question formation, and the social uses of modals. Even within the treatment of each grammar point, this text does not attempt to cover every detail or exception. The guiding principle is: "Is this point going to be useful for this student audience at this level?"

*Nitty Gritty Grammar* provides a much-needed supplementary text for composition students who need help with the kinds of grammar problems that tend to frustrate developing ESL writers. What the text does *not* do is provide instruction for rhetoric per se. It is assumed that the instructor will provide a separate rhetoric (or equivalent materials) for the students as the main text for the course.

What this book will do is support the teaching of rhetorical principles while focusing on sentence structure and the editing phase of the writing process. Writing assignments include instructions for the student to write a topic sentence, detailed and organized support, and a concluding statement.

## Organization

Most chapters start with a *sample paragraph* presented as a model for the structure to be covered. This sample may be an excerpt from literature or another contextualized piece. Difficult vocabulary is glossed. Occasionally, a cartoon will lead off the chapter. (The last two chapters vary somewhat from the general pattern.) In all cases, the chapter opener serves as a means to help the student focus on the structure(s) presented in the chapter.

The readings come from a variety of sources, such as literature, newspapers, texts, student writing, and author-generated material. Contextualized passages are occasionally recycled in the text as examples for additional grammar points or as exercises. The rationale for repeating certain passages is that students can focus more effectively on the given grammar point within an already familiar context.

Following the chapter opener is the *Essential Information* section, often with an inductive analysis, which then leads students to discover rules independently. Clear explanations, charts, and examples reinforce the students' conclusions.

*Relevant Information* sections, when appropriate, supplement the discussion with additional information.

*Exercises* help students practice the points that have been presented. The exercises generally progress from more controlled to more open-ended practice, thus allowing students to express their own thoughts within a contextualized framework. The material for each exercise is usually related to a sample paragraph presented earlier. Some exercises are designated as "group/pair" tasks; these can easily be converted to tasks for individual work. Similarly, exercises designated as individual tasks can be adapted to tasks for groups or pairs.

*Editing Exercises* give students valuable practice in recognizing and correcting errors in the editing stage of the composing process. In many cases, paragraphs of authentic student writing are used in the editing exercises. (Instructions on how to edit are included in Chapter One.)

*Writing Assignments* appear at points in the text where a sample paragraph or other context provides a natural trigger for the topic. In many cases, the writing assignments will naturally generate the grammatical points presented in the given chapter; in a few instances, however, this may not be so. In the latter case, since composing is the primary goal in a developmental writing class, we capitalize on good writing topics, especially ones that naturally spin off from engaging reading passages.

Since reading and writing are closely related skills, we have placed the writing assignments immediately following the readings that have triggered them. In this way, the related readings are still fresh in the student's mind. One approach to handling the writing assignments, then, is to assign them immediately after the readings. As an alternative, the instructor may choose to return to the writing assignments at a later point. In this case, it is recommended that the students review the connected reading before beginning the writing assignment.

*Reviews* reinforce the material from the previous section(s). *Chapter Reviews* review and reinforce the material from the entire chapter.

The *Food for Thought* section at the end of each chapter provides an optional challenge for students. The puzzle-like questions in these sections offer the students the opportunity to do some innovative thinking, inviting them to apply in a creative way what they've learned.

Each chapter concludes with the *Classroom Assessment Technique* (*CAT*) to give both instructors and students an opportunity to check progress. Students are encouraged to review what they've learned and to formulate any questions they may still have. Instructors receive feedback from students so that they can evaluate the success of the teaching–learning process and follow up with any appropriate additional activities.

## How to Use This Text

This text is to be used as a flexible workbook–text. It is recommended that instructors cover the material on an as-needed basis.

The following point cannot be overemphasized: *It is not our intention for the students of any class to cover every page of this text.* (We shudder at the very thought!) Rather, we are offering instructors and their writing students a variety of grammar points and exercises that can be selected as they are needed. For extra assistance the text is accompanied by an instructor's manual.

## Acknowledgments

We would like to thank the people at St. Martin's Press, who backed us up at every stage of the project. First, thanks are in order to Kathleen Keller, our acquisitions editor, who initially recognized the merit of our project. Next, we thank Naomi Silverman, who ably and congenially guided us through all the stages of textbook publishing despite a personal tragedy. We also thank Sarah Crowley and Sarah Picchi, whose help with the day-to-day details during the early manuscript stage kept us on track. Finally, we thank Amy Horowitz, our project editor, whose gentle input, helpful attention to detail, and effective guidance helped turn our manuscript into an attractive published text.

The next group of people we owe thanks to consists of former instructors. We both want to thank Marianne Celce-Murcia, a fireball of energy, whose passion for the vagaries of American English was infectious. Robert would like to acknowledge the influence of two more of his professors at UCLA: the late William Bull, who had the knack for reducing a difficult concept, such as the subjunctive in Spanish, to palatable bite-size pieces, and Evelyn Hatch, whose forte was turning a student query into a question of her own that challenged the students to come up with their own answers. Ann would like to express gratitude to the following: Diane Larsen-Freeman, whose class on second-language acquisition at UCLA opened her eyes to the incredible challenges second-language learners face, and William Rutherford, who served as her "grammar mentor" at USC during her first year of college/university teaching and whose discussions led her to look at grammar from a variety of perspectives.

Closer to home, we thank our colleagues at El Camino College who field tested the text in its earlier forms over several years. Their support and comments were much appreciated.

Thanks are also due to our students, who inspired us throughout the years as we developed the material. We appreciate their candid feedback. Even with our inevitable "hits" and "misses" along the way, our students continued to encourage us. In addition to their honest comments, their expressive faces told us clearly when we were on track as well as when we were not.

Finally, we want to thank our families for putting up with the ups and downs of living with a textbook writer. It wasn't always easy, but they supported us at every turn.

"The unexamined life is not worth living." Likewise, "the unexamined manuscript is not worth publishing." With this in mind, we thank those reviewers who had a hand in shaping the content of *Nitty Gritty Grammar:* Charlotte Al-Jamal (Kelly Al-Jamal) Director, International Institute of Languages; Patrick Aquilina, Columbia University–American Language Program; James Coady, Ohio University; Gilbert Couts, The American University; Baruch Elimelech, Long Beach Community College; Tess Ferree, Columbia University–American Language Program; John Gayle, Old Dominion University; James Gillis, Pacific Lutheran University; Isabel Y. Jennings, San Antonio College; Judith Paiva, Northern Virginia Community College; Jerry Schwartz, The American University; and a number of anonymous reviewers.

We sincerely hope that instructors and their students enjoy using the materials in this text.

A. Robert Young
Ann O. Strauch

# BRIEF TABLE OF CONTENTS

# CONTENTS

# NITTY GRITTY GRAMMAR

Sentence Essentials
for Writers

# 1

# Sentence Essentials

## ≡ SUBJECTS AND VERBS

▶ **Sample Paragraph**

In the following paragraph based on Joseph Krumgold's *. . . and now Miguel,* Miguel describes the birth of a lamb on his family's sheep ranch in New Mexico. The subjects and verbs appear in italic letters.

### The Birth of a Lamb

°**lamb:** baby sheep
°**ewe:** adult female sheep

°**resembles:** looks like

  The *birth* of a lamb° *is* a remarkable event. First, the *ewe*° *lies down.* After a short time, the *ewe pushes* the lamb's head out into the light. To me, the *lamb resembles*° an airplane. The *"nose"* of the "airplane" *is* all glass. The "pilot's *eyes" look* out from behind the round glass. This *"pilot" is,* of course, a new lamb. In a few minutes, the whole *head* of the lamb *appears*. *It does* not *resemble* an airplane anymore. Then the "round *glass*" *breaks*. The lamb's *mother pushes* the entire body of the lamb out of her body. The *world receives* its new lamb. Immediately, the *mother licks* her new baby clean. A few minutes later, the *lamb finds* its legs. *It stands up. It tries* to walk. This *event is* a miracle° of nature.

°**miracle:** wonderful event outside the laws of nature

 **Essential Information: WHAT ARE SUBJECTS AND VERBS?**

Every sentence in "The Birth of a Lamb" is a simple sentence or, in other words, one independent clause. A clause must have a subject and a verb, and every sentence, no matter how long, must have at least one independent clause. The *subject* of a sentence tells what the sentence is about.[†]

### Examples

subject
|
After a short time, the *ewe* pushes the lamb's head out into the light.

subject
|
To me, the *lamb* resembles an airplane.

The *verb* says something about the subject. It has tense (in the above examples, present tense), and it often has different forms that agree with the subject of the sentence.

verb
|
The lamb *resembles* an airplane.

verb
|
The ewe *pushes* the lamb's head out into the light.

verb
|
This event *is* a miracle of nature.

In the above examples, *resembles*, *pushes*, and *is* are in the present tense to indicate present time, and the "s" form ending is singular to agree with a singular subject.

### *Relevant Information: Other Information in Sentences*

A subject and a verb are essential in a sentence, but other information may appear at various places, especially after the verb. In the following examples, the other information is in italic letters.

other information
|
The lamb resembles *an airplane*.

---

[†]**Note:** Commands, however, have no expressed subject in English. Example: Stand up.

other information

The ewe pushes *the lamb's head out into the light*.

To summarize, a sentence in English follows the general pattern:

> Subject + Verb + (Other Information)

# SUBJECTS: NOUNS AND PRONOUNS

 **Essential Information: NOUNS AS SUBJECTS OF SENTENCES**

The subject of a sentence can be a noun. Nouns name people, places, things, concepts, or activities.

**Examples**

|            | Related to the Sample Paragraph | From a School Setting                       |
|------------|---------------------------------|---------------------------------------------|
| People     | Miguel                          | teacher, student                            |
| Places     | New Mexico, ranch               | Miami Dade Community College, the library   |
| Things     | lamb, light, airplane           | pencil, notebook                            |
| Concepts   | miracle                         | education, knowledge                        |
| Activities | birth                           | exercise, writing                           |

**Example sentences**

*Miguel* lives on a sheep ranch.

The *lamb* resembles an airplane.

The *birth* of a lamb is a remarkable thing.

 **Exercise**   Identifying Noun Subjects in Proverbs

Underline the subject of each sentence.

**Example**

<u>Variety</u> is the spice of life. (American proverb)

1. The <u>pen</u> is mightier than the sword. (Edward Bulwer-Lytton)

2. Curiosity killed the cat. (American proverb)

3. Haste makes waste. (English proverb)

4. Still waters run deep. (English proverb)

5. A friend in need is a friend indeed. (English proverb)

6. Absence makes the heart grow fonder. (Thomas Haynes Bayly)

7. Two wrongs don't make a right. (English proverb)

 **Writing Assignment:** *Proverbs*

Select one of the proverbs from the previous exercise, and write a paragraph to explain what this proverb means to you. Start your paragraph with a topic sentence that gives the proverb and presents the general meaning. Put quotation marks around the proverb.

**Example**

> The English proverb "Misery loves company" means that people who are basically unhappy look for friends who are also basically unhappy.

Support your topic sentence with plenty of specific details that explain what the proverb means to you. (You may agree or disagree with the proverb.) Write a concluding sentence that gives a feeling of finish to your paragraph.

 **Essential Information: PRONOUNS AS SUBJECTS OF SENTENCES**

The subject of a sentence can be a pronoun.

pronoun
|
Miguel lives on a sheep ranch. *He* helps his parents take care of the lambs.

---

The following *personal pronouns* are used as subjects.

|  | Singular | Plural |
|---|---|---|
| First person | I[†] | we |
| Second person | you | you |
| Third person | he | they |
|  | she |  |
|  | it |  |

†The pronoun *I* is always a capital letter.

---

 **Exercise**   Identifying Nouns and Pronouns as Subjects of Sentences

Underline the subjects. Write *N* above the nouns and *P* above the pronouns.

### Examples

George Washington Carver was an agricultural scientist.

He developed hundreds of uses for the peanut.

1. Harriet Tubman was a slave in the nineteenth century.

2. She escaped from her master.

3. Later she helped hundreds of other slaves to freedom.

4. They took the underground railroad to the North.

5. Houses served as the underground railroad.

 **Essential Information: COMPOUND SUBJECTS**

When the subject consists of more than one noun or pronoun, it is a *compound subject*. The word *and* connects the two parts of a compound subject.

Pedro likes to fish for trout in the river.
Miguel likes to fish for trout in the river.
*Pedro and Miguel* like to fish for trout in the river. (compound subject)

 **Exercise**   Identifying Compound Subjects

The following sentences are based on Joseph Krumgold's . . . *and now Miguel*. Combine each pair of sentences into one sentence with a compound subject. Make any other changes necessary in the new sentence.

1. Miguel helps his father on the ranch.
   His older brother Gabriel helps his father on the ranch.

   *Miguel and his older brother Gabriel help their father on the*

   *ranch.*

2. Pedro is younger than Miguel.
   Faustina is younger than Miguel.

   Pedro and Faustina are younger than Miguel.

   _____

3. Miguel is too young to take the sheep to the mountains in the summer.
   Pedro is too young to take the sheep to the mountains in the summer.

   Miguel and Pedro are too young to take the
   sheep to the mountains in the summer

4. Miguel's mother wants him to stay at home with the women and children.
   Miguel's father wants him to stay at home with the women and children.

   Migel's parents want him to stay
   at home with the women and children

5.  Uncle Bonifacio goes with Miguel's father and Gabriel to the meadow.
    Uncle Eli goes with Miguel's father and Gabriel to the meadow.

    _____

    _____

6.  Miguel wants to go with the men to the mountains.
    Pedro wants to go with the men to the mountains.

    _____

    _____

# ≡ VERBS

 **Essential Information: VERB FORMS**

A verb may consist of one word, or it may consist of one or more auxiliary verbs plus the main verb, forming a verb phrase. Examples of sentences with verbs that consist of one word:

---

**1. Present**

  *Wedding Song* **is** the story of a young man in Cairo, Egypt.

**2. Past**

  Last month we **read** *So Far from the Bamboo Grove.*

---

Examples of sentences with verbs that consist of an auxiliary verb plus a main verb (i.e., a verb phrase):

---

**1. Present Progressive** (auxiliary verbs = *am/is/are*)

  In my ESL class this month, we **are reading** about Abbas and his day-to-day life.

**2. Past Progressive** (auxiliary verbs = *was/were*)

  Before that, I **was reading** *Gone with the Wind*, but I did not finish it.

**3. Present Perfect** (auxiliary verbs = *have/has*)

  We **have read** several excellent novels this semester.

**4. Modals** (*can, will, must, should . . .*) and **Phrasal Modals** (*be going to, have to . . .* )

  I **can read** a lot better now.
  I **am going to read** more books for pleasure.

---

*Note: The examples given in this section present a brief preview of a variety of verbs. Later chapters in this text cover verbs in greater detail.*

### *Relevant Information:* Be + ing

Look again at the examples of the progressive verbs (1 and 2 above).

. . . are reading . . .
. . . was reading . . .

What verb appears before the *-ing* form of the main verb?

_____

> A form of *be* must be used with the *-ing* form of a verb.

 **Exercise** Writing Verbs—The People in Your Life

Throughout your lifetime, you've known many people. In this exercise, you will tell about some of these people. In the following, only the subjects of the sentences appear. Write the verbs and the rest of these sentences. Circle the verbs.

**Example**

My neighbors come from Pakistan.
They speak Urdu.

1. The people in my family _____

   They _____

2. My closest friend _____

   We _____

3. The first person that I met in this class _____

   He (or she) and I _____

4. My classmates _____

   They _____

 **Essential Information: COMPOUND VERBS**

A simple sentence may contain one main verb, or it may contain two (or more) main verbs. A sentence that contains more than one verb has a *compound verb*. The word *and* usually appears between the two verbs.

**Examples**

        verb          verb
         |             |
Miguel *watches* the sheep and *gives* them food.

verb                    verb
|                       |
He *counts* the sheep and *checks* them for possible illness.

 **Exercise**   Compound Verbs—Toronto's International Festival

Combine each pair of sentences into one sentence with a compound verb.

**Example**

Each June in Toronto, international business owners *have* a special "open house." They *invite* people to visit.

Each June in Toronto, international business owners *have* a special "open house" and *invite* people to visit.

1.  People buy "passports." They attend special demonstrations at several businesses.

    *People buy "passports" and attend special demonstrations at several businesses.*

2.  Some people learn new things such as Japanese flower arranging. They develop an appreciation for Asian art.

    _____

    _____

3.  Other people taste foreign food. They discover delicious new dishes such as *baklava.*

    _____

    _____

4.  Still others watch new dances such as the limbo. They even try them.

    _____

    _____

5.  Other cities in Canada have similar festivals each year. They draw many people to their celebrations.

    _____

    _____

## REVIEW: SUBJECTS AND VERBS

 **Exercise A**   Identifying Subjects and Verbs—"Love"

The following sentences give a summary of Jesse Stuart's short story "Love." The story takes place on a corn farm. Underline the subjects once and the verbs twice.

**Example**

The <u>sun</u> <u>was shining</u> brightly in the late afternoon sky.

1.  My <u>father</u> and <u>I</u> <u>were walking</u> in the fields on our farm.

2.  Bob (our dog) walked with us.

3.  My father hated snakes.

4.  He saw one on the path.

5.  He told Bob to kill it.

6.  Bob attacked the snake.

7.  He took the snake by the neck.

°**whipped:** shook violently

8.  He whipped° the snake's body in the air.

9.  Blood poured from the snake's throat.

10. Then something hit my legs.

11. It was snake eggs from the snake's body.

12. Bob grabbed the snake again.

13. He threw her to the ground.

14. She lay dead.

15. We counted thirty-seven eggs.

16. Near sunset, the three of us went home.

17. My father and Bob were satisfied.

18. I felt sad.

19. I was thinking about birth and death.

20. The next morning, we returned to the same place.

21. In the same spot, I found the dead snake with another snake by her side.

22. It was the dead snake's mate.

23. He came to comfort his partner.

24. At that moment, I understood the meaning of love.

 **Exercise B**   Writing Compound Subjects and Verbs—
Three Exciting Days in Vancouver

Combine the following simple sentences. These combined sentences produce simple sentences with compound subjects or compound verbs. You may need to make changes in other parts of the combined sentences. Write the sentences in paragraph form on a separate piece of paper. Include the example sentences and remove the numbers.

**Examples**

Pat saw a lot on his vacation in Vancouver last summer.
Chris saw a lot on her vacation in Vancouver last summer.

Pat and Chris saw a lot on their vacation in Vancouver last summer.

They spent three days in this interesting city.
Their teenagers Molly and Claude spent three days in this interesting city.

They and their teenagers Molly and Claude spent three days in this interesting city.

On their first day, they flew into Sea Island Airport.
They took the Hustle Bus downtown.

On their first day, they flew into Sea Island Airport and took the Hustle Bus downtown.

The beginning of your paragraph should look like this:

Three Exciting Days in Vancouver

Pat and Chris saw a lot on their vacation in Vancouver last summer. They and their teenagers Molly and Claude spent three days in this interesting city. On their first day, they flew into Sea Island Airport and took the Hustle Bus downtown. That day . . .

Now finish the story using the following sentences.

1. That day Pat explored the city on foot.
   Molly explored the city on foot.

   *That day Pat and Molly explored the city on foot.*

2. Chris took a bus trip to Simon Fraser University.
   Claude took a bus trip to Simon Fraser University.

   _____

3. The next morning, the family got up early.
   They took a taxi to Stanley Park.

   _____

4. At the park, Pat visited the aquarium.
   The kids visited the aquarium.

   _____

5. Chris went to see the Indian ruins.
   She met the family later at the zoo.

   _____

6. On the third day, the four rented a car.
   They went to Mount Seymour Provincial Park.

   _____

7. Later, they drove to Gastown.
   They looked around in the Old World shops.

   _____

8. That night they had dinner in Chinatown.
   They finished their evening at the Hot Jazz Society.

   _____

9. By the time they got home, Chris was tired.
   By the time they got home, Pat was tired.

   _____

# CAPITALS AND ENDING PUNCTUATION

 **Essential Information: CAPITALS AND ENDING PUNCTUATION**

A sentence starts with a capital letter. It ends with one of three punctuation marks:

A statement ends with a period. (.)

A question ends with a question mark. (?)

A sentence expressing strong emotion (happiness, surprise, fear, anger) may end with an exclamation point. (!)

**Examples**

There is a snake in the path.

Do you see it?

It's ready to strike!

> A sentence begins with a capital letter and ends with appropriate punctuation.

 **Exercise** Capitals and Ending Punctuation

Cross out any letter that should be capitalized and write the correction above. Also, provide the correct punctuation at the end.

1. I said nothing.

2. what did my father say

3. he did not say anything, either

4. i was still thinking about the beautiful snake and her babies

5. they were dead

# ADDITIONAL INFORMATION ON SUBJECTS

 ### Essential Information: AVOIDING REPEATED SUBJECTS

Do not use a subject pronoun along with its subject noun. Read the following examples with repeated subjects. The following sentences are <u>not correct</u>.

*Harriet Tubman she was an escaped slave in the nineteenth century.[†]

*This brave woman she helped hundreds of slaves to freedom.

*The slaves they took the underground railroad to the North.

*The houses they served as the underground railroad.

 ### Exercise   Avoiding Repeated Subjects—American Cultural Literacy

Correct any errors in the following sentences by crossing out unnecessary words.

1. Clara Barton ~~she~~ started the American Red Cross in the 1880s.

2. Bonnie and Clyde they were two outlaws in the 1930s.

3. Al Capone was a leader of organized crime in Chicago in the late 1920s. He went to prison in the 1930s for income tax problems.

4. Martin Luther King he had a dream.

5. Amelia Earhart she was the first woman to fly an airplane across the Atlantic Ocean.

 ### Essential Information: FILLER SUBJECTS

The words *it* and *there* can serve as filler subjects. A filler subject appears in the normal subject position, but it has no content meaning.

*It* is a beautiful day.

*There* are a lot of people outside enjoying the nice weather.

 ### Essential Information: *IT* AS A FILLER SUBJECT

The filler *it* does not refer to anything previously mentioned. The main uses of the filler *it* are to express time, day, date, distance, weather, and temperature. *It* is always singular, followed by a singular verb form.

| | |
|---|---|
| Time: | It is 8:00. |
| Day: | It is Tuesday. |
| Date: | It is October 8. |
| Distance: | It is five miles to school. |
| Weather: | It was cloudy and rainy last week in Atlanta. |
| Temperature: | It was too hot last weekend. |

[†]Throughout this book, an asterisk (*) indicates incorrect usage.

**Exercise** The Filler *It*

Write a few sentences about the following topics. Use the filler *it*.

1. The present time, day, and date.

   *It's 9:20.*

   _____

   _____

2. The typical weather for different times of the year in your hometown.

   _____

   _____

   _____

3. The weather on your last trip or vacation.

   _____

   _____

   _____

4. The distances between places you go frequently—home, school, favorite place to shop—and the length of time it takes to get to each place.

   _____

   _____

   _____

 **Essential Information: *THERE* AS A FILLER SUBJECT**

The filler *there* does not refer to a place. It signals the existence of something. The real subject follows the verb. The verb agrees with the real subject.

   The singular verb forms *is* and *was* are used with a singular subject. The plural verb forms *are* and *were* are used with a plural subject.

   There *were* many *things* to do on our trip in Vancouver.
   There *was* a *concert* at Stanley Park.
   There *were* several *exhibits* at the aquarium.
   There *were* many interesting *shops* in Gastown.
   There *was* a great *restaurant* in Chinatown.
   There *are* many *pictures* in my photo album of our trip to Vancouver.

 **Exercise** The Filler *There*—What a Mess!

On a separate piece of paper, write three or four sentences describing one of the following situations. Use the filler *there*.

1. A living room after a party

2. A messy car

3. A crowded park on a Sunday afternoon

4. An overfilled refrigerator

5. A back yard after a strong windstorm

## REVIEW: SUBJECTS AND FILLER SUBJECTS

 **Exercise A**   The Fillers *It* and *There*—One Day Last August

In the following sentences, add the filler *it* or the filler *there*.

1. _____ was mid-August.

2. _____ was early in the morning.

3. _____ wasn't a cloud in the sky.

4. _____ was a hot day.

5. _____ was a snake on the path.

 **Exercise B**   Subjects—Nouns, Pronouns, and Filler Subjects—
A Typical ESL Classroom

The sentences in the following exercise describe a typical ESL classroom and the people in it. Add the missing subjects. Use nouns, pronouns, or the filler *there*.

A typical ESL classroom in some schools is fairly large.

1. _____ has a few windows for light and air.

2. _____ are many desks arranged in rows or in a circle.

3. _____ sit down at the beginning of class.

4. _____ is also a stand for the instructor's books and materials.

5. _____ usually arrives early.

6. _____ calls the roll at the beginning of class.

7. _____ is a chalkboard behind the instructor.

8. _____ often writes on the chalkboard to show the students the important points.

# ☰ EDITING

 **Essential Information: EDITING**

The writing process includes editing your own work. When you edit, you make corrections as you finish a draft. When you edit, you can . . .

Cross out words or letters you want to eliminate.

Use a caret (^) to add words above the caret.

Correct any other errors.

**Example**

### BOLIVIA

The geography of Bolivia has a couple of unusual features. First of all, Bolivia is in the central area of South America. It is one of two landlocked countries in South America. Also, Bolivia has a very famous lake. It is called Lake Titicaca. It is the highest body of water for boats in the world. I hope to visit this unique country someday.

 **Exercise A**    Editing—India

**Part One**
Edit the following.

**Example**
The largest city in India is Calcutta.

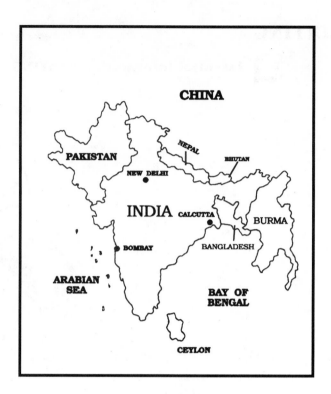

1.   $\overset{W\ are}{\wedge}$ We going to learn about the geography of India.

2.   first of all, occupies a large area of South Asia

3.   its capital New Delhi

4.   several groups of islands also form part of the republic

5.   they in the Arabian Sea and in the Bay of Bengal

6.   India's largest neighbor China

7.   lies to the northeast

8.   India it has five other neighbors

9.   one of them Bhutan

10.   You might already know the other four

11.   They Burma and Bangladesh to the east, Pakistan to the west, and Nepal to the north.

**Part Two**

Rewrite the edited sentences from Part One correctly in paragraph form on a separate piece of paper. Give your paragraph a title based on the main idea of the paragraph.

 **Exercise B**   Editing—Who Says "You Can't Take It with You"?

Edit the following paragraph.

**Who Says "You Can't Take It with You"?**

My grandfather ~~he~~ hated to spend money. He ^was^ very cheap. Every week put

at least 25 percent of his paycheck under his mattress. He didn't trust banks. The   2

day before he died, made his wife promise to put the money in his coffin with

him. He wanted to buy his way into heaven. My grandmother she promised to   4

do as he requested. The next morning took about $37,000 to the bank. Then

deposited it into her account. After that, wrote a check for $37,000. She put the   6

check in my grandfather's coffin. My grandmother very smart.

 **Exercise C**   Writing a Second Draft—
Who Says "You Can't Take It with You"?

Rewrite the paragraph "Who Says 'You Can't Take It with You'?" with the
corrected sentences.

 **CHAPTER REVIEW**

## REVIEW CHART: SUBJECTS AND VERBS

The following chart shows how subjects and verbs work together with other
information to form complete simple sentences.

| Subject         +    | Verb         +   | (Other Information)                          |
|----------------------|------------------|---------------------------------------------|
| The **nose** of the airplane | is        | all glass.                                  |
| The pilot's **eyes** | **look out**     | from behind the round glass.                |
| This **pilot**       | is               | a new lamb.                                 |
| In a few minutes, the whole **head** of the lamb | **appears**. |                          |
| It                   | **does** not **resemble** | an airplane anymore.               |
| Then the round **glass** | **breaks**.  |                                             |
| The lamb's **mother** | **pushes**      | the entire body of the lamb out of her body. |
| The **world**        | **receives**     | its new lamb.                               |

**Exercise A**    Identifying Subjects and Verbs—"Love"

In the following sentences based on Jesse Stuart's short story "Love," a boy, his father, and his dog "Bob" are returning home after a walk on their farm. They have just chased a snake and killed it. The father is happy they have killed it because he hates snakes, but the boy is beginning to feel sad about the snake's death. In the following paragraph, underline the subjects once and the verbs twice.

°**panting:** taking quick, short breaths
°**shaggy:** covered with long, rough hair
°**flecks:** small amounts
°**foam:** whitish mass of bubbles

°**chestnut:** tree that produces reddish nuts
°**ridge:** long, narrow top of a hill
°**lark:** bird

Bob was panting°. He was walking ahead of us back to the house. His tongue was out of his mouth. He was tired. He was hot under his shaggy° coat 2 of hair. His tongue nearly touched the dry dirt. White flecks° of foam° dripped from it. We walked toward the house. I said nothing. My father said nothing. I 4 still thought about the dead snake. The sun was going down over the chestnut° ridge°. A lark° was singing. It was late for a lark to sing. The red evening clouds 6 floated above the pine trees on our pasture hill. My father stood beside the path. His black hair moved in the wind. His face was red in the blue wind of day. His 8 eyes looked toward the sinking sun.

 **Exercise B**    Identifying Subjects and Verbs—
                            Computer Madness

In the following paragraph, underline the subjects once and the verbs twice.

### Computer Madness

Pat and Chris are crazy about computers these days. Pat went to the store and bought a new computer six months ago. He brought it right home and set 2 it up. He and Chris tried it out right away. Chris and the children practiced on a tutorial program for a few days. The next week Pat and Chris went back to the 4 store and bought a laser printer. A few days after that, they ordered six new programs and picked out a modem. Last month the children asked for a com- 6 puter system of their own. The entire family has gone crazy over computers. Now Pat and Chris are thinking of adding a room on to their house for all their 8 computer equipment.

 **Exercise C**    Writing Sentences and Checking for
                            Subjects and Verbs—Proverbs

Earlier in this chapter, you read several proverbs from various sources.

**Examples**

> Variety is the spice of life. (American proverb)

> A friend in need is a friend indeed. (English proverb)

On a separate piece of paper, write three to five proverbs, in English, that come from your own language. Don't worry if the translation is not "exact." Draw one line under the subject of each sentence and two lines under each verb.

When you finish, exchange your sentences with a partner. Check each other's sentences for subjects and verbs.

 **Exercise D**    Editing—Bicycles throughout the World

Edit the following paragraph.

### Bicycles throughout the World

Bicycles contribute to good health. Also, save gas. Some areas of the world take advantage of the benefits of bicycles more than other areas do. There two $\quad$ 2 bicycles for every car in the world. In China, the ratio of bicycles to cars is 250 to one. In the U.S.A., are 100 million bicycles to 137 million cars. In Tianjin, China, $\quad$ 4 people use bicycles for 77 percent of their trips downtown. In Manhattan, New York, use them for 8 percent of their trips downtown. The Netherlands has many $\quad$ 6 special roads for bicycles. They on mostly flat land. In the Netherlands, people they use bicycles for almost 50 percent of their trips downtown. in the U.S.A., $\quad$ 8 both Davis and Palo Alto in northern California encourage the use of bicycles. Both of them they college communities. In Davis, people use bicycles for almost $\quad$ 10 25 percent of their trips downtown. Maybe Davis students smarter than other people in the United States. $\quad$ 12

 **Exercise E**    Writing Sentences—Mobile Computing

Write four sentences based on the following picture of a speedy computer user. You may want to use some of the following vocabulary.

| Nouns | Verbs | Adjectives |
|---|---|---|
| computer (laptop) | break the law | clever |
| helmet | pay attention | dangerous |
| keyboard | ride a bicycle | impossible |
| monitor | save time | impractical |
| | speed | practical |
| | | ridiculous |

1. _____

2. _____

3. _____

4. _____

 **Writing Assignment A:** *Interviewing a Classmate*

Interview a partner. Take notes during the interview. Some topics you may want to cover in an interview include the following:

*Basic background information:* name, country, time in this country
*Family:* in native country, in this country
*Goals:* career, family, other
*Spare time:* hobbies, interests, vacations
*Preferences:* music, food, shopping places
*Opinions about this country:* language, people, customs
*General:* dislikes, personal philosophies

Write about your partner. In the first sentence, give your partner's name and tell how you know him or her.

### Example

Sung Lee is one of my classmates in my ESL Writing and Grammar class this semester.

Next, tell what else you found out about your partner during the interview. Write a concluding sentence that gives a feeling of "finish" to the paragraph. Edit your work. Exchange paragraphs with your partner and check each other's work.

 **Writing Assignment B:** *A Possession from the Past*

Write about a possession that was important to you in the past. It could be a toy, a musical instrument, a pet, or other possession. Explain why this possession was so important to you. Include how you felt about it.

Start your paragraph with a topic sentence. Support your topic sentence with plenty of specific details. Write a concluding sentence that gives a feeling of finish to your paragraph.

**Example Topic Sentence**

When I was a small child, my favorite possession was my bicycle.

Edit your work. Exchange paragraphs with a partner and check each other's work.

The following is a sample student paragraph.

### MY FIRST PIANO

My first friend was a piano. She came to my house when I was seven years old. One Friday afternoon, I came back from school as usual. My mother said, "You got a new friend, Sachi." I opened the door of the living room, and I found her. She was standing in the corner of the living room and shining. I touched her black and white keys, and she whispered softly, "Nice to meet you." Why did my parents give me a piano? They gave it to me because I was a tone deaf girl. I couldn't sing a song well, so they decided to buy it for me. They thought if I developed an interest in music through playing the piano, my singing talent would have to get better. After some time, it came true. I got an A in my music class when I was nine years old. Also, I was chosen as a member of the student orchestra. Now, I miss my friend very much. I'm sure she is waiting for me at my parents' house. I'm going to take a vacation to go back to Japan next summer, of course, to spend time with my first friend.

Adapted from a paragraph by Sachiko Ishii

## FOOD FOR THOUGHT

The following was written at the bottom of a one-page newspaper advertisement for IBM.

"One in a series from IBM. Another will appear in this newspaper tomorrow."

How many sentences appear inside the quotes? _____

## CLASSROOM ASSESSMENT TECHNIQUE (CAT)

### THE ONE-MINUTE PAPER

Take a minute or two to write answers to the following questions. Write your answers on a separate piece of paper without your name.

1. What are the most important points that you have learned in this chapter?

2. What questions remain in your mind at the end of this chapter?

*Note: Use this exercise to help you get answers to any questions you still have. Ask these questions to anyone who might be able to help you, such as another student or your instructor.*

# CHAPTER 2

# Clauses and Sentence Types

## ≡ CLAUSES

▶ **Sample Paragraphs**

The following paragraphs are based on a passage from the novel *Danny* by Roald Dahl. In these paragraphs, Danny is giving a loving description of his tiny trailer home. Read each paragraph and answer the questions that follow.

### Home Sweet Home (I)

°**tucked:** covers folded in
°**lumps:** pieces
°**snug:** comfortable

I really loved our gypsy trailer. I loved it especially in the evenings. I was tucked° in my bed. My father was telling me stories. The kerosene lamp was turned low. I could see lumps° of wood in the old stove. They were glowing red-hot. It was wonderful to be lying there. I was snug° and warm in my bed. I was in a little room. I went to sleep. I had a wonderful feeling. My father would still be there, very close to me. He was sitting in his chair by the fire. Sometimes he was lying in the bed above my own.

### Home Sweet Home (II)

I really loved our gypsy trailer. I loved it especially in the evenings when I was tucked in my bed and my father was telling me stories. The kerosene lamp was turned low, and I could see lumps of wood glowing red-hot in the old stove. It was wonderful to be lying there snug and warm in my bed in that little room. Most wonderful of all was the feeling that when I went to sleep, my father would still be there, very close to me, sitting in his chair by the fire or lying in the bed above my own.

1. Do both paragraphs give you the same information? _____

2. Which paragraph is better? Discuss this with another student or with your instructor.

 ## Essential Information: CLAUSES

> A clause is a group of related words that contains a subject and a verb.

### Examples

subject    verb
   |        |
*I* really *loved* our gypsy trailer.

subject  verb
   |  |
*It was* wonderful there.

"Home Sweet Home (II)" is better than "Home Sweet Home (I)," because it contains a variety of sentences. Many of the sentences in (II) combine information from the shorter sentences in (I). Some of the sentences with combined information have one clause, and others have more than one clause.

 ## Essential Information: COMBINING IDEAS

Often, the information from two sentences can be combined to create a new sentence. The new sentence may contain only **one independent clause**.

**Examples**

    subject    verb
       |       |

1a.      *I could see* lumps of wood in the old stove.

    subject      verb
      |        |

1b.  *They were glowing* red-hot.

    subject    verb
       |      |

1c.     *I could see* lumps of wood glowing red-hot in the old stove.

  subject  verb           subject   verb
    |   |                |  |

2a.     *It was* wonderful to be lying there. *I was* snug and warm in my bed.

    subject  verb
      |   |

2b.     *I was* in a little room.

    subject  verb
      |  |

2c.     *It was* wonderful to be lying there snug and warm in my bed in that little room.

   subject        verb
    |       /   \

3a. *My father would* still *be* there, very close to me.

   subject verb
    |     |

3b. *He was sitting* in his chair by the fire.

       subject verb
        |    |

3c. Sometimes *he was lying* in the bed above my own.

    subject     verb
     |     /  \

3d. *My father would* still *be* there, very close to me, sitting in his chair by

     the fire or lying in the bed above my own.

In other cases, the new sentences may contain **two clauses**.

**Examples**

    subject  verb
      |   |

1a.     *I loved* it especially in the evenings.

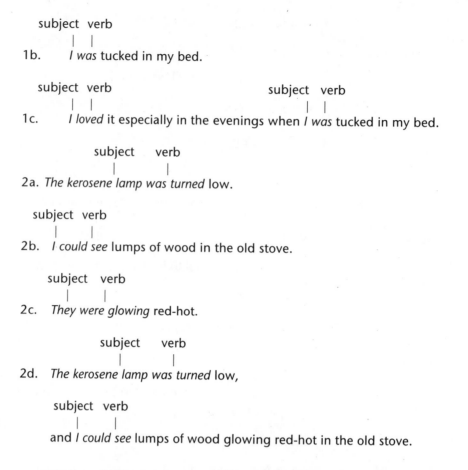

```
                subject  verb
                  |      |
1b.        I was tucked in my bed.
```

```
           subject  verb                    subject   verb
             |      |                          |       |
1c.        I loved it especially in the evenings when I was tucked in my bed.
```

```
                  subject     verb
                    |          |
2a.  The kerosene lamp was turned low.
```

```
             subject  verb
               |      |
2b.   I could see lumps of wood in the old stove.
```

```
              subject  verb
                |      |
2c.   They were glowing red-hot.
```

```
                  subject     verb
                    |          |
2d.   The kerosene lamp was turned low,
```

```
              subject  verb
                |      |
      and I could see lumps of wood glowing red-hot in the old stove.
```

---

## Writing Assignment A: A Childhood Memory

Describe a situation from your childhood in which you felt very content with one or both parents. As an option, you may write about any other adult who was important to you in your childhood. Start your paragraph with a topic sentence that identifies the person, the situation, and your feeling about the person and situation. Support your topic sentence with plenty of specific details. Write a concluding sentence that gives a feeling of finish to your paragraph.

**Exercise**   Identifying Clauses—*So Far from the Bamboo Grove*

The following sentences are from Yoko Kawashima Watkins' *So Far from the Bamboo Grove*. In this passage, the Japanese author is describing the air raids she experienced in North Korea near the end of World War II. Identify the number of clauses in each sentence. Write "1" or "2" in the blank space.

1.  __1__ Night after night the alert siren woke us.

2.  _____ Because it was dark inside and out, the air raids seemed more eerie.

3.  _____ The night planes flew very low.

4.  _____ They shook the whole earth.

5. _____ I could hear the bamboo making crackling noises.

6. _____ Everyone lost sleep, and everyone looked very tired the next day.

 **Writing Assignment B:** *A Frightening Experience*

In the previous exercise, you read parts of Yoko Watkins' frightening experience as she and her family tried to escape from the Communists in North Korea at the end of World War II.

Write about an experience that you found frightening, either as a child or as an adult. Start your paragraph with a topic sentence that identifies the situation and how you felt about it. Support your topic sentence with plenty of specific details. Write a concluding sentence that gives a feeling of finish to your paragraph.

 **Essential Information: INDEPENDENT AND DEPENDENT CLAUSES**

English has two types of clauses: *independent clauses* and *dependent clauses*. An *independent clause* can stand alone as a sentence.

### Examples

I am proud of my brother and sister.

Both are taking ESL classes at Queens College in New York.

They also work.

My sister works twenty hours a week.

My brother works twenty-five hours a week.

It's not easy to work and go to school at the same time.

> A sentence must have at least one independent clause, and it may have one or more dependent clauses.

A *dependent clause* cannot stand alone as a sentence in standard written English.

### Examples

When my brother finishes at Queens College, . . .

Since my sister loves science, . . .

. . . because she studies hard.

If she continues getting good grades, . . .

Dependent clauses must be attached to independent clauses.

When my brother finishes at Queens College, he is going to transfer to Columbia University.

Since my sister loves science, she wants to get into a good pre-med program.

She gets good grades because she studies hard.

If she continues getting good grades, I am sure she will succeed.

Most dependent clauses are introduced by a subordinator. Common subordinators include the following:

| TIME | CAUSE/EFFECT | CONDITION | CONTRAST | PURPOSE |
| --- | --- | --- | --- | --- |
| when | because | if | even though | so that |
| after | since | unless | although | |
| before | | | though | |
| while | | | | |
| as soon as | | | | |
| whenever | | | | |
| until | | | | |
| as | | | | |
| just as | | | | |

 **Exercise A**   Writing Independent and Dependent Clauses

Using information from "Home Sweet Home," the sample paragraph presented at the beginning of the chapter, write the missing clause.

### Part A

1. Danny loved the gypsy trailer especially in the evenings when _____
   _____.

2. While his father was telling him stories, _____
   _____.

3. Danny felt wonderful in his bed because _____
   _____.

### Part B

Now, write about your experience reading the paragraph by filling in the missing clauses.

4. I felt like Danny when _____
   _____.

5. I enjoyed reading about Danny because _____
   _____.

# SENTENCE TYPES

 **Essential Information: THREE BASIC SENTENCE TYPES**

English has three basic sentence types—simple, compound, and complex—depending on the clauses they contain.

A *simple sentence* has one independent clause.

Magic Mountain is an amusement park in Valencia, California.

It has a lot of scary rides.

A *compound sentence* has two independent clauses connected by a coordinator. Common *coordinators* include the following:

and        but        so

I didn't want to ride on Free Fall, but my sister convinced me.

She rode it first, so I agreed to ride it.

A *complex sentence* has one independent clause and one (or more) dependent clause(s).

When the ride started, I panicked.

If I ever return to Magic Mountain, I will go without my sister.

 **Writing Assignment:** *A Visit to an Amusement Park*

Write a paragraph about a visit to an amusement park or a similar place. Start your paragraph with a topic sentence that identifies the place and how you felt about it. (Suggested details include when you went, who you went with, and other relevant information.) Support your topic sentence with plenty of specific details. Write a concluding sentence that gives a feeling of finish to your paragraph.

# SIMPLE AND COMPOUND SENTENCES

 **Exercise** Identifying Simple and Compound Sentences—The Child's Nest

The following is based on Alice Taylor's autobiography *To School Through the Fields*. The author is telling about her childhood in rural Ireland and describing her family.

Identify the sentences as *simple* (S) or *compound* (CD). Write *S* or *CD* in the blank after each sentence. As a reminder, a simple sentence may have a compound subject or a compound verb.

## The Child's Nest

Our parents were a blend of opposites. __S__ My mother was kind and

gentle. _____ She had a far-seeing wisdom and expected only the best from her

fellow human beings. _____ My father was a man with a high level of intelli-

gence, but he had a low level of tolerance. _____ Patience was not one of his

°**virtues:** good qualities of
people

virtues°. _____ He loved trees, birds, and all his farm animals. _____ He appreci-

ated nature to the fullest, but he viewed his fellow human beings with a suspi-

cious eye. _____ He never expected too much from them. _____

There were seven children in the family, and we grew up as free as birds.

_____ We were far away from the outside influence of the city, so we grew up in

a world of simplicity. _____ Our farm was our world, and nature was our educa-

tor. _____ We absorbed the natural order of things and were free to grow up at

our own pace in a quiet place close to the earth. _____

---

 **Writing Assignment:** *Describing Your Parents*

Write about your parents' personalities. If they are similar, explain their similarities. If they are different, explain their differences. As an alternative, write
about two other people you know well, such as brothers, sisters, cousins, or close
friends.

Start your paragraph with a topic sentence that shows whether you are
writing about your parents' similarities or differences. Support your topic sentence
with plenty of specific details. Write a concluding sentence that gives a feeling of
finish to your paragraph.

 **Essential Information: COMBINING SIMPLE
SENTENCES INTO COMPOUND SENTENCES**

In order to create a compound sentence, combine simple sentences (independent
clauses) into one sentence that has two clauses with a coordinator between them.

| Simple Sentence | + | Coordinator | + | Simple Sentence |
|---|---|---|---|---|
| | | ,and | | |
| Independent clause | | ,but | | Independent clause |
| | | ,so | | |

*and* = the addition of a closely related idea

*but* = contrasting ideas

*so* = result

A comma usually appears before the coordinator in compound sentences.

### Examples

My father had a quick sense of humor.
The family loved his jokes.

My father had a quick sense of humor, and the family loved his jokes.

My father had a degree from UCLA.
My mother did not finish college.

My father had a degree from UCLA, but my mother did not finish college.

My mother valued education.
She took night classes.

My mother valued education, so she took night classes.

### *Relevant Information: Avoiding Several Independent Clauses in One Sentence*

Which of the following examples is better, and why?

1. My father had a degree from UCLA, but my mother did not finish college, and my mother valued education, so she took night classes.

2. My father had a degree from UCLA, but my mother did not finish college. My mother valued education, so she took night classes.

Your answer: _____

 **Exercise**   Combining Simple Sentences into Compound Sentences

The following sentences are from Yoko Kawashima Watkins' *So Far from the Bamboo Grove*. In this passage, the author is describing her family's rushed preparations to flee in the middle of the night from the Communists.

Write the sentences in paragraph form on a separate piece of paper, combining appropriate sentences. Start your paragraph with a topic sentence such as the following: I was completely confused.

°**dragged:** pulled along

°**staggered:** walked unsteadily, stumbled
°**yanked:** pulled suddenly

1. I dragged° six canteens toward the kitchen.
2. My head was dizzy.
3. I staggered°.
4. Ko yanked° the canteens from me.
5. She rushed to the kitchen pump.
6. I tried to walk toward the entrance to grab my emergency bag.
7. I seemed to be on a boat on an angry sea.

**Essential Information: RELATED IDEAS
IN COMPOUND SENTENCES**

The ideas you combine into the same sentence should be logically related. Study the following examples and discuss the differences between *related* and *not related* ideas with your classmates.

Not related

> My father just turned sixty-five, and my sister plays tennis on the weekends.

Related

> My father just turned sixty-five, and he's still active in sports. He plays soccer twice a week. My sister is also athletic. She plays tennis on the weekends, and she's on a volleyball team.

Not related

> My brother is a very busy stockbroker, and he has a dog named Big Bucks.

Related

> My brother is a very busy stockbroker, but he takes time to relax on the weekends. His favorite way to relax is to take his dog Big Bucks on long walks, and he also unwinds by listening to classical music.

 **Exercise**  Logically Related Ideas

Identify the sentences that contain logically related ideas. Write *OK* for good sentences and *NO* for not okay.

*No*  1. My mother is an attorney, and my sister is a teenager.

_____  2. My mother is an attorney, and she enjoys her work.

_____  3. My sister is a teenager, and she went to Sea World last year.

_____  4. My sister is a teenager, and she attends Lincoln High School.

_____  5. My sister loves marine animals, so she went to Sea World last year.

_____  6. My brother is a snake trainer, but he hates fried chicken.

_____  7. My brother likes fried snake, but he hates fried chicken.

# ≡ COMPLEX SENTENCES

 **Essential Information: COMBINING IDEAS
INTO COMPLEX SENTENCES**

An excellent way to combine ideas and express them well in college-level writing is to write complex sentences. To create a complex sentence, use two clauses in one sentence. One is independent, and the other is dependent.

<pre>        dependent                       independent</pre>

1.  When my parents moved to Los Angeles, **they lived with my grandparents for a few months.**

<pre>        independent                     dependent</pre>

2.  **Later, they moved to the suburbs** because they did not like the city.

<pre>        dependent                       independent</pre>

3.  After my family settled in Manhattan Beach, **I was born.**

---

## Writing Assignment: *A Childhood Relationship*

Write about a sister, a brother, a cousin, or another relative who was important to you in your childhood. (As an option, you may write about a close friend.) Describe your relationship with this person, and explain why this person was important to you. Tell about this person's personality and include activities you did together.

Start your paragraph with a topic sentence that names the person and explains what this person's relationship to you was/is. Support your topic sentence with plenty of specific details. Write a concluding sentence that gives a feeling of finish to your paragraph. Your instructor may ask you to make sure to include several compound and complex sentences.

**Exercise**   Identifying Clauses in Complex Sentences—
"The Most Important Endangered Species"

Circle the independent clauses in the following passage. Underline the dependent clauses.

### The Most Important Endangered Species

°**vital:** absolutely necessary

Plants are vital° to human existence. When most people see "endangered species," they think of animals. We sympathize with animals because they live 2 and breathe and have families. Whenever an animal species is endangered, people become very worried. In contrast, when we "kill" plants, no one seems 4 concerned. However, many plants are on the endangered list because humans have changed the plants' environment. Plants are important because they 6

°**convert:** change

convert° the sun's energy into food. Also, when the leaves of trees in tropical regions breathe, they send large amounts of water into the air. Furthermore, 8 we need plants because they produce oxygen. If we kill all our plants, animal life will cease. 10

**Essential Information: THE ORDER OF CLAUSES IN COMPLEX SENTENCES**

Refer back to the previous exercise with complex sentences. In some sentences, the independent clause is first. In other sentences, the dependent clause is first. Either order is acceptable.

1. Animal life will cease if we kill all our plants.

2. If we kill all our plants, animal life will cease.

As a general rule, if the dependent clause comes before the independent clause, a comma is used between the clauses. If the independent clause comes before the dependent clause, however, no comma is used.

| Independent clause | Dependent clause. |
|---|---|

OR

| Dependent clause | , | Independent clause. |
|---|---|---|

 **Exercise A**   Identifying Sentence Types—Proverbs

Identify the following sentences as S = simple, CD = compound, or CX = complex.

1. __*CX*__ When I had money, everyone called me brother. (Polish proverb)

2. _____ Chance makes our parents, but choice makes our friends. (Delille)

3. _____ The best is the cheapest. (Ben Franklin)

4. _____ Speech is silver, and silence is golden. (German proverb)

5. _____ There's no place like home. (J. Howard Payne)

6. _____ If you're not jealous, you're not in love. (St. Augustine)

7. _____ Strong and bitter words indicate a weak cause. (Victor Hugo)

°**bayonet:** knife at the end of a rifle

8. _____ I fear three newspapers more than a hundred thousand bayonets°. (Napoleon)

9. _____ You should never answer a letter while you're angry. (Chinese proverb)

10. _____ If you throw a lucky man into the sea, he will come up with a fish in his mouth. (Arab proverb)

11. _____ If you want to be a writer, write. (Epictetus)

12. _____ Prejudice° is the child of ignorance°. (William Hazlitt)

13. _____ I have made this letter longer than usual because I don't have the time to make it shorter. (Pascal)

14. _____ Our true nationality is humankind. (H. G. Wells, *The Outline of History*)

°**prejudice:** unfavorable opinion for no good reason
°**ignorance:** not knowing

## Writing Assignment: *Writing about a Proverb*

Select one of the proverbs from the previous exercise and write a paragraph to explain what this proverb means to you. Start your paragraph with a topic sentence that gives the proverb and the general meaning. Put quotation marks around the proverb.

### Examples

The Vietnamese proverb "A needle wrapped in a rag will be found in the end" means that sooner or later all lies are discovered.

"Helping each other, even boys can hold back a lion" (Ethiopian proverb) reminds us of the importance of cooperating with each other in order to accomplish difficult goals.

Support your topic sentence with plenty of specific details. Write a concluding sentence that gives a feeling of finish to your paragraph.

**Exercise B**   Writing Simple, Compound, and Complex Sentences—
*So Far from the Bamboo Grove*

The following sentences are from Yoko Kawashima Watkins' *So Far from the Bamboo Grove*. In this passage, the author is describing her escape from the Communists in North Korea. She is traveling in a hospital train with her family. Only Yoko and her family have enough food.

On a separate piece of paper, write the following sentences in paragraph form. Combine the sentences that appear in the same number.

1. Somehow that day passed.

2. Evening came. I was hungry.

3. I had eaten nothing since leaving home.

4. I fumbled° through my sack. Mother stopped me.

5. The others, too, had not eaten in all that time. It would not be fair to them if I ate.

°**fumbled:** looked for carelessly

**Exercise C**   Writing Compound and Complex Sentences—
"The Unicorn in the Garden"

Combine the following pairs of simple sentences. Write your answers in paragraph form on a separate piece of paper. Most of the resulting sentences will be compound and complex. Answers will vary.

°**irony:** opposite result from what is expected

°**unicorn:** imaginary horse-like animal with one horn

Irony° in the Story "The Unicorn° in the Garden"

*Topic sentence:* James Thurber's "The Unicorn in the Garden" is an imaginative short story with a humorous, surprise ending.

1. The husband looks out his window one sunny morning. He sees a unicorn in the garden. *The husband looks out his window one sunny morning and sees a unicorn in the garden.*

2. He tells his wife about the unicorn. She doesn't believe him.

3. The husband speaks politely. The wife answers very rudely.

°**psychiatrist:** medical doctor who treats mental illnesses

4. The husband leaves. The wife calls the police and a psychiatrist°.

5. She is very excited. She wants to get rid of her husband.

6. The police and the psychiatrist arrive. They ask some questions.

7. They ask the husband about the unicorn. He denies everything about this mythical animal.

8. They take the wife away. They think she is the crazy person.

9. I really enjoyed "The Unicorn in the Garden." The ending is so ironical.

10. I was expecting the police and the psychiatrist to take the man away. They end up taking the wife away instead.

11. I also like the ending. The rude wife doesn't succeed in her plan to get rid of her husband.

12. He's polite. She's rude.

13. She gets what she deserves. He lives happily ever after.

# ADDITIONAL INFORMATION ON USING COORDINATORS AND SUBORDINATORS

 **Essential Information: CORRECTING A COMMON MISUSE**

Do not use both a coordinator and a subordinator to connect two clauses.

 The following sentences are *not correct*:

    subordinator                  coordinator
       |                                |
\**Although* my mother spoke Tagalog, *but* my father did not.

      subordinator                  coordinator
        |                               |
\**Even though* my father had a college degree, *but* my mother did not.

The following sentences are *correct*:

  subordinator
     |
*Although* my mother spoke Tagalog, my father did not.

                coordinator
                  |
My mother spoke Tagalog, *but* my father did not.

   subordinator
     |
*Even though* my father had a college degree, my mother did not.

             coordinator
             |
My father had a college degree, *but* my mother did not.

 **Exercise** Editing for Correct Use of Coordinators and Subordinators

Edit the following.

1. Although my father was a man of high intelligence, ~~but~~ he had a low level of tolerance.

2. Even though my father appreciated nature, he viewed his fellow human beings with a suspicious eye.

3. My brother likes fried snake, but he hates fried chicken.

4. Although my sister is a very busy lawyer, but she takes time to relax on the weekends.

5. Even though my grandparents never went to school, but they managed to learn enough English to get by.

---

## REVIEW: SIMPLE, COMPOUND, AND COMPLEX SENTENCES

 **Exercise**   Writing about Your Home and Family

At the beginning of this chapter you read about Danny and his father in their tiny trailer home. Write six sentences about your family and home. Make the first two simple sentences, the second two compound sentences, and the last two complex sentences.

When you finish, exchange your work with a partner, and check your partner's sentences. (Check only for the correct sentence type. Do not worry about other kinds of errors for now.)

Simple:

1. _____

2. _____

Compound:

3. _____

4. _____

Complex:

5. _____

6. _____

---

## CHAPTER REVIEW

 **Exercise**   A Lesson in Salesmanship

Combine the following pairs of simple sentences. Write your answers in paragraph form on a separate piece of paper. Most of the resulting sentences will be compound and complex. Answers will vary.

A Lesson in Salesmanship

*Topic Sentence:* According to the old English proverb, "A fool and his money are soon parted."

1. Someone reminded me of this proverb recently. It made me think of my cousin Hank.

2. Hank's mother died not long ago. She left him a dining room set along with a few other items.

3. He didn't want to sell the set. He really needed the money.

4. He decided on a low price. He wanted to sell it fast.

5. He put an ad in the newspaper. He got a few calls.

6. A minister from a neighborhood church called. He asked about the furniture.

7. Apparently, his church needed a table and chair set very badly. The church members were donating money.

8. Hank was asking $200. The minister could pay only $120.

9. My cousin agreed to consider this low price. The minister sounded very kind.

10. The minister and another person came to look at the table. They were very friendly.

11. My cousin began to feel embarrassed about asking money from a minister. He donated the table and chairs to the church.

12. The people left. Hank called the church.

13. He offered the lady on the phone another chair to go with the dining room set. She sounded confused.

14. She then handed the phone to the minister. He said that something was wrong.

15. The church didn't need any furniture. He hadn't left the church at all that day.

16. Now, I don't really think my cousin was a fool. Maybe he was a little too trusting.

 **Writing Assignment:** *A Teacher You Had in the Past*

Write a paragraph about a teacher you had in elementary school or high school. Start your paragraph with a topic sentence that identifies the teacher, the school level, and your feeling about the experience. Support your topic sentence with plenty of specific details. Write a concluding sentence that gives a feeling of finish to your paragraph.

**Example Topic Sentence**

Mr. Lee was the most hard-working teacher I had during my high school years.

## FOOD FOR THOUGHT

True or false?

All sentences are clauses, and all clauses are sentences.

Your answer: _____

## CLASSROOM ASSESSMENT TECHNIQUE (CAT)

### THE ONE-MINUTE PAPER

Take a minute or two to write answers to the following questions. Write your answers on a separate piece of paper without your name.

1. What are the most important points that you have learned in this chapter?

2. What questions remain in your mind at the end of this chapter?

*Note: Use this exercise to help you get answers to any questions you still have. Ask these questions to anyone who might be able to help you, such as another student or your instructor.*

# Run-On Sentences and Sentence Fragments

---

## ≡ RUN-ON SENTENCES

▶ **Sample Paragraph**

Read the following paragraph about a student who considers it important to include exercise in his schedule. Underline any errors.

**Too Busy to Exercise**

Last Friday I didn't have enough time for everything on my schedule.

That morning the alarm rang at 6:00, I jumped right out of bed. Then I got

2

dressed and ran out the door. I got to school late, I couldn't find a parking

place. I parked five blocks from campus. I had to walk quickly with a heavy          4

book bag I got tired fast. After school I raced to my car, I had to go to work

at McBuns. At work, my boss told me to work overtime. For the next nine          6

hours, I fried hamburger patties and unloaded delivery trucks. I didn't get

home until 9:30 that night. My body ached I felt terrible. I was disappointed,          8

I didn't have time to go to karate practice.

 ## Essential Information: CORRECT SENTENCES VERSUS RUN-ON SENTENCES

The three basic sentence types are simple, compound, and complex.

> Simple sentence—one independent clause
>
> > My brother and I are taking an elementary writing class together.
> >
> > The class meets twice a week.
> >
> > It starts at 10:00 and ends at 12:20.
>
> Compound sentence—two or more independent clauses connected by a coordinator
>
> > We arrive five to ten minutes early, and the instructor arrives a little before 10:00.
>
> Complex sentence—one independent clause and one (or more) dependent clause(s)
>
> > When the instructor arrives, she takes the roll.
> >
> > She starts the lesson as soon as the students are ready to begin.

For a list of common subordinators, see page 28. If you connect two clauses correctly, you will have either a compound sentence or a complex sentence. If you connect two clauses incorrectly, you will have a run-on sentence.

> A run-on sentence consists of two (or more) independent clauses without correct punctuation between them.

### Run-on sentences

> *We arrive five to ten minutes early, the instructor arrives a little before 10:00.
>
> *The instructor arrives, she takes the attendance.
>
> *She starts the lesson the students are ready to begin.

***Note:*** *See the previous examples for the corrected versions of these run-ons.*

**Exercise**   Identifying Run-On Sentences—"The Unicorn in the Garden"

The following paragraph is a summary of James Thurber's short story "The Unicorn in the Garden." Some sentences are correct. Others are run-on sentences. Write the symbol *RO* over the place where the two clauses are joined incorrectly.

### Irony° in the Story "The Unicorn° in the Garden"

°**irony:** opposite result from what is expected

°**unicorn:** imaginary horse-like animal with one horn

°**psychiatrist:** medical doctor who treats mental illnesses

James Thurber's "The Unicorn in the Garden" is an imaginative short

story with a humorous, surprise ending. The husband looks out his window     2

one sunny morning *RO* he sees a unicorn in the garden. He tells his wife about

the unicorn, she doesn't believe him. Even though the husband speaks politely,   4

the wife answers very rudely. As soon as the husband leaves, the wife calls the

police and a psychiatrist°. She is very excited, she wants to get rid of her hus-   6

band. When the police and the psychiatrist arrive, they ask some questions.

They ask the husband about the unicorn, he denies everything about this       8

mythical animal. They take the wife away they think she is the crazy person.

I really enjoyed "The Unicorn in the Garden" because the ending is so ironical.   10

I was expecting the police and the psychiatrist to take the man away, they end

up taking the wife away instead. I also like the ending because the rude wife    12

doesn't succeed in her plan to get rid of her husband. He's polite, but she's

rude. She gets what she deserves, he lives happily ever after.                  14

**Essential Information: CORRECTING RUN-ON SENTENCES**

A run-on sentence consists of independent clauses with

1. NO PUNCTUATION

   or

2. ONLY A COMMA between them.

You can correct run-on sentences in the following ways.

**Run-On Sentences**

| | |
|---|---|
| *He's polite she's rude. | ERROR |
| *He's polite, she's rude. | ERROR |

1. CREATE TWO SIMPLE SENTENCES:

   He's polite. She's rude.          CORRECT

2. CREATE A COMPOUND SENTENCE:

   He's polite, but she's rude.          CORRECT

3. CREATE A COMPLEX SENTENCE:

   Even though he's polite, she's rude.          CORRECT

 **Exercise A**   Correcting Run-On Sentences

Go back to the paragraph at the beginning of the chapter, "Too Busy to Exercise." On a separate piece of paper, rewrite the paragraph with the corrections.

 **Exercise B**   Correcting Run-On Sentences

Go back to the exercise in the preceding section—"The Unicorn in the Garden." On a separate piece of paper, rewrite the paragraph with the corrections.

 **Exercise C**   Identifying and Correcting Run-Ons—"The Thrill of So Many Beautiful Cars"

**Part One**

Read the following paragraph, and identify the run-on sentences. Write *RO* above the place where the clauses are connected incorrectly. (One "sentence" has two run-ons.) Later, your instructor may ask you to do Part Two—rewriting the paragraph without the run-ons.

°**thrill:** excitement

°**amazement:** great surprise

### The Thrill° of So Many Beautiful Cars

My first reaction to Los Angeles was amazement° at all the gorgeous cars.

My uncle picked me up in a huge Cadillac. The back seat was enormous, it felt          2 so comfortable. We left the airport, I became fascinated with the traffic. My

uncle told me to look out back, I didn't see anything at first, then a shiny blue      4

Porsche sped past us. We got off the freeway, I continued to be interested in

all the glamorous automobiles. We were waiting at a red light, I looked out       6

the window and saw nothing but huge tires. I looked up and saw a gigantic

pickup truck. The pickup then made a right-hand turn, I was captivated even      8

after it disappeared. Soon we drove up to my uncle's house and parked in

front. My uncle was curious, he asked me how I liked the United States so far.      10

I answered, "I'm already in love with this country," my eyes weren't meeting

his. My heart was pounding, my attention was glued to a silver gray Mercedes      12

that was driving smoothly past us.

### Part Two

Rewrite the paragraph "The Thrill of So Many Beautiful Cars" on a separate piece
of paper. Correct the run-on sentences by creating simple, compound, or complex sentences.

## Writing Assignment A: *Your First Impressions of a New Environment*

Write about your first reactions to or your first impressions of a new environment.
This new environment may be a new city or a new country. Start your paragraph
with a topic sentence that identifies the new place and includes your reaction to
or impression of the place. Support your topic sentence with plenty of specific
details. Write a concluding sentence that gives a feeling of finish to your
paragraph.

### Exercise D   Correcting Run-Ons—Sightseeing in Toronto

Edit the following passage. Find the run-on sentences, and mark them with *RO*
above the place where the sentences are joined incorrectly. Next, on a separate
piece of paper rewrite the paragraph correctly with simple, compound, or complex
sentences.

### Sightseeing in Toronto

°**landmark:** easily recognized object such as a
building

Toronto, Canada, has several fascinating places to visit. The first landmark°

you will notice in Toronto is the CN Tower, it's the tallest free-standing building      2

in the world. The view is spectacular from the CN Building's Space Deck, for

example, on a clear day you can see Niagara Falls. Next, the Metro Toronto Zoo      4

has a modern idea for zoos. The emphasis is on showing nature as a whole, here you can see the animals in their natural environment. The African Pavilion is          6

°**greenhouse:** glass building for growing plants

the largest and most interesting, it is like being inside a huge greenhouse°.

Another place worth visiting is the Royal Ontario Museum. This famous          8

museum was once part of the University of Toronto, it's now independent.

°**archaeology:** study of how people lived in the past

At the Royal Ontario Museum the visitors can enjoy art, archaeology°, and the          10

natural sciences. These are just a few of the many exciting places to visit and

enjoy in Toronto.          12

 **Writing Assignment B:** *Sightseeing*

Write about a city or tourist spot that you have visited, and describe places you enjoyed. Start your paragraph with a topic sentence that identifies the city or tourist spot and how you felt about the places you visited there. Support your topic sentence with information about three specific places. Use plenty of supporting details. Write a concluding sentence that gives a feeling of finish to your paragraph.

## ☰    REVIEW: RUN-ON SENTENCES    ☰

 **Exercise A**   Identifying Run-On Sentences—"Living in an Apartment"

Write *RO* above the incorrect punctuation in run-on sentences.

### Living in an Apartment

People often ask me why my family and I would rather live in an apart-

ment than a house. First, we can't afford to live in a house. In my family, only          2

my father works, so we have to save money by living in an apartment. The rent

is reasonable, we don't pay for the water. Next, we feel much safer about living          4

in an apartment than we would in a house. One of my father's friends who lives

in a house has gotten robbed several times, so we like the idea of having neigh-          6

bors in the same building. When we go out, we ask our neighbors to keep an

eye on our place, we don't want to take any chances. Finally, we don't have to          8

spend our time keeping the apartment in good condition. When something is

broken, we call the manager to fix it. Also, we don't have to mow the lawn,          10

when the manager thinks it's necessary, he does it. For these reasons, we like living in our apartment, we think living in an apartment is especially good for          12

newcomers to the United States.

Adapted from a paragraph by Min Jung Kim

 **Exercise B**   Correcting Run-Ons—"To Risk and Live Freely"

Edit the following passage. Find the run-on sentences, and correct them by creating simple, compound, or complex sentences. Your instructor may ask you to do this as an editing exercise. Or your instructor may ask you to rewrite the corrected paragraph on a separate piece of paper.

°**risk:** take a chance

"To Risk° and Live Freely"

In Tim Timmons' article "To Risk and Live Freely," the author describes

several ways people can take risks in life. His main idea is that we must take          2

risks in order to enjoy life to its fullest. In my own life I can see how risk has

played a big part, for example, learning how to drive was a major risk for me.          4

When I was in Egypt, I didn't drive, it's shameful for a woman to drive in Egypt.

Also, the traffic is terrible, the drivers don't follow the traffic rules. I moved to          6

California, I promised myself to take a risk and learn how to drive. Immediately,

I started saving money for a car, I began studying the traffic laws. I even went          8

to driving school, in two months I passed the course. Shortly after that, I got my

license. As a result, driving gives me the freedom to go to school, get a job, and          10

shop at my convenience, I'm an independent person now. Most importantly,

 this small success has given me greater confidence in myself and my future in          12

my new country. It has also proved to me the wisdom of Tim Timmons' philoso-

phy and shown me that I must continue to take risks in life in order to live the          14

best I possibly can.

Adapted from a paragraph by Enas Shafik

## ≡ SENTENCE FRAGMENTS

▶ ### Sample Paragraph

Read the following paragraph. The groups of words in italic letters are *not sentences.*

A Reaction to "To Risk and Live Freely"

In Tim Timmons' article "To Risk and Live Freely," the author insists that
a person should take risks in life in order to live freely and successfully. I abso-

lutely agree with this philosophy. *Because of my experience when my younger sister and I were in elementary school.* Giving money to young children is a risk for parents. However, my parents took the risk and gave us an allowance once a month to train us to spend the money usefully. Needless to say, when we got the money the first month, *spent it all on useless things. Such as junk food.* As time passed by, though, we learned how to spend our money wisely. *And even how to save a portion of it.* If our parents hadn't taken the risk, we wouldn't have learned this valuable lesson. As Tim Timmons suggests, taking a risk might lead a person to a good result, but not taking a risk leads to no result at all.

Adapted from a paragraph by Min Jung Kim

## MISSING SUBJECT FRAGMENTS

 **Essential Information: MISSING SUBJECTS IN INDEPENDENT CLAUSES**

With your classmates, discuss the following **incomplete** and **complete sentences**.

Incomplete

> Chris Evert took the tennis championship away from Billie Jean King. *After that, became the top all-around female athlete.

Complete

> Chris Evert took the tennis championship away from Billie Jean King. After that, she became the top all-around female athlete.

Incomplete

> Bruce Lee was an outstanding talent in the martial arts. *Combined the Chinese yin/yang principle with the sport. *Also started his own movie production studio.

Complete

> Bruce Lee was an outstanding talent in the martial arts. He combined the Chinese yin/yang principle with the sport. He also started his own movie production studio.

What is missing in the incomplete sentences above?

_____

 **Exercise**  Adding Missing Subjects—Pele

**Part One**

Edit the following paragraph.

### Pele

Pele is one of the most famous soccer stars in history. *He c*ame from a poor

family. Was born on October 23, 1940, in a small town in Brazil. All the people   2 in the town were poor. Didn't have enough money to buy food every day. Of

course, was not enough money to buy a soccer ball. But Pele's father was very     4

inventive. Tied some old clothing together to form a ball. The young Pele and

the other boys in the neighborhood joyfully played soccer with this rag ball.     6

Played barefoot until the sun went down every day. Later, Pele played soccer

on an organized team. Soon became the best player on the team. Before Pele     8

turned thirty, became a millionaire.

**Part Two**
Rewrite the paragraph about Pele on a separate piece of paper, adding the missing
subjects.

 **Essential Information: MISSING SUBJECTS
IN DEPENDENT CLAUSES**

With your classmates, discuss the differences between the following **incomplete**
and **complete** sentences.

Incomplete

   *Pele became a millionaire before turned thirty.

Complete

   Pele became a millionaire before he turned thirty.

What is missing in the incomplete sentence above?

_____

> Every clause in English must have a visible subject.

 **Exercise**   Missing Subjects in Dependent Clauses—A Boring Job

Amado Muro describes a job he had as a teenager in the following adaptation from
his short story "Cecilia Rosas." Edit the paragraph.

### A Boring Job

   I got a job hanging up women's coats at La Feria Department Store when $\overset{I}{\wedge}$

was in the ninth grade at Bowie High School in El Paso. It wasn't the kind of     2

job that had much appeal for a Mexican boy or for boys of any other nationality

either. The work was really boring although gave me some spending money.     4

I stood around the Ladies' Wear Department all day waiting for customers to

finish trying on coats so could hang them up.     6

**Essential Information: MISSING SUBJECTS
IN ADJECTIVE CLAUSES**

Read the following sentences taken from Judy Brady's "I Want a Wife." The
adjective clauses appear in italics.

1.  I want a wife *who will pick up after me.*

2.  I want a wife *who cooks the meals.*

3.  I want a wife *who will keep my house clean.*

4.  I want a wife *who takes care of the children when they are sick.*

Like other clauses, adjective clauses must have both a *subject* and a *verb*. What word
serves as the subject in the adjective clauses in the previous examples? _____

The following words are used as subjects in adjective clauses:

    that = for people or things

     who = for people

   which = for things

*Note: Some instructors recommend using* who *for people and* that *for things.*

### Examples

Ronald Reagan is the only American president *who* used to be a movie
actor.

The Smithsonian is a group of over twelve museums *that* contains a large
collection of historical items.

If the subject is missing, the clause is incomplete. It's a fragment. The following
sentence contains a missing subject fragment.

*Susan B. Anthony was a reformer fought for women's rights. (The subject
*who* is missing.)

Here is the correct sentence.

Susan B. Anthony was a reformer *who* fought for women's rights.

 **Exercise**   Missing Subjects in Adjective Clauses—Cultural Literacy

Edit the following sentences. Add the missing *who*, *that*, or *which*, as necessary.

*Note: Some instructors may recommend using only* who *or* that *in this exercise.*

### Example

who

The only American president˄resigned from office was Richard Nixon.

1. The Peace Corps is an agency *that* sends American volunteers to work in foreign countries.

2. Uncle Sam is a figure represents the government of the United States.

3. The person caused the first major incident of the civil rights movement was Rosa Parks.

4. Franklin D. Roosevelt is the only president served four terms.

5. Al Capone killed any man opposed him.

6. The draft is a system enrolls young men for possible military service.

7. Helen Keller was a blind and deaf author showed tremendous courage throughout her life.

8. Watergate was the incident led to Richard Nixon's resignation.

9. Margaret Mead was an American anthropologist revolutionized her field.

10. Lee Iacocca is an American businessman became extremely successful.

11. Ralph Nader is a lawyer with an Arabic background became a supporter of consumer rights.

# DEPENDENT CLAUSE FRAGMENTS

 **Essential Information: DEPENDENT CLAUSES AS SENTENCE FRAGMENTS**

In conversations, people often use dependent clauses as sentences because they are involved in a dialogue. Notice what Bob says in this dialogue:

*Amy:* Why are you looking so sad?

**Bob:** **Because I messed up on my history test.**

*Amy:* How do you know?

**Bob:** **Because Joe, the class genius, said my answers were all wrong.**

*Amy:* When will you know for sure?

**Bob:** **When I get the test back on Monday.**

The use of dependent clauses in conversation is common because the other person supplies the independent clauses in the questions. In writing, however, there is only one person communicating ideas. Therefore, dependent clauses cannot normally exist as sentences in standard written English. They must be joined to independent clauses to form complex sentences.

> A dependent clause standing alone is a sentence fragment. It must be joined to an independent clause to form a complete sentence.

The following examples are correct sentences based on the above dialogue:

> I'm looking sad *because I messed up on my history test.*

> I know *because Joe said my answers were all wrong.*

> I'll know for sure *when I get the test back on Monday.*

 **Exercise A**   Identifying Dependent Clause Fragments

Are the following groups of words sentences or fragments?

**Part One**

Write *C* or *F* on the line before each number.

C = correct

F = fragment

_F_   1. When I go on vacation.

_____   2. I like to have plenty of money.

_____   3. Nice hotels are expensive.

_____   4. When I stay in a cheap hotel, I don't feel comfortable.

_____   5. Because they are often on noisy streets.

_____   6. I don't sleep well.

_____   7. When I don't sleep well.

_____   8. I can't enjoy daytime activities such as sightseeing, shopping, and visiting museums.

_____   9. If you don't have plenty of money for your vacation.

_____ 10. Stay at home.

_____ 11. Until you save up enough for an enjoyable trip.

**Part Two**

On a separate piece of paper, write the sentences in the previous exercise in paragraph form. Combine sentences where possible. Give your paragraph the title "Think Twice."

 **Writing Assignment: *Your Worst Vacation or Trip***

Write about your worst (or one of your worst) vacations or trips. Start your paragraph with a topic sentence that identifies the vacation or trip and tells how you feel about it. Support your topic sentence with plenty of specific details. Write a concluding sentence that gives a feeling of finish to your paragraph.

**Exercise B**    Editing for Dependent Clause Fragments—My Algebra Test

Edit the following paragraph for dependent clause fragments. On a separate piece of paper, rewrite the paragraph with the corrections.

### My Algebra Test

I didn't do well on my algebra test. *Frag* Because I didn't have enough time to study. When I got home yesterday afternoon. There was a message on my        2

answering machine. My boss wanted me to work that evening. Because one of

my co-workers was sick. If this situation happens again. I will tell my boss "no!"    4

 **Essential Information: ADJECTIVE CLAUSES AS DEPENDENT CLAUSE FRAGMENTS**

Earlier, you practiced adjective clauses with subjects and verbs.

                              S       V

Al Capone killed any man *who opposed* him.

Adjective clauses, like other dependent clauses, must be attached to independent clauses. If not, a fragment will result. Read the following examples of fragments. The adjective clauses are in italics.

1.  *The things *that hit my leg*.

2.  *The male snake *that showed up the next day*.

The adjective clauses in the above examples contain a subject and a verb, but they are not attached to independent clauses. Read the following corrected fragments. The adjective clauses are in italics.

1.  The things *that hit my leg* were snake eggs.

2.  The male snake *that showed up the next day* was the father.

 **Exercise A**    Identifying Adjective Clause Fragments

Underline the adjective clause fragments.

1.  The house <u>that my neighbors bought.</u>

2.  The apartment that my cousin moved into has two bedrooms.

3.  The condominium that I'd like to buy.

4.  The room that my cousin rents.

5.  The townhouse that my sister and her husband just sold.

**Exercise B**   Correcting Adjective Clause Fragments—
Using Your Imagination

Correct the following fragments by completing the sentences. These are silly sentences with crazy ideas. Have fun and use your imagination.

### Example

The dinosaur that was jogging on the beach *was wearing a yellow polka dot bikini.*

1.  The spaceship that landed in my back yard

    _____

2.  The snake lips that we ate

    _____

3.  The king who came to dinner at my house last night

    _____

4.  The teenager who became president of the United States

    _____

Now write your own silly sentences. Include an adjective clause in each sentence.

5.  _____

6.  _____

# ADDED DETAIL FRAGMENTS

 **Essential Information: ADDED DETAIL FRAGMENTS**

Another type of fragment occurs when a writer wishes to add details. If the writer puts the details in a group of words without its own subject and verb in a "sentence" of its own, a fragment results.

### Examples

1.  It's not unusual for a person born into a poor family eventually to become rich. *For example, Pele. (fragment)

    It's not unusual for a person born into a poor family eventually to become rich. For example, Pele was born into poverty and later became a millionaire. (correct)

2.  Pele kicked the ball. *Into the goal. (fragment)

    Pele kicked the ball into the goal. (correct)

Notice that in the first corrected example, a verb and other information were added to the subject "Pele." In the second example, the phrase with details was simply added to the previous sentence.

**Exercise** Correcting Added Detail Fragments

Rewrite any of the following that have added detail fragments.

1. Muhammad Ali was born Cassius Clay on January 17, 1942. In Louisville, Kentucky.

   *Muhammad Ali was born Cassius Clay on January 17, 1942,*

   *in Louisville, Kentucky.*

2. Cassius showed an early interest in boxing. For example, by taking boxing lessons when he was twelve years old.

   _____

   _____

3. In 1960 Cassius won a gold medal in boxing at the Olympics in Rome. This success launched him into a career in professional boxing.

   _____

   _____

4. In 1964 Cassius became the world champion heavyweight boxer. Beating Sonny Liston in the sixth round.

   _____

   _____

5. Then in a rematch, he beat Liston again. This time by a knockout in the first round.

   _____

   _____

6. Soon afterward, Cassius became a Black Muslim. And changed his name to Muhammad Ali.

   _____

   _____

 **REVIEW: FRAGMENTS**

 **Exercise A**    Editing for and Correcting Fragments—
                    Family Arguments

Edit the following paragraph to eliminate the fragments: missing subjects, dependent clauses, and added details. Your instructor may ask you to write the paragraph, with corrections, on a separate piece of paper.

### Family Arguments

My family members argue a lot. For example, my father and my sister Sue
last weekend. This sister is the only one loses complete control of herself. Even         2
though all my family members like to argue. In a rage, Sue slammed the bedroom door. With a lot of force. Then opened it slowly. Ten minutes later. It              4
wobbled. And then fell off the hinges. My father angrily ordered Sue to talk
with him. In five minutes. As Sue was running out the door, replied that she             6
would return later. She claimed that she had to leave right away. To go to work.
Then my father shouted that it would have to be much later—after repaired the            8
door. Or bought a new one. I'm tired of family arguments. Quarrels that are
such a disgrace for the entire family!                                                   10

 **Exercise B**   Editing for and Correcting Fragments—
                     My First Day at College

Edit the following paragraph. Review the list of subordinators on page 28 before
you begin.

### My First Day at College

My first day of classes at Miami Dade Community College was a disaster.
Everything was fine on the way to campus. Until I turned into the parking lot            2
on Twenty-Seventh Avenue. All of the parking places were completely filled.
Since I wanted to be on time, panicked and parked in a staff space. Near the            4
Administration building. As I ran toward the English classrooms, looked back
and saw the campus police giving me a ticket. Next, I discovered that didn't            6
have my class schedule with me. Was in my car, and were only a few seconds
before the class was supposed to start. In a greater panic, ran back to the car.        8
As fast as I could. When I reached into my pocket for my keys, were not there!
I had locked them in my car! As a result, I missed my class. In the future, plan        10
to arrive at school early. With plenty of time to spare.

 **Writing Assignment:** *A Disaster*

Write about a disaster you experienced at some time in the past. Start your
paragraph with a topic sentence that identifies the situation and your dominant

feeling about it. Support your topic sentence with plenty of specific details. Write a concluding sentence that gives a feeling of finish to your paragraph.

 **Exercise C**   Editing for and Correcting Fragments—Halloween

Edit the following paragraph.

### Halloween

Halloween is a festival to celebrate autumn. Just as May Day is a festival to celebrate spring. The ancient religious leaders in Europe called Druids started                2
the custom. Said that the underground gods searched for victims. At midnight on October 31. The god represented death loved to terrify people. Wanted to                4
gather all the wicked souls had died during the year. Of course, this idea frightened the people of that time. When went out at night. This is where the idea                6
of witches and ghosts came from. Soon the people began to enjoy this custom gave them an opportunity for fun and excitement. All over Europe. Children                8
started telling scary stories and frightening each other. As soon as got dark. Is how the modern custom of Halloween began.                10

## CHAPTER REVIEW

 **Exercise**   Editing for Run-Ons and Fragments—The Tiger's Whisker

Edit the following folk story from Korea for run-on sentences and fragments. Your instructor may ask you to rewrite the paragraphs. The story contains twelve errors.

### The Tiger's Whisker

"The Tiger's Whisker" is a famous Korean folk story about how a young wife named Yun Ok received some advice from an old man. Yun Ok was un-                2
happy in her marriage. Because her husband did not treat her kindly. Her husband didn't talk to her often and when he did, talked to her impolitely. Yun                4
Ok became so desperate that she decided to ask an old man for advice.

This man was famous for helping people with problems. For example,                6
marital problems and other types of family problems. The unhappy young woman explained her situation to the old man, he thought very carefully. And                8
then answered.

°**shivered:** shook

The old man told Yun Ok that he could solve her problem if she first          10

brought him the whisker of a living tiger. At first Yun Ok shivered° with fear

after a few minutes she bowed her head and agreed to do as she was asked.          12

Later that night, Yun Ok went out to the mountainside and found the

cave of a ferocious tiger lived there. She placed a bowl of delicious food at the          14

entrance of the cave, and then she waited nearby. For several months, Yun Ok

brought food for the tiger, gradually the tiger got used to seeing Yun Ok close          16

by. Little by little, she moved closer to the tiger until could touch the beast.

Finally, Yun Ok asked the tiger for one of his whiskers, he agreed. As soon as          18

she could, she raced back to see the old man. In her hand, she held the tiger's

whisker. The valuable whisker that would surely provide the cure for her un-          20

happiness.

Yun Ok handed the treasured whisker to the man, he immediately tossed          22

it into the fire. She cried out in desperation, "What are you doing? You've

thrown away my last hope!"          24

"No," answered the old man. "If you know how to tame a vicious tiger,

surely you can do the same with your husband."          26

Yun Ok returned home slowly, thinking about the old man's advice.

Answer the following questions. Your instructor may ask you to discuss your
answers in small groups.

1.  What's the main idea of the old man's advice?

    _____

    _____

2.  In your opinion, who is responsible for the husband's unkind behavior: the
    husband or his wife?

    _____

    _____

3.  Do you agree or disagree with the old man's advice? Explain why or why
    not.

    _____

    _____

**Writing Assignment: Summary and Reaction—"The Tiger's Whisker"**

Write a *summary and reaction* paragraph based on the folk story "The Tiger's Whisker." Start your paragraph with a *topic sentence* that includes the title, the source, and the main idea of the story. (Use the first sentence of the story as a model.) Write a *brief summary* of the story. Next, write a *reaction* with the following parts:

In one sentence, write what the old man's advice was.

State whether or not you agree with this advice.

Explain why you agree or disagree with the old man's advice. Develop your ideas and be specific.

Write a *concluding sentence* that gives a feeling of finish to your paragraph.

## FOOD FOR THOUGHT

Read the following paragraph by Jane Myers, a staff reporter with *The Ann Arbor Times*. It tells about the convenience of having clothing with many pockets.

All the equipment essential to running the world. And held close to the body. Easily available. Neatly classified. Pen in the inside coat pocket. Keys in the back left trouser pocket. Efficiency. Order. Confidence.

How are the sentences in the paragraph structured?

## CLASSROOM ASSESSMENT TECHNIQUE (CAT)

### THE ONE-MINUTE PAPER

Take a minute or two to write answers to the following questions. Write your answers on a separate piece of paper without your name.

1. What are the most important points that you have learned in this chapter?

2. What questions remain in your mind at the end of this chapter?

*Note: Use this exercise to help you get answers to any questions you still have. Ask these questions to anyone who might be able to help you, such as another student or your instructor.*

# CHAPTER 4

# The Present Tense and the Present Progressive Tense

## THE PRESENT TENSE

▶ **Sample Paragraph**

The following paragraph is from *Fountain and Tomb* by Naguib Mahfouz. It describes a typical hot summer night in Cairo, Egypt. The verbs appear in italics.

### Summer Night on the Roof

On a hot summer night we *spread* mats and cushions out on the roof and *stay up* very late, our light the light of the stars or the moon. The cats *cavort*° among us, and the clucking of our chickens *keeps* us company. Sometimes the wife and three daughters of our Syrian neighbor, Hag Bisheer, *join* us. They *enjoy* singing their mountain songs, and I *listen* with a thirst almost as strong as my craving° for light skin and blue eyes. The mother and daughters, the oldest of whom *is* ten, *bewitch*° me, and I *insist* upon being allowed to listen. The music *makes* me light, and I *join in* and *sing* so well our neighbor *says*, "What a lovely voice you *have*, my boy!"

°**cavort:** jump about noisily

°**craving:** very strong desire
°**bewitch:** have a magical effect on

 **Essential Information: THE FORM OF PRESENT TENSE VERBS**

The verbs in "Summer Night on the Roof" are in the present tense. Write the missing verbs.

Group A

. . . we _____ our mats . . .

The cats _____ among us . . .

. . . and I _____ with a thirst . . .

Group B

. . . the clucking of the chickens _____ us company.

The music _____ me light . . .

What's the difference in form between the verbs in Group A and Group B?

The base form of the verb is used for all persons except the third person singular form. The third person singular refers to one person, place, thing, or concept.

|  | **Singular** | **Plural** |
|---|---|---|
| First person | I sing | we sing |
| Second person | you sing | you sing |
| Third person | he sings<br>she sings<br>it sings<br>Pat sings<br>the bird sings | they sing |

**Examples**

On a typical evening . . .

    . . . my brother *watches* TV.

    . . . my neighbor's dog *barks* at our cats.

    . . . my mother *listens* to the radio.

> Use the *S* form of the verb for the third person singular.

## Writing Assignment: *A Summer Night*

Write about a typical summer night in the town where you grew up or in the town where you live now. Paint a picture with words. Help your reader experience the heat, the cool, the smells, and the sounds.

    Start your paragraph with a topic sentence that identifies the town, the season, and the main idea. Support your topic sentence with plenty of specific details. Write a concluding sentence that gives a feeling of finish to your paragraph.

**Exercise**  Writing the Present Tense Form—The Costs of a Used Car

The following paragraph is based on information from the pamphlet "Buying a Used Car" (see Consumer Information from the Federal Trade Commission, 1990). Write the correct present tense form of the verbs in the blanks.

**The Costs of a Used Car**

Before you (look) _____*look*_____ for a used car, think carefully about the

costs. Remember, the real cost of a car (include) _____ more than the

purchase price: it (include) _____ loan terms°, such as interest rates°

and the length of the loan. If you (plan) _____ to finance° the car, you

(need) _____ to know how much money you can put down° and how

much you can pay monthly. Car dealers and banks (offer) _____ a

variety of interest rates and payment plans, so you will want to shop around. If,

for example, you (need) _____ low monthly payments, consider

making a large down payment° or getting financing that will stretch your

payments over five years, rather than the usual three. Of course, this longer

payment period (mean) _____ paying more interest and a higher total

cost.

°**loan terms:** amount, frequency, and percent of loan
°**interest rates:** percent charged for a loan
°**finance:** pay for over a period of time
°**put down:** pay first amount at time of buying

°**down payment:** amount of first payment at time of buying

☞ **Essential Information: SPELLING RULES FOR THE THIRD PERSON SINGULAR FORM OF THE VERB**

Read the following examples and answer the questions that follow each group of examples.

**Group I**

| Base Form | Third Person Singular Form |
|---|---|
| sing | sings |
| keep | keeps |
| make | makes |
| include | includes |
| plan | plans |
| need | needs |
| mean | means |

What is the general rule for writing the third person singular form of the verb?

_____

**Group II**

| | |
|---|---|
| stretch | stretches |
| finish | finishes |

| | |
|---|---|
| smash | smashes |
| wash | washes |
| watch | watches |
| kiss | kisses |
| mix | mixes |
| buzz | buzzes |

If the verb ends in a sibilant sound, what is added to the base form in order to produce the third person singular form? (Sibilant sounds are hissing sounds that are often spelled with *s*, *z*, *sh*, *ch*, and *x*.)

_____

**Group III**

| | |
|---|---|
| use | uses |
| rise | rises |
| cause | causes |
| freeze | freezes |
| idolize | idolizes |

If the simple form of the verb already ends in an *e*, what is added to the base form in order to produce the third person singular form?

_____

**Group IV**

| | |
|---|---|
| study | studies |
| carry | carries |
| try | tries |
| fly | flies |

If the verb ends with a consonant + *y*, how is the third person singular form written?

_____

**Group V**

| | |
|---|---|
| buy | buys |
| play | plays |
| employ | employs |

If the verb ends with a vowel + *y*, what is added to the base form in order to produce the third person singular form?

_____

**Note:** *Some verbs are irregular.*

| | |
|---|---|
| be | is |
| have | has |
| do | does |

**Exercise**  Writing the Correct Present Tense Form—Jason's Parents

Write the correct form of the verbs in the following paragraph.

### Jason's Parents

Six-year-old Jason (idolize) _____*idolizes*_____ his parents, David and Hideko.

1

David (own) _____ a computer software business. Hideko (study)

2

_____ business management at the University of Southern California.

3

When Hideko (finish) _____ her classes, she (go) _____

4                    5

home. After she (greet) _____ Jason and (have) _____ a

6                    7

snack with him, she (study) _____ for an hour. After David (arrive)

8

_____ and (visit) _____ with his family, he (spend)

9              10

_____ a short time on his computer. Later, David (fix) _____

11                                 12

dinner with Hideko. After dinner, Jason often (wash) _____ the dishes

13

with one of his parents. Later, David usually (tell) _____ Jason a story

14

or (play) _____ a game with him. Sometimes Jason (watch)

15

_____ the news on television with his mother and (fall)

16

_____ asleep in her arms. David (carry) _____ Jason to bed

17                                 18

and (kiss) _____ him good-night.

19

# THE MEANING OF THE PRESENT TENSE: HABITUAL ACTION

 ### Essential Information: THE PRESENT TENSE

Reread the paragraph "Summer Night on the Roof" at the beginning of the chapter.

> The present tense often expresses habitual action.

 ### Essential Information: TIME MARKERS USED WITH THE HABITUAL PRESENT TENSE

Common time markers include the following:

| | |
|---|---|
| always | every day, week, month |
| frequently | once a day, week, month |
| often | twice a day, week, month |
| usually | three times a day |
| sometimes | |
| seldom | |
| rarely | |
| never | |

**Examples**

Julia *usually* starts her day with a cup of coffee.

She *rarely* has more than two cups.

*Once a week* she goes out with friends for breakfast.

 **Writing Assignment A:** *The Habitual Present Tense—Your Typical Weekend*

Write about what you usually do on weekends. Include some time markers commonly used with the present tense. Start your paragraph with a topic sentence such as . . .

On a typical weekend, I usually follow the same basic routine. First, . . .

Continue describing your activities, using plenty of specific details. Write a concluding sentence that gives a feeling of finish to your paragraph.

 **Writing Assignment B:** *The Habitual Present Tense—A Typical Day in a Classmate's Life*

Work with a partner. Find out what he or she does on a typical weekday (or a typical weekend day). Write about what you found out about your partner. Include some time markers commonly used with the present tense.
    Start your paragraph with a topic sentence such as . . .

My classmate (name) often follows the same routine every weekend morning. First, . . .

Continue describing your partner's activities, using plenty of specific details. Write a concluding sentence that gives a feeling of finish to your paragraph.

## ☰  REVIEW: HABITUAL ACTION  ☰

 **Exercise A**  Present Tense Verbs—Hi and Lois

Read the following cartoon. Why did the authors include this cartoon in the text at this point?

(Reprinted by special permission of King Features Syndicate.)

<hr />

 **Exercise B**   Habitual Present Tense—A Typical Workday in Tokyo

The following paragraph describes what Hiroki Tanaka does on a typical workday in Tokyo. In each blank, write the correct verb from the list. Make sure you use the *s* form, as appropriate.

| follow | start | stop |
|--------|-------|------|
| need | be | get |
| arrive | sip | ignore |
| go | shop | return |
| buy | play | settle down |

### A Typical Workday in Tokyo

In Tokyo, Hiroki Tanaka _____ the same basic routine every

workday. He _____ his day with a one-hour subway train ride. He
        2

usually _____ for coffee at a downtown coffee shop. While he
        3

_____ his coffee, he _____ the loud noises from the traffic
     4                              5

and crowds. After he _____ at his job, he _____ to a nonstop
                          6                              7

morning of work. At noon, Hiroki _____ lunch at a carryout counter,
                                        8

°**Pachinko:** Japanese slot machine game

and after lunch, he _____ a short game of Pachinko° in a nearby
<sub>9</sub>

parlor. In the afternoon, Hiroki _____ to several more busy hours of
<sub>10</sub>

work. At night, he _____ back home on the train. Sometimes he
<sub>11</sub>

_____ on the way home in one of the underground shopping arcades
<sub>12</sub>

connected to the subway stations. By the time Hiroki _____ home, he
<sub>13</sub>

_____ tired and ready to go to sleep. He _____ his rest for
<sub>14</sub>                                                    <sub>15</sub>

the next busy workday.

## Writing Assignment A: *The Habitual Present—An Imaginary Person*

Imagine a typical day in the life of one of the following people: a king, a queen, a movie star, a famous singer, a billionaire, a spy, or other person in your imagination. Write a paragraph to tell about what you imagine a typical day for this person is like.

Start your paragraph with a topic sentence such as . . .

King Faisal's typical day usually starts out with . . .

Continue describing the person's activities, using plenty of specific details. Write a concluding sentence that gives a feeling of finish to your paragraph.

As an alternative, pick a famous person and pretend that you are that person. Write a paragraph or several sentences to tell about a typical day in your life as that person.

### Example

I am Rod Stewart. As soon as I get up in the morning, I call my live-in hair dresser to fix my hair.

## Writing Assignment B: *The Habitual Present—A Holiday or Ceremony*

Write a paragraph about a typical holiday or ceremony in your country. Start your paragraph with a topic sentence that identifies the holiday or ceremony. Describe the holiday or ceremony using plenty of specific details. Write a concluding sentence that gives a feeling of finish to your paragraph.

### Example Topic Sentence

On the Fourth of July, people like to spend the day outdoors having fun.

# THE MEANING OF THE PRESENT TENSE: GENERAL TRUTH

▶ **Sample Paragraph**

In his essay, "My Friend, Albert Einstein," Banesh Hoffman writes the following:

> He was one of the greatest scientists the world has ever known, yet if I had to convey° the essence° of Albert Einstein in a single word, I would choose "simplicity."

°**convey:** show, express
°**essence:** central or basic quality

Hoffman then goes on to give an example of this simplicity in Einstein's explanation of why our feet sink into dry sand or in sand immersed in water.

> When sand *is* damp, Einstein explained, there *are* tiny amounts of water between grains. The surface tension° of these tiny amounts of water *pulls* all the grains together, and friction *makes* them hard to budge°. When the sand *is* dry, there *is* obviously no water between grains. If the sand is fully immersed°, there is water between the grains, but no water surface to pull them together.

°**surface tension:** liquid molecules holding together
°**budge:** move
°**immersed:** put under water

 **Essential Information: THE PRESENT TENSE**

> The present tense often expresses general truth.

 **Exercise**   General Truth—Second-Hand Smoke

Write the correct form of the verbs in the blanks.

## Second-Hand Smoke

Second-hand cigarette smoke (harm) _____*harms*_____ nonsmokers. Much
<sub>1</sub>

of this smoke (rise) _____ off the end of a burning cigarette. Scientists
<sub>2</sub>

(call) _____ it sidestream smoke. This type of smoke (contain)
<sub>3</sub>

_____ twice the amount of tar and nicotine than the smoker (inhale)
<sub>4</sub>

_____. The smoker (puff) _____ through a filter, but
<sub>5</sub>                                   <sub>6</sub>

sidestream smoke (do) _____ not (go) _____ through a
<sub>7</sub>                              <sub>8</sub>

filter. Recent studies (warn) _____ us of the dangers of second-hand
<sub>9</sub>

smoke. It (kill) _____ about 53,000 nonsmokers in the United States
<sub>10</sub>

each year. It (cause) _____ about 37,000 deaths a year from heart
<sub>11</sub>

disease. It also (bring) _____ about 20 percent of all lung cancers in

nonsmokers. As a result of the recent studies, many people (want)

_____ stricter laws against smoking in public buildings.

## Writing Assignment A: *General Truth—Sports*

Write a paragraph about a game or a sport that you're familiar with. Start your paragraph with a topic sentence. Support your topic sentence with plenty of specific details. Write a concluding sentence that gives a feeling of finish to your paragraph.

### Examples

#### AMERICAN FOOTBALL

American football follows some simple rules and guidelines. A coin toss determines who kicks off and who defends each goal. Teams change sides after the first and third quarters. In college and pro football, a quarter lasts fifteen minutes. Time stops at various points throughout the game. The game ends after four quarters. The team that scores the highest number of points wins.

#### KARATE

Karate is a popular sport for several good reasons. It builds your body and helps you control your mind. This assists your mind and body in working together. Karate also allows you to defend yourself against attack. It makes you a faster runner and a stronger athlete. It also helps you think faster and work longer. It is not surprising that karate is so popular.

*Option: Your instructor may ask you to do some research on a sport. Include the information from your research in your paragraph.*

## Writing Assignment B: *General Truth—Television*

Write a paragraph about why television is so popular. Start your paragraph with a topic sentence. Support your topic sentence with plenty of specific details. Write a concluding sentence that gives a feeling of finish to your paragraph.

You may start your paragraph with the topic sentence and first point given below.

Television is one of the most popular forms of home entertainment. First, it relaxes people.

# PRESENT PROGRESSIVE: THE MOMENT OF COMMUNICATION

 **Essential Information: THE PRESENT PROGRESSIVE TENSE**

In the following material, the present progressive verbs appear in italic. These are the verbs that consist of . . .

*am/is/are + verb + ing*

What is happening at this moment in the classroom?

The instructor *is talking* about verbs.

The instructor *is* also *explaining* "the moment of communication."

The students in the classroom *are reading* the textbook.

Other students outside *are walking* by the classroom door.

Some birds in the trees *are singing*.

Some cars on the street *are* occasionally *honking*.

What else *is happening* right now in your classroom?

_____

_____

> The present progressive form of the verb is used for the moment of communication.

Common time markers often used with the *moment of communication* include the following:

now
right now
at the/this (very) moment

*Note: Contractions are common with the verb "to be":*

| I'm | we're |
|-----|-------|
| you're | you're |
| he's<br>she's<br>it's | they're |

 **Exercise** Activities at the Moment of Communication

On a separate piece of paper, write five sentences using present progressive verbs to describe what is happening in the following picture.

**Writing Assignment:** *Activities at the Moment of Communication in the Real World*

Find a comfortable place in public where you can sit and write while you observe people's actions. Some suggestions include a cafeteria, the library, the beach, or the park. Write a paragraph describing the actions around you.

Start your paragraph with a topic sentence that identifies the location you are describing. Use plenty of specific details to describe what you see. Write a concluding sentence that gives a feeling of finish to your paragraph.

### Relevant Information: Restrictions on the Progressive— Stative and Dynamic Meanings of Verbs

How does the following sentence sound to you?

   *I'm having a headache because I'm owning three cars and they are all needing repairs.

_____

The present progressive cannot be used in the above sentence. Why?

_____

English verbs can be divided into two uses—*stative* and *dynamic*.

The meaning of *stative* verbs can be compared to a lake: the nature of both is relatively constant, expressing little change. In the following sentences, the meanings of the verbs express *stative* usage:

I *have* a headache.

I *own* three cars.

My cars *need* repairs.

The meaning of *dynamic* verbs can be compared to a river: the nature of both includes the idea of energy, expressing change. This change can range from slight to intense.

The word *dynamic* comes from the Greek word for *energy* or *power*. The word *dynamite* also comes from this Greek root, clearly showing its root meaning of *energy*. In the following sentences, the meanings of the verbs express *dynamic* usage:

I *am getting* a headache.

I *am selling* one of my three cars.

My mechanic *is fixing* the other two cars.

> When a verb expresses a stative rather than a dynamic meaning, it is not used in the progressive.

# ≡ TEMPORARY HABIT

### ▶ Sample Paragraph

Read the following paragraph and pay particular attention to how the present progressive verbs are used.

**My Friend Yoshie**

When I ran into my high school friend Yoshie at the Galleria Center in Houston, Texas, last month, we had a chance to catch up on news with each other. First, she is living with her sister and brother-in-law near Rice University. She is attending day classes at the university on Monday, Wednesday, and Friday. Most of the classes she is taking are general education requirements. She is only taking one class in her major, computer science. In the evenings and on weekends, she is working part-time at a computer software store in the Galleria Center. That's how we ran into each other again. I went into the software store because I was looking for a new word processing program. Shortly after we talked, she helped me get a job at the same computer store.

 **Essential Information: USING THE PRESENT PROGRESSIVE TENSE TO EXPRESS TEMPORARY HABIT**

> The present progressive often expresses a temporary habit. However, the action is not necessarily happening at the moment of communication.

Common time markers used with the present progressive tense to express *temporary habit* include the following:

> now, right now, for now
> today
> these days
> nowadays
> this summer, winter
> this week, month, year, semester, quarter, term

 **Exercise A**   Temporary Habit—Questions

Answer these questions using complete sentences. For questions three and four, you will need to get the information from the classmates sitting near you.

1.   Are you taking a math course this semester?

   _____

2.   What other classes are you taking this semester?

   _____

3.   What is the person next to you studying this semester?

   _____

4.   What is another person next to you studying this semester?

   _____

 **Exercise B**   Writing about a Temporary Habit

On a separate piece of paper, write several sentences about some activities you are temporarily involved with. When you finish, exchange your sentences with a partner. Read your partner's sentences and edit the verbs for any possible errors.

**Example**

   This week I am taking an antibiotic for a minor infection.

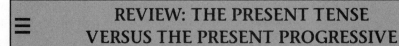
## REVIEW: THE PRESENT TENSE VERSUS THE PRESENT PROGRESSIVE

 **Exercise A**     Selecting the Correct Verb Form—
                    Laura's Heavy Schedule

Write the correct form of the verbs. In some cases, more than one answer is possible.

**Laura's Heavy Schedule**

Laura (have) _____ a heavy schedule this semester. She (take)
<sub>1</sub>

_____ a chemistry class, two English classes, an art class, and a busi-
<sub>2</sub>

ness class. Also, she (watch) _____ her neighbor's house for a month,
<sub>3</sub>

and she (babysit) _____ her sister's children. At this moment it (be)
<sub>4</sub>

_____ 8:00 on Thursday evening, and Laura (have) _____ a
<sub>5</sub> <sub>6</sub>

chemistry test tomorrow. Right now, she (try) _____ to study and keep
<sub>7</sub>

an eye on the kids at the same time. The kids (watch) _____ cartoon
<sub>8</sub>

videos. However, Laura (not concentrate) _____ on her chemistry text.
<sub>9</sub>

Instead, she (watch) _____ the cartoons.
<sub>10</sub>

 **Exercise B**   Selecting the Correct Verb Form—Louise

Write the correct form of the given verbs in the blanks.

**Louise**

This week Louise (do) _____ something entirely different from
<sub>1</sub>

what she usually (do) _____ in her daily routine. In her normal rou-
<sub>2</sub>

tine, Louise (get up) _____ at 6:00 A.M. on weekdays. She almost
<sub>3</sub>

always (have) _____ breakfast at 7:00 and (read) _____ the
<sub>4</sub> <sub>5</sub>

newspaper while she (eat) _____ . She (say) _____ goodbye
<sub>6</sub> <sub>7</sub>

to her family before 7:45. She usually (go) _____ to work with a few
<sub>8</sub>

co-workers and (spend) _____ the entire day at the office. This week,
<sub>9</sub>

however, Louise's schedule (be) _____ entirely different. To start with,
<sub>10</sub>

she (get up) _____ and (have) _____ breakfast at 10:00 or
<sub>11</sub> <sub>12</sub>

later, and she (not read) _____ the newspaper. Instead, she (read)
<sub>13</sub>

_____ a detective novel. Also, she (spend) _____ all her time
<sub>14</sub> <sub>15</sub>

with her husband and family. They (swim) _____ in the ocean every
<sub>16</sub>

day and (go out) _____ to dinner every night. You have probably
<sub>17</sub>

guessed that Louise (be) _____ on vacation this week.
<sub>18</sub>

**Writing Assignment:** *Mixed Verb Forms—Routine vs. Vacation*

Write a paragraph that includes two parts. In the first half describe your normal weekday routine. In the second half, describe your dream vacation as if it were happening right now. Use the paragraph above about Louise as a model.

# ≡ FUTURE TIME

▶ **Sample Paragraph**

Read the following paragraph about a trip planned for the future. The present tense and present progressive verbs in italics refer to future time.

### A Trip to Washington, D.C.

I am ready for my trip to Washington, D.C. My plane flight *leaves* tomorrow at 9:00 A.M. and *arrives* in Washington, D.C. at 6:20 P.M. I *am staying* for three nights at the Embassy Suites Hotel near the Capitol. The next morning, the tour to Mount Vernon *leaves* at 9:30 and *returns* to the Capitol at 4:45 in the afternoon. After that, I *am playing* it by ear.

 **Essential Information: THE PRESENT AND THE PRESENT PROGRESSIVE**

> Both the present and the present progressive can be used to refer to a planned activity or event in the future.

**Exercise**　Future Time

Write several sentences about a scheduled or planned activity that will take place in the near future.

**Example**

> I am taking Lucy out to a movie downtown this Saturday afternoon. It starts at 4:00. After the movie, we are going to her cousin's house for a birthday party.

　　**CHAPTER REVIEW**　　

## CHART: REVIEW OF VERBS

| THE PRESENT TENSE AND THE PRESENT PROGRESSIVE TENSE | | |
| --- | --- | --- |
| | THE PRESENT TENSE | THE PRESENT PROGRESSIVE TENSE |
| FORMS | base form or *S* form with third person singular | *am/is/are + verb + ing* |
| HABITUAL ACTION | Joe *gets up* late on Sundays. | |
| GENERAL FACT/TRUTH | Water *freezes* at 32 degrees Fahrenheit. | |
| MOMENT OF COMMUNICATION | | Joe *is studying* for his chemistry test. |
| TEMPORARY HABIT (NOT NECESSARILY AT THE MOMENT OF COMMUNICATION) | | Joe *is taking* a chemistry class this semester. |
| FUTURE—SCHEDULED OR PLANNED EVENT | Susan's flight *arrives* . . . | . . . *is arriving* at 7:00 tonight. |

 **Exercise**　Test Anxiety

**Part One: Preparation for Editing**

The following paragraph is an excerpt from "Help Your Child Improve in Test-Taking," a publication of the Office of Educational Research and Improvement (U.S. Department of Education).

Fill in the correct forms of the present tense. (Most, but not all, of the verb forms should be in the third person singular form.)

A student who (suffer) _____ from test anxiety (tend)
                               1

_____ to worry about success in school, especially doing well on tests.
       2

He (worry) _____ about the future and (be) _____ ex-
                 3                                              4

tremely self-critical. Instead of feeling challenged by the prospect of success, he

(become) _____ afraid of failure. These problems (make)
                5

_____ him anxious about tests and his own abilities. Ultimately, he
       6

(become) _____ so nervous that he (feel) _____ incompe-
                7                                            8

tent about the subject matter of the test.

## Part Two: Editing

The following exercise is based on information on how to avoid test anxiety, taken from "Help Your Child Improve in Test-Taking." This paragraph tells about Thanh, who has good study habits that help him avoid test anxiety. Edit for verb errors.

### No More Test Anxiety

Thanh avoids test-taking anxiety by following the suggestions he read

about last year in "Help Your Child Improve in Test-Taking," a publication by        2

the Office of Educational Research and Improvement. First of all, Thanh space

his studying over days or weeks. He knows that real learning occurs through        4

studying that take place over a period of time. He makes sure he understands

the information and relate it to what he already knows. He also review several        6

times. Second, he avoid "cramming" the night before. He know that cramming

increase anxiety, which interferes with clear thinking. Instead, he get a good        8

night's sleep. Third, on the test day Thanh look quickly at the entire test to see

what types of questions are included (multiple-choice, true/false, essay, etc.).        10

This help him pace himself. Next, when he takes an essay test, he read all the

questions first and uses the margin for noting phrases that relates to the        12

answers. These phrases helps him in writing the essay answer. Last, if Thanh has

trouble with a certain answer to a question, he skips it and go on. He mark it        14

for later identification. If he have time at the end of the test, he returns to the

unanswered question(s). By following the tips Thanh learned in the brochure,        16

he has improved his grade point average by a point and a half.

**Part Three: Writing about Your Study Skills**

On a separate piece of paper, write several sentences about changes you can make in your study skills in order to avoid test-taking anxiety.

 **Writing Assignment A: *Present Tense—Customs***

Write a paragraph about the customs visitors follow when they visit someone's home in your native country (or another country). Use present tense verbs as much as possible. Start your paragraph with a topic sentence such as

> A visitor to someone's home in Taiwan follows several customs.

Support your topic sentence with plenty of specific details.

**Example**

> People usually remove their shoes before entering a home.

Write a concluding sentence that gives a feeling of finish to your paragraph.

*Option: Your instructor may ask you to do some research on your country (or another country). Include the information from your research in your paragraph.*

 **Writing Assignment B: *Present Tense—Classroom Procedures***

Write a paragraph about classroom procedures in your native country (or another country). Use present tense verbs as much as possible. Start your paragraph with a topic sentence such as

> Instructors and students follow several procedures in a classroom in Peru.

Support your topic sentence with plenty of specific details.

**Examples**

> In Afghanistan, the instructor does most of the talking.
>
> In Mexico, students call the teacher "teacher."
>
> In Korea, students stand up when the instructor enters the room.

Write a concluding sentence that gives a feeling of finish to your paragraph.

 FOOD FOR THOUGHT

What is the difference in meaning in these two sentences?

> My sister has a baby.
>
> My sister is having a baby.

## ☰ CLASSROOM ASSESSMENT TECHNIQUE (CAT) ☰

### THE ONE-MINUTE PAPER

Take a minute or two to write answers to the following questions. Write your answers on a separate piece of paper without your name.

1. What are the most important points that you have learned in this chapter?

2. What questions remain in your mind at the end of this chapter?

*Note: Use this exercise to help you get answers to any questions you still have. Ask these questions to anyone who might be able to help you, such as another student or your instructor.*

# The Past Tense and the Past Progressive Tense

## ≡ THE PAST TENSE

### ▶ Sample Paragraphs

Read the following paragraphs. The past tense verbs appear in italics.

°**legend:** old story, probably not true
°**kingdom:** country ruled by a king or queen

**An Irish Legend °**

A long time ago, an aging king *ruled* a large kingdom° in Ireland. He *had* three sons and *wanted* to leave his kingdom to the most intelligent of the three.

One day, the king *took* his eldest son with him on a long trip. After several hours, he *said* to his son, "Son, shorten the road for me." The son *had* no idea how to answer, and the disappointed king *turned* around and *returned* home with his son.

The next day the king *left* with his next son on the same trip, and the same thing *happened*.

On the third day, the king *took* his youngest son, and after a few hours *said* to his son, "Son, shorten the road for me."

 **Stop reading here.** Discuss with your classmates what you think the third son did. Then continue reading.

Right away the youngest son *began* to tell his father a long and entertaining story. The king *became* so interested in the story that he never *noticed* the length of the journey. When they *arrived* at their destination, the king *handed* his youngest son the crown° to his kingdom.

°**crown:** head decoration of a king or queen

 **Essential Information: THE PAST**

The most common use of the past tense is to refer to past time.

 **Essential Information: SPELLING RULES FOR THE REGULAR PAST TENSE FORMS**

Read the following examples and answer the questions that follow each group of examples.

**Group I**

| Base Form | Past Tense |
|-----------|-----------|
| turn | turned |
| hand | handed |
| want | wanted |

What is the general rule for forming the regular past tense form of the verb?

_____

**Group II**

| | |
|------|--------|
| rule | ruled |
| notice | noticed |
| arrive | arrived |

What is the rule for forming the past tense of verbs that end in an *e*?

_____

**Group III**

| | |
|--------|-----------|
| stop | stopped |
| refer | referred |
| wrap | wrapped |
| permit | permitted |

The base forms in this group have the following characteristics:

1. They end in one vowel and one consonant.

2. The verbs with more than one syllable are stressed (in spoken English) on the last syllable.

What is the rule for forming the past tense of the verbs in this group?

_____

**Note:** *Final* x *and final* w *are exceptions.*

|       |         |
|-------|---------|
| relax | relaxed |
| flow  | flowed  |

Why don't we double the final consonant in the following verbs?

|        |          |
|--------|----------|
| open   | opened   |
| talk   | talked   |
| remain | remained |
| invent | invented |

_____

**Group IV**

|       |         |
|-------|---------|
| try   | tried   |
| study | studied |
| reply | replied |
| carry | carried |

The base forms in this group end in a consonant and a *y*. What is the rule for forming the past tense of the verbs in this group?

_____

How do you explain the *y* in the past tense of the following verbs? *Hint:* Do these verbs have a vowel or a consonant before the *y*?

|       |         |
|-------|---------|
| play  | played  |
| spray | sprayed |

_____

**Group V**

|      |      |
|------|------|
| have | had  |
| take | took |
| say  | said |

Is there a rule for forming the past tense forms of the words in this group?

_____

**Exercise**   Spelling Practice for Past Tense Verbs—King Sejong

## 세종 대왕은 15세기에 한국에서 훌륭한 통치자였다.

King Sejong was a great ruler in Korea in the fifteenth century.

Write the correct past tense forms for the verbs in the following paragraph. Eleven of the verbs are regular, and five of the verbs are irregular.

### King Sejong

King Sejong (be) _____*was*_____ a great ruler in Korea in the fifteenth
                         1

century. He (accomplish) _____ many things for his people. First of all,
                                 2

he (start) _____ a new, easier writing system for Koreans. Many years
                3

ago Korean writing (use) _____ Chinese characters. It (have)
                                 4

_____ thousands of picture words, and it (be) _____ very
        5                                                          6

hard to learn. In 1443, however, King Sejong the Great (ask) _____
                                                                      7

Korean scholars to invent a new Korean alphabet. He (want) _____ an
                                                                    8

easier system for his people to learn and use. Out of these efforts, Koreans

(develop) _____ a new writing system: *Hangul.* This system (permit)
                9

_____ the common people to get an education. But King Sejong
        10

(accomplish) _____ a lot more than this. He (study) _____
                    11                                                  12

the sciences. While he (be) _____ king, Koreans (invent)
                                    13

_____ the sundial and a water clock. They also (make) _____
        14                                                                  15

maps of the solar system. They even (invent) _____ ways to measure
                                                        16

daily rainfall and to write and read music. The world has certainly benefited from

the generous and scholarly efforts of this great king.

---

### Writing Assignment: *A Historical Figure*

Write about a historical figure from your native country. Your instructor may suggest that you draw information from a book or article. Start your paragraph with a topic sentence that identifies the person. (Use the paragraph about King Sejong as a model.) Support your topic sentence with plenty of specific details. Write a concluding sentence that gives a feeling of finish to your paragraph.

 **Essential Information: NEGATION**

Read the examples of the negative forms of the past tense verbs.

| POSITIVE | NEGATIVE |
| --- | --- |
| lived | didn't live   (didn't = did not) |
| went | didn't go |
| ate | didn't eat |

1.  What form of the verb follows the auxiliary?

_____

2.  Correct the following verbs.

   a.  *didn't lived    _____

   b.  *didn't went    _____

   c.  *didn't ate      _____

 **Exercise A**    Practicing the Past Tense and Summary Writing—
                      Glory at What Price?

The following exercise is based on the fascinating story of one of America's best-loved heroines of the twentieth century: Amelia Earhart.

The entire exercise consists of five steps. In Steps One and Three, you will read the first and second part of the Amelia Earhart story. Fill in the blanks with the past of the verbs in parentheses. This will give you practice in writing the irregular forms of common verbs. (Most of the verbs in the story are irregular. You may need to use a dictionary.)

After you finish Steps One and Three, your instructor may ask you to do Steps Two, Four, and Five—writing a summary of what you read.

**Step One**

Fill in the blanks in the following with the correct past tense verb.

### Glory at What Price? (Part I)

Amelia Earhart (capture) ___*captured*___ the attention of the world in
                                   1

1928. In that year, Amelia (become) _____ the first woman to cross
                                              2

the Atlantic Ocean by air. After that, people frequently (read) _____
                                                                          3

about her in newspapers throughout the world over the next decade.

In 1932 Amelia (fly) _____ across the Atlantic solo. She (be)
                              4

_____ the first woman and second person to do so. (Charles
    5

Lindbergh was the first.) Later, in 1935, Amelia (become) _____ the
                6

first person to fly solo across the Pacific Ocean, from Honolulu, Hawaii, to Oak-

land, California. Also, she (set) _____ the women's record for the
           7

fastest nonstop transcontinental flight (Los Angeles, California to Newark, New

Jersey). Later, she (break) _____ her own transcontinental record. In
        8

1934 she (win) _____ the Harmon Trophy as America's Outstanding
      9

Airwoman for the third year in a row.

  In March 1937 Amelia Earhart (begin) _____ her first attempt at
              10

an around-the-world flight. Soon after the plane (take off) _____, it
                 11

(go) _____ into loops and (hit) _____ the ground.
   12          13

**Step Two**

On a separate piece of paper, write a summary of "Glory at What Price? (Part I)."

**Step Three**

Fill in the blanks in the following with the correct past tense verb.

### Glory at What Price? (Part II)

  In June 1937 Amelia (leave) _____*left*_____ on her second attempt to fly
            1

around the world. The second to the last leg of the flight (be) _____ the
               2

most dangerous, from Lea, New Guinea, to Howland Island (northwest of Hawaii).

  Lea Airport personnel (think) _____ Amelia Earhart (have)
            3

_____ enough fuel when she (take off) _____ from Lea,
  4             5

New Guinea. Unfortunately, in one of the last radio communications with

Amelia, she (say) _____ her gas (be) _____ low. Soon
       6        7

afterward, the radio crew (lose) _____ contact with Amelia. No one
          8

(know) _____ what had happened to her.
    9

  Bad weather (make) _____ visibility difficult that day. Thus, one
         10

theory is that the plane (speed) _____ right past Howland Island.
         11

And if the plane (run out) _____ of gas, it probably (strike)

<sub>12</sub>

_____ the surface of the sea and (sink) _____.

<sub>13</sub>                                               <sub>14</sub>

    No one ever (find) _____ Amelia's airplane, and no one knows

<sub>15</sub>

for sure what (happen) _____ to Amelia Earhart.

<sub>16</sub>

## Step Four

On a separate piece of paper, write a summary of "Glory at What Price? (Part II)."

## Step Five

Write a summary of the entire story "Glory at What Price? (Parts I and II)" on a separate page.

    The length of the complete summary should be approximately the same length as *one* of the individual summaries you wrote for Parts I and II. Therefore, you will need to condense your ideas even more than you did in Steps Two and Four. You can do this by focusing only on the main ideas in the story.

    Start your summary with a topic sentence. Support your topic sentence with *main ideas only. Do not give unnecessary details.* Write a concluding sentence that gives a feeling of finish to your paragraph. Your concluding idea might express your personal opinion of or reaction to the story.

 **Exercise B**   Editing for Correct Past Tense Verbs—
Two Heads Are Better Than One

Edit the verbs in the following paragraph.

### · Two Heads Are Better Than One ·

    "Two heads are better than one." This is an English proverb about wisdom.

It means that working together is better than working alone so that a person   2

can get more ideas from other people. I agree with this saying. At work a few

years ago, my boss use a new network system to connect all the computers in   4

the business. After she complete the installation, only two computers work. At

first, my boss tries to find out what was wrong by herself, but she couldn't find   6

the problem. Then she ask me to help her. When my boss explains to me how

she had connected the machines, I notice that the order of the steps was incor-   8

rect. When I tell her about my discovery, we both make the necessary changes.

After we finished, all the computers in the system work fine. This experience   10

showed me that two people working together can solve a problem better than one person working alone. It's important to cooperate and work as a team          12

because in this way more talents and skills can be applied in any situation.

Adapted from a paragraph by Sue Sedor

## Writing Assignment A: *An Early School Experience*—To School through the Fields

In the following paragraph from Alice Taylor's *To School through the Fields*, the author describes her early memories of school in Ireland. As you read the paragraph, allow it to take you back to your early school days.

### To School through the Fields

°**bearable:** something you're able to accept or put up with

°**glinting:** giving off flashes of light

°**ramble:** walk about aimlessly

Going to school and coming back was so enjoyable that it made school itself bearable°. My main objection to school was that I had to stay there. It was the first experience to interfere with my freedom, and it took me a long time to accept that there was no way out of its trap. I could look out through a window in the back wall of the schoolhouse and see my home away in the distance, with the fields stretching out invitingly and with the Darigle river glinting° in the valley. I made many an imaginary journey home through that window. It was not that I wished to be at home so much, but that I wanted to be free to ramble° out through the fields. I envied the freedom of the crows on the trees outside the window, coming and going as they pleased.

This paragraph may have helped you start thinking about an early school experience. Write a paragraph about an early school experience you had. It could be your first day, a pleasant experience, or an unpleasant experience.

Start your paragraph with a topic sentence that identifies the time, place, and type of experience you are writing about. Continue with specific supporting details in time order. Write a concluding sentence that gives a feeling of finish to your paragraph.

## Writing Assignment B: *The Joy of Discovery*

Mario Puzo, the author of *The Godfather*, describes the joy of discovering something wonderful in his narrative "Italians in Hell's Kitchen." Read the paragraph and experience his joy.

### The Joy of Discovery

°**conception:** idea

°**pasture:** fields where animals eat grass
°**darted:** ran quickly from one point to another
°**waded:** walked in water
°**hay:** dried grass for feeding animals

As a child, I knew only the stone city. I had no conception° of what the countryside could be. When I got to New Hampshire, when I smelled grass and flowers and trees, when I ran barefoot along the dirt country roads, when I drove the cows home from pasture°, when I darted° through fields of corn and waded° through clear brooks, when I gathered warm brown speckled eggs in the henhouse, when I drove a hay° wagon drawn by two great horses—when I did all these things—I nearly went crazy with the joy of it. It was quite simply a fairy tale come true.

From your experience, write a paragraph about the joy of discovery or another joyful event. Make the reader feel your joy. For some, it might be a graduation day, the birth of a child, winning a prize, returning to your homeland, or seeing some natural wonder for the first time.

Start your paragraph with a topic sentence that identifies the time, place, and type of experience you are writing about. Continue with specific supporting details in time order. Write a concluding sentence that gives a feeling of finish to your paragraph.

### *Writing Assignment C: Memory of a Childhood Vacation—Our Playground–The Sea*

In the following paragraphs from Alice Taylor's *To School through the Fields*, the author describes her childhood memories of the sea. As you read the paragraph, allow it to help you remember a vacation experience from your childhood.

### Our Playground—The Sea

°**nostrils:** the two openings of the nose
°**trotting:** running slowly
°**eerie:** causing fear because of strangeness

The first smell of the sea was heaven to our nostrils°, and we saw donkey carts with their loads of seaweed trotting° along the strand. Sunbathing bored us. We climbed the rocks and investigated damp eerie° caves and packed the long warm day with endless activities. We headed straight for the strand after breakfast and with the exception of mealtimes we never left again till dark.

To us the sea was great fun, where we splashed and dived under waves and got mouths full of salt water. There was a huge cluster of rocks called the Black Rocks which were covered by the full tide, but when it was out, it left warm pools which sheltered many little sea creatures. We loved investigating all of these and gathering shells and sea grass.

Choose a favorite childhood vacation spot and write a paragraph about why you enjoyed it so much. Start your paragraph with a topic sentence that identifies the time, place, and type of experience you are writing about. Continue with specific supporting details in time order. Write a concluding sentence that gives a feeling of finish to your paragraph.

## THE PAST PROGRESSIVE

### ▶ Sample Paragraph

Read the following paragraph about a frightening situation. The past progressive verbs appear in italics.

### The Man at the Door

I had a frightening experience a few months ago when my husband was out of town on a business trip. I wanted to have a relaxing evening, so after dinner I decided to watch television. While my tiny daughter and I *were watching* a detective movie, I noticed a noise at the front porch. Someone *was trying* to open the door! My heart started to race. I *was staring* at the door in fright when I heard the person at the door knock forcefully. Then he began tapping rapidly. The next thing I knew was that the door *was opening* slowly. As I *was running* for the kitchen with my child in my arms, I heard the familiar voice of my husband. He *was calling* out to me, "Hi, Honey! I thought I forgot my keys!"

 **Essential Information: THE FORM OF THE PAST PROGRESSIVE**

The past progressive consists of a past form of *be* plus the *-ing* form of the verb.

> Was/Were + Verb + ing

 **Essential Information: THE USE OF THE PAST PROGRESSIVE**

Read these sentences again from the paragraph "The Man at the Door."

> While my tiny daughter and I *were watching* a detective movie, I noticed a noise at the front porch.

> Someone *was trying* to open the door!

> The next thing I knew was that the door *was opening* slowly.

> He *was calling* out to me, "Hi, Honey! I thought I forgot my keys!"

> The past progressive tense refers to an action in progress in the past.

***Note:*** *Stative verbs, however, cannot be used in the progressive form. For information on stative and dynamic verbs, refer back to Chapter Four, page 72, Relevant Information: Restrictions on the Progressive—Stative and Dynamic Meanings of Verbs.*

 **Exercise**   What Were You Doing . . . ?

Write answers to the following questions, using the past progressive tense.

1.  What were you doing last night when the sun set?

    _____

2.  What was your family doing yesterday when you got home?

    _____

3.  What were you doing when the teacher arrived at class?

    _____

4.  What was your teacher doing when you arrived at class?

    _____

5. What were you doing at 7:15 this morning?

## CHAPTER REVIEW

**Exercise**  Editing for the Past and Past Progressive—
The Joy of Country Life

Edit the verbs in the following paragraph.

### The Joy of Country Life

When I was eight years old, my parents took a trip with me and my sister
to my uncle's house in the country, and this was my first opportunity to enjoy    2
rural life. Was there any pleasure greater than being able to enjoy the refreshing
country air in the middle of the summer along with the discovery of so many    4
kinds of wildlife? Not for me. In the late afternoons, my sister and I enjoy the
cool breezes while we run and laughed and catch insects such as fireflies. We    6
also see many new kinds of beautiful birds (but we didn't catch any). One day
we went fishing in the lake with my uncle. This was our first time, so our uncle    8
teached us how to do it. The fish were bit very well that summer, and we catch
twenty fish in three hours. This really add to my joy. Because of this wonderful    10
experience filled with many new discoveries for me, my opinion about the
country changed. Now, I firmly believed that the country is a much more enjoy-    12
able place for a vacation than the city.

Adapted from a paragraph by Hsin-Mei Lee

### Writing Assignment A: A Frightening Experience

Write a paragraph about a time you had a frightening experience. Start with a topic
sentence that identifies the time, place, and type of experience you are writing
about. Continue with specific supporting details in time order. Write a concluding
sentence that gives a feeling of finish to your paragraph.

### Writing Assignment B: An Imaginary Event

The following is a colorful description of an imaginary event in the past. It is
from Roald Dahl's *James and the Giant Peach*. As you read it, pay attention to the

verbs and the details. Perhaps it will inspire you to think of your own imaginary event.

### Chocolate Heaven

This building happened to be a famous factory where they made chocolate, and almost at once a great river of warm melted chocolate came pouring out of the holes in the factory wall. A minute later, this brown sticky mess was flowing through every street in the village, oozing° under doors of houses and into people's shops and gardens. Children were wading° in it up to their knees, and some were even trying to swim in it, and all of them were sucking it into their mouths in great greedy gulps° and shrieking° with joy.

°**oozing:** flowing, moving slowly
°**wading:** walking in
°**gulps:** quick, deep swallows
°**shrieking:** screaming

Write a description of an imaginary event in the past. Possible topics include:

The day Disney World allowed people in free

The day I had one million dollars to spend in one day

The day a flying saucer landed near my house

As an alternative, you may write about a disaster you witnessed or something exciting you witnessed.

Start your paragraph with a topic sentence that identifies the time, place, and type of experience you are writing about. Continue with specific supporting details in time order. Write a concluding sentence that gives a feeling of finish to your paragraph.

 **Writing Assignment C:** *What Happened Next?*

The following is a paragraph from Raymond Chandler's detective novel *The Lady in the Lake*. Philip Marlowe, the detective, had a nightmare. Later, he was lucky enough to fall back to sleep. Now it is late in the morning, and he is waking up naturally. Read the paragraph and then, on a separate piece of paper, write what happened next. Use your imagination.

It was nine o'clock when I woke up again. The sun was on my face. The room was hot. I showered and shaved and partly dressed and made the morning toast and eggs and coffee in the dinette. While I was finishing up, there was a knock at the apartment door.

 **Writing Assignment D:** *A Childhood Memory*

In the following passage from Alice Taylor's *To School through the Fields*, the author tells how she and her younger brother Connie spent their days before they went to school.

°**grove:** group of trees

°**left to our own devices:** left alone

**In the Grove° behind the House**

Connie and I spent our days in the grove behind the house. The others were gone to school, so we were left to our own devices°. We played imaginary games beneath the trees where the ground was soft with the fallen leaves and pine needles of many years. One old tree had a huge hole in its trunk, and into this we sat and pretended that we were traveling to many strange places. Because we could not see the top of this tree, we believed that it grew into heaven. Heaven in those days was very real.

Write a paragraph about the ways you spent your free time when you were a child. Start your paragraph with a topic sentence that identifies the time, place, and type of experience you are writing about. Support your topic sentence with plenty of specific supporting details. Write a concluding sentence that gives a feeling of finish to your paragraph.

## FOOD FOR THOUGHT

Explain the difference in the meaning of the verbs in the following sentences.

1. I bought the sweater and then noticed that it had a hole in it.

2. I was buying the sweater when I noticed that it had a hole in it.

_____

1. When the alarm rang, I got out of bed.

2. When the alarm rang, I was getting out of bed.

_____

## CLASSROOM ASSESSMENT TECHNIQUE (CAT)

## THE ONE-MINUTE PAPER

Take a minute or two to write answers to the following questions. Write your answers on a separate piece of paper without your name.

1. What are the most important points that you have learned in this chapter?

2. What questions remain in your mind at the end of this chapter?

*Note: Use this exercise to help you get answers to any questions you still have. Ask these questions to anyone who might be able to help you, such as another student or your instructor.*

# 6 The Present Perfect Tense and the Present Perfect Progressive Tense

≡≡≡ **THE PRESENT PERFECT**

▶ **Sample Paragraph**

Read the following paragraph about how the microchip has changed modern life. The present perfect verbs appear in italics.

**Any Program You Want**

Many new conveniences *have found* their way into people's homes since the development of the microchip. First, many people *have added* video cassette recorders to their home entertainment centers. With a VCR, anyone can program the machine to tape television programs at any time for later viewing. Also, telephones *have changed* a lot in recent years. Now people can program dozens of phone numbers into the machine for automatic dialing. Most importantly, of course, microchips *have brought* computers right into people's homes. Now everyone has easy access to an unlimited number of applications from financial planning and word processing to educational programs and even games. There is no doubt that the microchip *has made* significant changes in most people's lives because these tiny silicon marvels allow us to use information according to our needs.

 **Essential Information: THE FORM OF THE PRESENT PERFECT TENSE**

The present perfect consists of *have* or *has* plus the past participle of the verb.

> The Present Perfect = Have / Has + Past Participle

**Examples**

Many new conveniences *have found* their way into people's homes since the development of the microchip.

There is no doubt that the microchip *has made* significant changes in most people's lives.

The auxiliary verb *has* is used with the third person singular.

The microchip *has made* significant changes in most people's lives.

In informal writing, *have* or *has* are often written as contractions with pronouns.

|  | Singular | Plural |
|---|---|---|
| First person | I've | we've |
| Second person | you've | you've |
| Third person | he's | |
|  | she's | they've |
|  | it's | |

Many new conveniences have found their way into people's homes since the development of the microchip. As a result, *they've* changed our lives in many ways.

There is no doubt that the microchip *has made* significant changes in most people's lives. *It's* certainly *made* changes in my life.

Regular past participles are the same form as the simple past tense of the verb.

**Examples**

| BASE FORM | PAST TENSE | PAST PARTICIPLE |
|---|---|---|
| add | added | added |
| change | changed | changed |
| study | studied | studied |

Some irregular verbs have the same irregular form in the simple past tense and the past participle.

**Examples**

| BASE FORM | PAST TENSE | PAST PARTICIPLE |
|-----------|-----------|-----------------|
| find | found | found |
| buy | bought | bought |
| make | made | made |

Some irregular verbs have three different forms.

**Examples**

| BASE FORM | PAST TENSE | PAST PARTICIPLE |
|-----------|-----------|-----------------|
| go | went | gone |
| begin | began | begun |
| shake | shook | shaken |

# ≡ PAST TIME TO PRESENT TIME: THE PRESENT PERFECT TENSE

 **Essential Information: PAST TO PRESENT TIME**

One common use of the present perfect is to express past to present time.

> Past to Present Time = An Activity or Condition That Started in the Past and Continues up to the Present

PAST                 PRESENT

X————————————————————→

**Examples**

We *have covered* five chapters in this text so far.

You *have studied* four verb forms in some detail.

**!** Do *not* use the simple present for this time period.

*I live in Texas for two years.
*I have my car six months.

The above sentences are *not* correct English.

**!** Also, do *not* use the simple past tense for a time period that includes *past to present* (and possibly future).

I lived in Ottawa for two years.

The past tense verb indicates that the person left Ottawa and is no longer living there. It does not include the present.

I had my car two months.

The past tense verb indicates that the person no longer has the car. It does not include the present.

The two previous sample sentences with past tense verbs are correct English, but they do not express past to present time.

 **Exercise A**   Past to Present—Matrix

Look at the following matrix and the sentences based on it. These sentences are in the present perfect. After studying the example, you are going to draw your own matrix with important events in your life that have continued up to the present.

| | 1954 | 1969 | 1970 | 1972 | 1977 | 1981 | NOW |
|---|---|---|---|---|---|---|---|
| 1. Be in the U.S. | | | | | | | → |
| 2. Have his V.W. | | | | | | | → |
| 3. Know his wife | | | | | | | → |
| 4. Be married | | | | | | | → |
| 5. Have his job | | | | | | | → |
| 6. Live in his house | | | | | | | → |

1. Brian has been in the U.S. since 1954.

2. He has had his V.W. since 1969.

3. He has known his wife since 1970.

4. He has been married since 1972.

5. He has had his present job as an ESL instructor since 1977.

6. He has lived in his house in San Pedro since 1981.

What word is used before the dates in each sentence?

_____

Now it is your turn. Fill in important events after the numbers on the left, and write the dates on the top line of the matrix.

|  | 19___ | 19___ | 19___ | 19___ | 19___ | 19___ | NOW |
|---|---|---|---|---|---|---|---|
| 1. _____ _____ |  |  |  |  |  |  |  |
| 2. _____ _____ |  |  |  |  |  |  |  |
| 3. _____ _____ |  |  |  |  |  |  |  |
| 4. _____ _____ |  |  |  |  |  |  |  |
| 5. _____ _____ |  |  |  |  |  |  |  |
| 6. _____ _____ |  |  |  |  |  |  |  |

When you finish, exchange matrices with another student, and write sentences based on the information in your partner's matrix.

1. _____
2. _____
3. _____
4. _____
5. _____
6. _____

When you finish writing sentences about your partner, your instructor may ask you to write a sample sentence about your partner on the board.

 **Exercise B**   "... And the Winner Is ..."

Work in small groups of four to five students. In this exercise you will find out which person has been involved in the following activities for the longest time. In your answer, include the word *for* and an amount of time.

**Example**

Who has been married the longest?

Brian has been married for twenty-two years.

1. Who has lived in this state (or province) the longest?

   _____

2. Who has had his or her watch the longest?

   _____

3. Who has had a driver's license the longest?

   _____

4. Who has been at this school the longest?

   _____

5. Who has known the instructor the longest?

   _____

Write two questions of your own.

6. _____

   _____

7. _____

   _____

*Optional final step: Now that there is a "winner" for each group for each question, each winner for each group will stand up and announce his or her winning answer. Who is the winner for each question in the entire class? Write complete sentences.*

1. _____

2. _____

3. _____

4. _____

5. _____

### Relevant Information: For and Since with the Present Perfect Tense

As you saw in the previous exercises, *for* and *since* are often used with the present perfect to show time.

*For* refers to a period of time.

My wife and I have known each other *for thirteen years*.

We have been married *for ten years*.

*For* can usually be deleted.

We have lived in our house *six years*.

We have had our Chevy *three years*.

*Since* refers to a point in time. This point can be clock time, a date, or an event in the past expressed in a clause.

We have been in class *since 6:30*.

The instructor has been at this school *since 1985*.

She has had three jobs *since she graduated from college*.

 **Exercise A**  *For* and *Since*—About Amy

Fill in the blanks with *for* or *since*.

1.  Amy has been in Canada ___*for*___ three years.

2.  She has not seen her mother in China _____ 1988.

3.  Her parents haven't lived together _____ twenty years.

4.  They have lived in separate countries _____ 1974.

5.  Amy has been homesick _____ she came to Canada.

 **Exercise B**  *For* and *Since*—About You

Answer the following questions. Write complete sentences. As an alternative, your instructor may ask you to work with a partner and write your partner's answers to the questions.

How long have you . . .

1.  lived in this country?

   _____

2.  worked at your present job?

   _____

3.  lived at your current address?

   _____

4.  known the instructor?

   _____

5.  had your dictionary?

   _____

## REVIEW: PAST TO PRESENT TIME— THE PRESENT PERFECT TENSE

 **Exercise**   Using a Variety of Verb Tenses—Hoang Tran

Edit the following paragraph for correct verbs. It contains six verb errors. After you edit the paragraph, do the exercise that follows.

### Hoang Tran

Hoang Tran has lived in the United States for five years. When she first arrived in this country, she has lived in San Francisco for six months. Then she       2
and her family moved to Texas. She has lived in Dallas, Texas, for four and a half years. Her first job was in a restaurant. She worked as a waitress. Since       4
then, she had several other jobs, but she worked as a bookkeeper in a hotel for the last two years. Hoang studied English for the last seven years, and she is       6
still studying English at a community college near her home. She plans to continue classes in English and in accounting. She has met Vinh three semesters       8
ago in Accounting I, and they are sweethearts since then. In fact, they are talking about getting married next year.       10

**True or False?**

Identify the following statements as true or false, based on the information in the previous paragraph. Circle T for *true* or F for *false*. If the information is false, write the true statement.

T     F     1. Hoang Tran has lived in the U.S. for five years.

_____

T     F     2. She lives in San Francisco.

_____

T     F     3. She has lived in Dallas for four and a half years.

_____

T     F     4. She is a waitress.

_____

T     F     5. She worked in a hotel two years ago.

_____

**T     F     6.** She and Vinh were sweethearts for three semesters.

_____

**T     F     7.** They are getting married next year.

_____

# PAST TIME TO PRESENT TIME: THE PRESENT PERFECT PROGRESSIVE TENSE

### ▶ Sample Paragraph

Read the following paragraph, which is based on William Rathje's "Why We Throw Food Away." The present perfect progressive verbs appear in italics.

### Tucson's Food Waste

The people of Tucson throw away about fifteen percent of the food they buy. I know about Tucson's food waste because I work with a crew that *has been studying* the city's garbage for over a decade. We *have been sorting* it, *weighing* it, and *keeping* track of the relative volumes of this and that. If Tucson's pattern is typical across the United States, then this country throws away enough food to feed all of Canada.

 **Essential Information: THE FORM OF THE PRESENT PERFECT PROGRESSIVE TENSE**

The present perfect progressive consists of the present of *have* plus *been* plus the *-ing* form of the verb.

> Have/Has + Been + Verb + ing

### Examples

I work with a crew that *has been studying* the city's garbage for over a decade.

We *have been sorting* it, *weighing* it, and *keeping* track of the relative volumes of this and that.

The auxiliary verb *has* is used with the third person singular.

I work with a crew that *has been studying* the city's garbage for over a decade.

*Have* or *has* can be written as contractions with pronouns, especially in informal writing.

*It's been studying* the city's garbage for over a decade.

*We've been sorting* it, . . .

**Essential Information: PAST TO PRESENT TIME
WITH THE PRESENT PERFECT PROGRESSIVE**

Read the following pairs of sentences.

   A. *I've worked* for the city of Tucson for ten years.

   B. *I've been working* for the city of Tucson for ten years.

   A. *I've studied* the city's garbage for over five years.

   B. *I've been studying* the city's garbage for over five years.

   A. *I've learned* a lot about people's wastefulness.

   B. *I've been learning* a lot about people's wastefulness.

The sentences in A and B refer to the same reality—past to present time. The present perfect progressive, however, has a slightly different emphasis.

> The present perfect progressive places more emphasis on the in-progress nature of an action that started in the past and is in progress up to the present.

### *Relevant Information: Stative Verbs*

Stative verbs cannot be used in the progressive form. For information on stative and dynamic verbs, refer back to Chapter Four, page 72, Relevant Information: Restrictions on the Progressive—Stative and Dynamic Meanings of Verbs.

     Go back to the matrix on page 98. Which of these verbs can be used in the progressive form?

_____

 **Exercise**  Practicing the Present Perfect Progressive Tense—Steamed

Have you ever felt "steamed"? In other words, did you ever feel angry and annoyed about something that was happening nearby? (Of course, you have!)

     Write sentences in response to the following annoying situations. Use the present perfect progressive. Clues that you may use in your answers appear in parentheses in some cases.

1.  People are standing next to a parked car, and they are very annoyed.
    (car alarm ring)

    *The alarm has been ringing for over an hour.*

2.  An angry woman is standing at a bus stop on a windy, rainy day.
    (wait for bus)

    _____

3. A mother gets home from a busy day at work, but her kids haven't done their homework or their chores. (watch TV)

   _____

4. Gretchen took out the ironing board at noon. It's 3:00, and her back is aching.

   _____

5. Carlos is unemployed, but almost every day he leaves his house well dressed and comes back a few hours later, usually depressed.

   _____

# ═══ UNSPECIFIED PAST TIME

### ▶ Sample Paragraph

Read the following paragraph about the differences between psychologists and psychiatrists.

### Psychologists and Psychiatrists

Both psychologists and psychiatrists help people with psychological problems, but their training is quite different. Psychologists have training specifically in the field of psychology. They *have attended* graduate school in psychology and *completed* their training in a counseling office. They cannot prescribe drugs to their patients. On the other hand, psychiatrists have medical training. They *have attended* medical school and *obtained* the M.D. (doctor of medicine) degree. In addition, they *have completed* their training in a hospital. Because of their medical training, psychiatrists can prescribe drugs to their patients. Due to these differences in training, psychiatrists usually charge their patients more per hour than psychologists do.

 ### Essential Information: THE PRESENT PERFECT TENSE FOR UNSPECIFIED PAST TIME

> The present perfect tense can refer to unspecified past time.

 **Exercise**   The Present Perfect Tense for Unspecified Past Time— Training for Professionals

How much do you know about other professions? Work in a small group to do the following exercise.

What kind of training have the following professionals had? (If you're not sure, make a guess.) Write your answers in complete sentences.

1. A dentist

   *A dentist has graduated from dental school.*

2. A college instructor

   _____

3. An accountant

   _____

4. A registered nurse

   _____

5. A lawyer

   _____

6. A chef

   _____

 **Essential Information: UNSPECIFIED TIME VERSUS SPECIFIED TIME IN THE PAST**

Read the following paragraphs. Both refer to past time.

### JAPANESE PRISONS

°**hostage:** person held against his or her will

There *has* never *been* a hostage° crisis in a Japanese prison. There *has been* only one "prison disturbance." There *has* never *been* a reported case of homosexual rape or of prisoner gang wars. No inmate *has* ever *killed* a guard; there *has been* only one inmate death in the last ten years at the hands of another. There *have been* only thirty-five escapes from Japanese prisons in the last seven years.

Prison officials are highly trained. Last year, though two-thirds of those who *passed* the national qualifying test for prison guards *were* university graduates, only one-fourth *got* jobs as guards.

Even though the first paragraph refers to events in the past, the past tense does not appear. Instead, the *present perfect* appears because the paragraph is referring to *unspecified time in the past*. Why, then, do the italicized verbs in the second paragraph appear in the *past tense*?

_____

Which two words in the second paragraph helped you identify the time as "past"?

_____

Words such as "last year" express past time and are called *past time markers*. Other past time markers include:

| yesterday | two weeks ago | a long time ago |
| last night | last month | at 6:00 A.M. |
| last week | last year | in 1990 |

**Exercise**   Present Perfect Tense versus Past Tense—Exploring Space

Fill in the blanks with present perfect or past verbs.

1.  People (always, dream) *have always dreamed* about exploring space.

2.  In this century, we (accomplish) _____ this dream.

3.  In 1957 Russia (send up) _____ the first satellite, Sputnik I, to orbit Earth.

4.  On July 20, 1969, United States astronauts Neil Armstrong and Edwin Aldrin (become) _____ the first people to walk on the moon.

5.  In the 1970s the United States (launch) _____ a spacecraft to study the planets.

## Essential Information: TIME MARKERS AS SIGNALS FOR TENSE CHANGE IN A SERIES OF SENTENCES

A past time marker in one sentence often sets up a past time context for the sentences that follow. This past time context then calls for past tense verbs. In the following paragraph, notice that the past time marker "long ago" causes a change into the *past* in several of the sentences that follow.

### FAMOUS ASTRONOMERS

Astronomers study the stars. Many famous astronomers have helped us understand the universe. Most people have heard the names of two of the greatest astronomers: Copernicus and Galileo. *Long ago*, people *thought* that the Earth was the center of everything. They *thought* that the Sun and planets *revolved* around the Earth. Copernicus *said* that the Earth *wasn't* the center of things. He *showed* that the Sun *was* the center of the Solar System and that the Earth *moved* around it. Also, Galileo *said* that the Earth *revolved* around the Sun. Shortly afterwards, the government *put* him in jail. *Today* we *remember* Copernicus and Galileo as brilliant astronomers.

Look again at the five sentences in the previous paragraph (repeated below). Which verb tenses are used in each of these sentences and why?

1.  Astronomers *study* the stars.

    _____

2.  Many famous astronomers *have helped* us understand the universe.

    _____

3.  Most people *have heard* the names of two of the greatest astronomers, Copernicus and Galileo.

    _____

4.  Long ago, people *thought* that the Earth was the center of everything.

    _____

5.  They *thought* that the Sun and planets *revolved* around the Earth.

    _____

   Now look at the last sentence in the previous paragraph (repeated below). Which verb tense is used and why?

   Today we *remember* Copernicus and Galileo as brilliant astronomers.

_____

 ## Essential Information: THE LACK OF TIME MARKERS

### Part One: The Context Calls for the Past Tense

Past time markers are not always necessary to signal the past tense. The context alone may clearly indicate past time, which calls for the past tense.

### Examples

Context: A student is writing about a personal experience.

   He writes: "My first date with Kimiko was a disaster."

Context: A student spent spring break in Brazil.

   She writes: "My trip to Brazil was exhausting."

The context tells us that both the first date and the trip are events in the past.

### Part Two: Changing from the Present Perfect to the Past

At other times, writers establish an unspecified past tense context with the present perfect, and then they switch to the past tense for specific events within that context.

### Examples

   I have been to Tijuana. I bought this shirt there.

   I have read all the novels of Dick Francis. I especially liked his latest one. It was really exciting.

 ## Exercise  Cartoon

Why did the authors of this text include the following cartoon at this point in the book?

_____

_____

(Reprinted with special permission of King Features Syndicate)

## COMPLETED ACTION VERSUS IN-PROGRESS ACTION

 **Essential Information: DISTINGUISHING BETWEEN COMPLETED ACTION AND IN-PROGRESS ACTION**

What's the difference in meaning in each pair of sentences?

A. I've read *Of Mice and Men* for my term paper.

B. I've been reading *Of Mice and Men* for my term paper.

A. I've organized my term paper.

B. I've been organizing my term paper.

A. I've typed the final draft.

B. I've been typing the final draft.

Write your answer here:

_____

 **Exercise A** Completed Action versus In-Progress Action—Situations

Add an explanatory sentence to the following situations. Use the present perfect or present perfect progressive, depending on whether the action is complete or incomplete.

1. Donna is at home relaxed. The gifts for her family and friends are under the Christmas tree.

   *She has finished her Christmas shopping.*

2.  Pat is putting the ironing board away. The ironed clothing is in the closet.

    _____

3.  Paul is in his garage. He is covered with grease, and the front wheels of his car are on the ground.

    _____

4.  It's April first. Carla has a giant headache. Tax forms cover the top of her desk.

    _____

5.  David was working on his car engine when I walked by his house this morning. Now, he just called me to offer me a ride to soccer practice.

    _____

6.  Judy is putting her trigonometry book and calculator away.

    _____

7.  Walt is exhausted, but he's going back to the mall tomorrow with his Christmas shopping list.

    _____

8.  Susie can't buy any more books at the book fair.

    _____

9.  Gloria is rolling up the hose and putting the sponge, soap, and bucket away.

    _____

**Exercise B**   Practice in Pairs

Work with a partner. Ask each other the following questions.

1.  What have you been doing all semester (or quarter) in this class?

    _____

2.  How many compositions (or writing assignments) have you written?

    _____

3.  What has the instructor been emphasizing about writing compositions?

    _____

4.  What is the most important thing you have learned?

    _____

5.  Has your writing improved? In what way? Give an example.

    _____

6.  Has your attitude toward writing changed? Explain.

_____

7.  What grammar point has been giving you the most problems?

_____

## REVIEW: PAST VERSUS PRESENT PERFECT

 **Exercise A**   Identifying a Variety of Verbs—My Wife's Accident

Can you explain the uses of the verb tenses in the following short paragraph? Work with a partner to decide why each verb tense is used.

### My Wife's Accident

I *have* never *broken* a bone, but my wife *had* an accident on Memorial Day. First we *planted* some flowers on a hill. Then we *started* to come down from the hill. When she *stepped* off the retaining wall° onto a bench, the bench *broke*. She *fell* and *broke* her ankle. I *had* to take her to the emergency room at San Pedro Hospital, and now she *is* on crutches. I *have* never *had* such a memorable Memorial Day.

°**retaining wall:** a low wall that holds back earth

 **Exercise B**   Practicing the Past Tense and the Present Perfect Tense—No Fake Earthquake for Me!

Write the correct verbs—past tense or present perfect—in the blanks.

### No Fake Earthquake for Me!

I have visited most of the major tourist spots in Southern California. First, I have been to all of the large amusement parks with wild rides. The first amusement park I visited (be) _____ Disneyland my first month in Los Angeles. Later, I (go) _____ to Knott's Berry Farm and then to Magic Mountain. I (see, also) _____ all of the most well-known museums in the area. I (go) _____ to the Los Angeles County Museum a few years ago to see the exhibit of the Impressionists. Shortly after that, I (visit) _____ the Getty Museum, the Norton Simon Museum, and the Huntington Museum. There is only one tourist spot I have not seen yet, and that is Universal Studios in California. This tourist spot has a simulated earthquake ride that is supposed to

be very exciting and realistic. But I (experience, already) _____
$\overline{\phantom{xxxxx}6}$

a real California earthquake, so why would I want to visit Universal Studios to

pay for a phony earthquake ride?

 **Exercise C**  Practicing the Present Perfect Tense—Tourist Spots

In small groups, find out who has visited the following tourist spots by asking each
other questions based on the prompts given below. Write your group's answers in
complete sentences on a separate piece of paper. Make sure you use the correct verb
forms.

**Example**

   . . . (visit) a city that allows gambling?

    Who has visited a city that allows gambling?
               *or*
    Has anyone visited a city that allows gambling?

    Thanh and Suki have visited Las Vegas.

1.  . . . (see) a famous waterfall?
2.  . . . (go) to an amusement park such as Disneyland or Disney World?
3.  . . . (go camping) in a forest?
4.  . . . (hike) in a national park?
5.  . . . (visit) a large museum?
6.  . . . (attend) a concert in any big city?
7.  . . . (go) to a large zoo?
8.  . . . (travel) to a historical landmark?
9.  . . . (spend) a vacation at a beach resort?
10.  . . . (tour) the government buildings in any state or province?
11.  . . . (shop) in a large shopping mall in a large city?

CHAPTER REVIEW

## CHART: REVIEW OF VERBS

| | | PRESENT PERFECT TENSE | PRESENT PERFECT PROGRESSIVE TENSE |
|---|---|---|---|
| FORM | | HAVE/HAS + PAST PARTICIPLE | HAVE/HAS + BEEN + PAST PARTICIPLE |
| PAST TO PRESENT | **DYNAMIC** | Jake *has lived* in Ottawa for two years. | Jake *has been living* in Ottawa for two years. |
| | | | Jake *has been typing* his term paper for two hours. (in progress) |
| | **STATIVE** | Jake *has had* his computer for six months. | |
| UNSPECIFIED PAST | | Jake *has read* several books for his term paper. | |
| | | Jake *has typed* his term paper. (completed) | |

    **Exercise A**   Editing—The Courtship of Sue and Joe

Edit the following paragraph.

### The Courtship of Sue and Joe

Things have been getting serious between Sue and Joe recently. Sue has

lived in Miami since over four years. Joe lives there for two years. She and Joe        2

have been knowing each other for almost two years. They have taken several

classes together at Miami Dade Community College. Last year they have taken        4

two English classes together, and they have started dating regularly about six months ago. They didn't date anyone else since then. Lately, they have been      6

talking about getting married.

 **Exercise B**   Practicing a Mixture of Verbs—Leaving Your Birthplace

The questions in this exercise focus on the theme, "leaving your birthplace." Write complete sentences to answer the questions on a separate piece of paper.

1. When did you come to this country?

2. How old were you?

3. Who took you to the airport? (Or who did you come with?)

4. How did you feel when you left your country?

5. Have you met many people from your native country? How did you meet them?

6. Have you had any problems adjusting to a new culture? Explain.

7. Have you been happy here? Why or why not?

8. Have you ever regretted your decision to leave your homeland?

 **Exercise C**   Mixed Verb Tenses—The Real Thing

Fill in the missing verbs. You may use any of the following verb tenses:

present
present progressive

past
past progressive

present perfect
present perfect progressive

In several cases, more than one answer may be possible.

### The Real Thing

°**boom:** grow rapidly

°**boost:** increase
°**authentic:** the real thing; not copied

°**oyster:** flat shellfish that produces pearls

Right now business (boom)° _____ for Asian food in the United
                                      1
States. Immigrants (provide) _____ the biggest boost° for authentic°
                                    2
Asian food. In addition, Americans (develop) _____ more sophisticated
                                                    3
preferences. An example of the search for authenticity (be) _____ the
                                                                  4
Lee Kum Kee brand of oyster° sauce. The Hong Kong–based manufacturer's

traditional label (disappear) _____ briefly in the late 1980s when the
                                    5

U.S. importers (try) _____ to Westernize the image of the product to
<br>6

win more shelf space in big supermarkets. Now, however, Americans (prefer)

_____ products that (be) _____ more genuinely Asian in
<br>7                             8

°**prosper:** be successful     appearance and taste. Lee Kum Kee (prosper)° _____ in the United
<br>9

°**chains:** groups of related    States, and people (find) _____ its sauces in supermarket chains° in all
stores                                        10

fifty states. Even at some baseball stadiums, fans (buy) _____ Asian
<br>11

°**cuisine:** style of cooking    cuisine°. David Lee, the U.S. importer (explain) _____ the return to the
<br>12

original packaging this way: "We (try) _____ to move toward the
<br>13

°**mainstream:** usual or     mainstream°, but the mainstream (move) _____ toward us."
common way of acting                                      14

## Writing Assignment: Summary and Reaction–"The Ox and the Colt"

Read the following fable "The Ox and the Colt." In this story, an ox and a colt are
arguing over who should drink at the water hole first. The ox claims that he should
go first because he is older.

**The colt:**    Should I let you go first simply because you've grown old? The
world today belongs to the young. After all, young people haven't
made the mistakes your generation has!

**The ox:**    Then you should respect me because I've experienced more of life
than you.

**The colt:**    Do you think you've experienced more than I have just because
you've lived longer? You forget that the world has changed. What
have oxen done that's so great?

**The ox:**    They've worked in the fields of the kings!

**The colt:**    You've forgotten that horses have carried the kings themselves on
their backs for centuries! Really, your arguments have only made
me laugh so far!

°**vulture:** a large bird that   *(As soon as the two animals get ready to fight to the death, they notice several vultures°*
eats dead flesh.            *overhead waiting for the kill.)*

**The colt:**    We've overlooked an important fact here. There may be room for
us both to drink together.

**The ox:**    We've found a perfect solution.

*(As the ox and the colt drink water together, the vultures fly away.)*

What's the moral of this fable?

_____

Write a summary and reaction paragraph based on the story of the ox and the colt. In the first sentence identify the story. Next, in a few sentences, tell what happened in the story. Last, write your reaction to the story, based on the lesson this story teaches. Finish with a concluding idea.

## ≡    FOOD FOR THOUGHT    ≡

Read the following sentences spoken on election day. Answer the questions that appear after A and B.

    A: I've voted. Have you?

    B: I voted. Did you?

1. Are A and B possible on election day?

_____

2. Are A and B possible on the day after the election?

_____

## ≡    CLASSROOM ASSESSMENT TECHNIQUE (CAT)    ≡

### THE ONE-MINUTE PAPER

Take a minute or two to write answers to the following questions. Write your answers on a separate piece of paper without your name.

1. What are the most important points that you have learned in this chapter?

2. What questions remain in your mind at the end of this chapter?

*Note: Use this exercise to help you get answers to any questions you still have. Ask these questions to anyone who might be able to help you, such as another student or your instructor.*

# CHAPTER 7
# Nouns and Determiners (Articles)

(Reprinted with permission of Patrick Hardin)

## NOUNS

### ▶ Sample Paragraph

Read the following passage based on Lawrence Sanders' *The First Deadly Sin*. The nouns appear in italics.

#### Daniel Blank

*Daniel Blank* was a tall *man*, slightly over six *feet*, and was now slender. In *high school* and *college* he had competed in *swimming*, *track*, and *tennis*. These physical *activities* had given his *body* well-developed *shoulders* and *thighs*. Shortly after his *separation* from his *wife*, he had taken a "physical *inventory*" of

°**deterioration:** the
 process of getting worse

°**fanatic:** one who shows
 excessive enthusiasm
°**swear off:** quit

his naked *body* in the full-length *mirror* on the *inside* of his *bathroom door*. He saw that *deterioration*° had begun.

He had at once begun a strict *program* of *diet* and *exercise*. He bought several *books* on *nutrition* and *systems* of physical *training*. He was not a *fanatic*°. He did not swear off° *drinking* and *smoking*. But he cut his *alcohol intake* by half and switched to non-*nicotine cigarettes* made of dried *lettuce leaves*. He tried to avoid *starch, carbohydrates, dairy products, eggs,* and red *meat*. He ate fresh *fruit, vegetables,* broiled *fish, salads* with a *dressing* of fresh *lemon juice*. Within three *months,* he had lost twenty *pounds,* and his *ribs* and *hip bones* showed.

*Note: In the following noun phrases, the first noun modifies the second noun.*

bathroom *door*

alcohol *intake*

non-nicotine *cigarettes*

lettuce *leaves*

dairy *products*

lemon *juice*

hip *bones*

 ### Essential Information: NOUNS

Most nouns name people, places, or things. Some nouns name concepts or activities. Read the following examples, and write additional examples.

People:    Daniel, Mr. Blank, man

_____

Places:    bathroom, college

_____

Things:    shoulder, thigh, juice, month, fish

_____

Concepts:  separation, deterioration, nutrition, intake

_____

Activities: swimming, tennis, exercise, drinking

_____

 ### Exercise   Identifying Nouns

Underline the nouns in the following proverbs from countries throughout the world.

1. You can't have your <u>cake</u> and eat it too. (American)

2. To hide one lie, a thousand lies are needed. (Indian)

3. If you have to kill a snake, kill it once and for all. (Japanese)

4. With soft words, you can talk a snake out of its hole. (Iranian)

5. You cannot buy a true friend with money. (Russian)

6. If you chase two rabbits, you will not catch either. (Russian)

7. Whoever lies down with a dog will get up with fleas. (Hebrew)

8. No one calls his own buttermilk sour. (Iranian)

9. If you kick a stone because you are angry at it, you will only hurt your foot. (Korean)

10. It is better to have trouble at the beginning than at the end. (Indian)

11. It is the buyer who profits from the fight of two shopkeepers. (Korean)

12. Talk does not cook rice. (Chinese)

When you finish, exchange your work with a partner. Check your partner's work for underlined nouns.

 **Writing Assignment:** *Explaining a Proverb and Identifying Nouns*

### Step One

Discuss the meanings of the proverbs in the previous exercise with students in a small group or the entire class.

### Step Two

Select a proverb from the previous exercise and write a paragraph to explain its meaning. Start your paragraph with a topic sentence that includes the proverb, the country it comes from, and the meaning of the proverb.

### Example

The proverb "Step by step a person goes up the staircase" from Turkey means that a person can reach a goal little by little.

Explain in greater detail what this proverb means to you. Be specific. Include a personal experience. Write a concluding sentence that gives a feeling of finish to your paragraph.

## CHART: AN OVERVIEW OF NOUNS

The rest of this chapter covers the following categories of nouns, with particular emphasis on singular count nouns and their determiners (articles). (For a discussion of these terms, see page 121.)

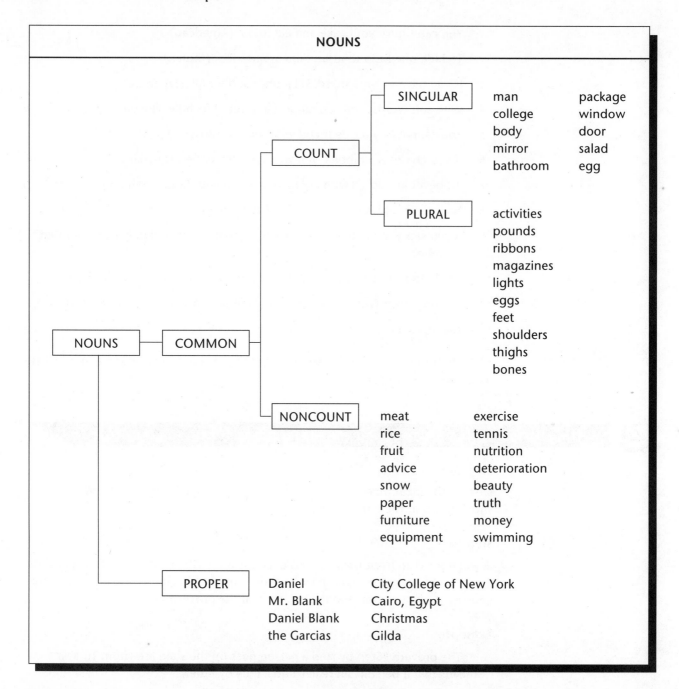

**NOUNS**

- NOUNS
  - COMMON
    - COUNT
      - SINGULAR

        man        package
        college    window
        body       door
        mirror     salad
        bathroom   egg

      - PLURAL

        activities
        pounds
        ribbons
        magazines
        lights
        eggs
        feet
        shoulders
        thighs
        bones

    - NONCOUNT

      meat       exercise
      rice       tennis
      fruit      nutrition
      advice     deterioration
      snow       beauty
      paper      truth
      furniture  money
      equipment  swimming

  - PROPER

    Daniel         City College of New York
    Mr. Blank      Cairo, Egypt
    Daniel Blank   Christmas
    the Garcias    Gilda

 **Essential Information: PROPER AND COMMON NOUNS**

Proper nouns refer to specific people, places, or things. They begin with a capital letter.

**Examples**

  Daniel, City College of New York, Nike

Common nouns do not refer to specific people, places, or things. They usually do not begin with a capital letter (unless, of course, they are the first word in a sentence or are part of a title).

**Examples**

> man, college, shoes

In the following sections, the discussion covers common nouns. Later in the chapter, the discussion returns to proper nouns.

 ### Essential Information: COUNT AND NONCOUNT NOUNS

Common nouns can fall into two categories: count and noncount nouns. A count noun can take two forms: singular or plural.

**Examples**

> Daniel bought a *book* on nutrition.
> *Book* = singular
>
> Daniel also bought two *books* on exercise.
> *Books* = plural

A noncount noun generally has only one form: singular.

**Examples**

> Gilda bought some brown *rice* yesterday.
>
> She is interested in better *nutrition*.
>
> She plans to give Daniel some *advice* on *rice* and good *nutrition*.

In English, noncount nouns cannot be counted. For example, people do not count *rice*. They can count *bags* of rice or *pounds* of rice. They can even count *grains* of rice—if they are very, very patient! But they cannot count *rice*.

# SINGULAR COUNT NOUNS AND DETERMINERS (ARTICLES)

 ### Essential Information: SINGULAR COUNT NOUNS AND DETERMINERS

Determiners are noun markers that signal that a noun will follow. The most commonly used determiners are articles.

Determiners are used with many types of nouns. In this presentation, however, the focus is on determiners—especially articles—with singular count nouns.

 **Exercise** Identifying Singular Count Nouns

What is a singular count noun?

Go back to the paragraph about Daniel at the beginning of the chapter. List five examples of singular count nouns.

1. _____*man*_____

2. _____

3. _____

4. _____

5. _____

 **Essential Information: DETERMINERS WITH SINGULAR COUNT NOUNS**

Read the following short paragraph and look for errors.

### Going to Son's Swim Lesson

Yesterday I had to take son to swim lesson. I helped him put on swimsuit and get towel. Then we got in car and drove to pool. We arrived five minutes before lesson began.

Explain the mistake that occurs repeatedly in the previous paragraph.

_____

Read the next short paragraph, which is grammatically correct.

### Going to My Son's Swim Lesson

Yesterday I had to take my son to his swim lesson. I helped him put on his swimsuit and get a towel. Then we got in the car and drove to the pool. We arrived five minutes before his lesson began.

Certain words are missing before the following nouns in the first paragraph:

| | | |
|---|---|---|
| son | swimsuit | car |
| lesson | towel | pool |

What do these nouns have in common?

_____

> Before a singular count noun, a determiner is normally used.

### *Relevant Information: Set Phrases*

In many set phrases with a preposition plus a noun, no article is used.

| | | | |
|---|---|---|---|
| at church | in uniform | on campus | for breakfast |
| at school | in business | on schedule | for example |

| at college | in person | on fire | for sale |
|------------|-----------|---------|----------|
| at lunch | in bed | on sale | |
| at night | in fact | | |
| at home | | | |

Daniel exercises *at home at night*.

He reads his exercise and nutrition books *in bed*.

He bought new exercise equipment *on sale*.

He eats brown rice and vegetables *for lunch*.

The following is a list of common *determiners* that can be used before singular count nouns.

1. articles: a, an, the

2. possessives: my, your, her, Pat's, Chris's

3. singular demonstrative adjectives: this, that

4. the number "one"

5. quantity words: another, every, each

(*Mother Goose and Grimm* by Mike Peters. Reprinted by permission: Tribune Media Services)

 **Essential Information: MODIFIERS BETWEEN DETERMINERS AND NOUNS**

A determiner is normally used before a singular count noun. However, a writer may use a modifier or a series of modifiers between the determiner and the noun.

| Determiner | Modifier | Modifier | Modifier | Modifier | Singular Count Noun |
|------------|----------|----------|----------|----------|---------------------|

Read the following description of a room from Raymond Chandler's *The High Window*. Notice how many modifiers appear between "an" and "room" in the last sentence.

°**musty:** with a bad smell
°**fusty:** a smell of decay;
  moldy

I went in. The room beyond was large and square and sunken and cool and had the restful atmosphere of a funeral chapel and something of the same smell. It didn't look as if anybody ever sat in it or would ever want to. *An* old musty°, fusty°, narrow-minded, clean and bitter *room.*

The following discussion and practice will help you identify determiners, nouns, and modifiers.

A. Often, one or several adjectives appear between the determiner and the noun.

> Daniel wrecked *his* Corvette.
> Daniel wrecked *his* new *Corvette*.
> Daniel wrecked *his* beautiful, new *Corvette*
>
> Acme Towing took *the car* away.
> Acme Towing took *the* smashed *car* away.

B. One or several nouns can modify another noun and appear between the determiner and the noun.

> Daniel visited *the shop*.
> Daniel visited *the* auto *shop*.
> Daniel visited *the* auto body *shop*.

C. Both an adjective and a noun can modify a noun and appear between the determiner and the noun.

> They installed *a fender*.
> They installed *a* new *fender*.
> They installed *a* fiberglass *fender*.
> They installed *a* new fiberglass *fender*.

 **Exercise A**    Identifying Nouns and Determiners in Sentences with Modifiers

Circle the determiners and the nouns they modify. Underline the modifiers that come between them.

1. Gilda had (a) small (accident) yesterday.

2. She broke the shower door.

3. She called the repair shop.

4. The repairman installed a new shower door.

5. Afterward, Gilda took a nice, long, steamy, hot, refreshing shower.

 **Exercise B**    Identifying Determiners—A Happy Day

In the following paragraphs taken from Naguib Mahfouz's *Fountain and Tomb*, circle the determiners and the nouns they modify.

**A Happy Day**

It's a happy day. I'm going with my mother to visit the wife of our local

police prefect. It pours down rain all morning, but it's nice again by noon; the        2

sun is shining.

She is an enormous woman, with a tattoo° in the dimple of her chin. Her        4

°**tattoo:** picture on the
skin

laughter is piercing°. The cat has thick fur of the purest white and purrs° con-

°**piercing:** unpleasantly
sharp

stantly.        6

°**purrs:** makes the sound
of a happy cat

She hugs my mother in welcome while I wait. She lifts me high into the air

and then crushes me to her breast. I sink into deep softness, a lush° mattress        8

°**lush:** thick and comfortable

which floods my being with warmth.

I play with the cat until it disappears under the sofa. Stuck on the wall        10

above two crossed swords is a bull's head. I stare at it and wish I could reach it.

°**yearn:** wish strongly

I yearn° for the warm hug at the end of the visit.        12

The conversation continues. She lights the gas lamp hanging from the

°**flits:** flies quickly

ceiling. A moth flits° around the light. I wonder: will it ever come, the moment        14

of leave-taking with its promise of warmth?

# ≡ THE ARTICLES *A(N)* AND *THE* BEFORE SINGULAR COUNT NOUNS

 **Essential Information: *A(N)* AND *THE***

The determiners that many students tend to forget to use in their writing are the articles *a(n)* and *the*. These words are among the most frequently used words in English.

*A(n)* is called the *indefinite article*. It is related to the word *one*.

*The* is called the *definite article*. It is related to the words *this* and *that*.

# ≡ THE INDEFINITE ARTICLE: *A(N)* PLUS SINGULAR COUNT NOUNS

 **Essential Information: *A* AND *AN***

*A* and *an* are regularly used with singular count nouns. They are used when the writer and the reader are introducing a noun into the context.

Use *a* before a consonant sound, and use *an* before a vowel sound. If an adjective comes between the article and the noun, the use of *a/an* depends on the first sound of the adjective.

**Examples from the Author Raymond Chandler**

| | |
|---|---|
| a pistol | an automatic pistol |
| an office | a dark office |
| an expression | a sad expression |
| a marriage | an unhappy marriage |
| a divorce | an uncontested divorce |
| a crime | an unusual crime |
| a room | an empty room |

 **Exercise**   Editing for Missing Indefinite Articles—Pele

Edit the following paragraph.

### Pele

Pele is one of the most famous soccer stars in history. He came from ᵃ

poor family. He was born on October 23, 1940, in small town in Brazil. All the      2

people in the town were poor. They didn't have enough money to buy food

every day. Of course, there was not enough money to buy soccer ball. But      4

Pele's father was very inventive. He tied some old clothing together to form

ball. The young Pele and the other boys in the neighborhood joyfully played      6

soccer with this rag ball. They played barefoot until the sun went down every

day. Later, Pele played soccer on organized team. Soon he became the best      8

player on the team. Before Pele turned thirty, he became millionaire.

## ≡ THE DEFINITE ARTICLE *THE* WITH SINGULAR COUNT NOUNS

### ▶ Sample Paragraph

Raymond Chandler created the famous private investigator Philip Marlowe. In the following passage from the novel *The High Window*, Marlowe is describing his office.

### The Office in the Cahuenga Building

I had an office in the Cahuenga Building, sixth floor, two small rooms at the back. One I left open for a patient client to sit in, if I had a patient client. There was a buzzer on the door which I could switch on and off from my private office.

I looked into the reception room. It was empty of everything but the smell of dust. I threw up another window, unlocked the communications door, and went into the room beyond. Three hard chairs and a swivel chair, a flat desk with a glass top, five green filing cases, three of them full of nothing, a calendar and a framed license on the wall, a phone, a washbowl in a stained cupboard, a hat rack, a carpet that was just something on the floor, and two open windows with net curtains that puckered in and out like the lips of a toothless old man sleeping. Not beautiful, not gay, but better than a tent on the beach.

I hung my hat and coat on the hat rack, washed my face and hands in cold water, lit a cigarette, and hoisted the phone book onto the desk. I wrote down Elisha Morningstar's address and the phone number that went with it and had my hand on the instrument when I remembered that I hadn't switched on the buzzer for the reception room. I reached over the side of the desk and clicked it on. Someone had just opened the door of the outer office.

 **Essential Information: THE DEFINITE ARTICLE *THE* AND COMMON FOCUS**

Communication takes place within an established context. In context, when writers use *the* before a noun, it is because the writers know that the readers are already familiar with the noun referred to. In other words, communicators use *the* when they have *common focus* on a particular noun.

The noun in focus may be a singular count noun, a plural noun, or a noncount noun. The most important point to keep in mind, however, is that a singular count noun almost always has a determiner—*the* or another determiner—before it.

**COMMON FOCUS:**

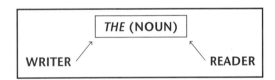

# ESTABLISHING COMMON FOCUS THROUGH FIRST MENTION

 **Essential Information: ESTABLISHING COMMON FOCUS THROUGH FIRST MENTION—THEN REPEATING THE SAME NOUN**

For the following material, refer to the Raymond Chandler reading on page 126. Find the first mention of the nouns given below and write them in the blanks in column I. Include the article that accompanies each noun.

The words in column II appear in the reading.

| I | II |
|---|---|
| 1. _____ | the buzzer |
| 2. _____ | the desk |
| 3. _____ | the hat rack |

Now write an explanation of why Chandler used *a* with the nouns in column I and *the* with the nouns in column II.

_____

_____

_____

Read another example from *The High Window:*

> A young blond man in a brown suit and a cocoa-colored straw hat with a brown and yellow tropical print band was reading. . . . The man in the brown suit drank Coca Colas and looked bored.

In the last sentence, why does Chandler switch from "A man in a brown suit" to "*The* man in *the* brown suit . . ."?

_____

 **Exercise**  First Mention Followed by the Same Noun

Write a sentence to follow the sentences given. In your sentence, repeat the noun that appears in italics in the first sentence.

**Example**

Gilda bought a *lamp* and a chair.

The lamp was blue and green to match her sofa.

1.  Daniel bought a *TV* and a stereo.

    *The TV was for his bedroom.*

2.  Gilda had a *sandwich* and a Coke for lunch.

    _____

3.  Daniel had a *salad* and a cup of coffee for lunch.

    _____

4.  Gilda saw a *movie* and visited friends last weekend.

    _____

5.  Daniel rented a *video* and invited a friend over last night.

    _____

 **Essential Information: FIRST MENTION FOLLOWED BY A SYNONYM**

For the following material, refer to the Raymond Chandler reading on page 126. Find the first mention of the nouns given below and write them in the blanks in column I. Include the article that accompanies each noun.

|                I                |          II           |
| ------------------------------- | --------------------- |
| 1. _____ | the instrument        |
| 2. _____ | the reception room    |

You can't find a previous mention of these nouns because they don't exist in the reading. Now, go back to see if you can find synonyms, and write them in column I. Include the article with each noun.

Can you explain why the author uses *the* with the nouns listed in column II?

_____

_____

A noun is often introduced and later referred to by a synonym. The first mention establishes common focus, and the definite article *the* is then used with the synonym.

Read another example from *The High Window:*

### THE SMALL ROOM

It was a small room looking out on the back garden. It contained what you would expect to find in a small office. A thin fragile-looking blondish girl in shell glasses sat behind a desk with a typewriter on it. She had her hands poised on the keys, but she didn't have any paper in *the machine.*

In the last sentence, why does Chandler use "*the* machine" for the first mention of that noun?

_____

**Exercise**    First Mention Followed by a Synonym

Write a sentence to follow the sentences given. In your sentence, use a synonym for the noun that appears in italics in the first sentence.

**Example**

Gilda gave her mother a *couch* and a sweater for Christmas.

The sofa matched her mother's recliner chair.

1. She gave her aunt a *photograph* and a scarf.

   *The picture was black and white.*

2. She gave her brother a *lamp* and a detective novel.

   _____

3. Daniel gave his mother a new *carpet* and a stereo.

   _____

4. He gave his sister a *novel* and a jacket.

   _____

5. He gave his best friend a *cap* and a belt.

---

 **Essential Information: FIRST MENTION FOLLOWED BY A PART OR OTHER CLOSELY-RELATED IDEA**

For the following material, refer to the Raymond Chandler reading on page 126. Find the first mention of the following nouns and write them in the blanks in column I. Include the article.

|  I  |  II |
| --- | --- |
| 1. _____ | the door |
| 2. _____ | the phone number |

Can you explain why the author used *the* with the nouns in column II?

---

     Read another example. In the following excerpt from *The Lady in the Lake* by Raymond Chandler, someone is following Philip Marlowe's car.

### THE HEADLIGHTS

     Westmore was a north and south street on the wrong side of town. I drove north. At the next corner I bumped over disused interurban tracks and on into a block of junk yards. Headlights glowed in my rear view mirror. They got larger. I stepped on the gas, reached for the keys from my pocket, and unlocked the glove compartment. I took a .38 out and laid it on the seat close to my leg.

The following appear in the reading:

    the gas

    the glove compartment

    the seat

Can you explain why the author used *the* with the above nouns?

---

You can't find a previous mention of the nouns. However, because the reader knows that Philip Marlowe is driving a car, there is common focus on all of the related parts of the car, and *the* is used.

 **Exercise**  First Mention Followed by a Part or Other Closely Related Idea

Write a sentence to follow the given sentences. In your new sentence, use a part of the noun that appears in italics.

**Example**

My brother bought a new *television*. (screen)

The screen had a small crack in it.

1. My aunt bought a large, new *house*. (kitchen)

   *The kitchen is ultra-modern.*

2. Akbar rented a *car* from Rent-A-Wreck. (battery)

   _____

3. Mrs. Henderson leased a *computer system* from Acme Computers. (printer)

   _____

4. Tran rented a *stereo system* from Abby Rents. (speakers)

   _____

5. Abdul borrowed a *suitcase* from me. (lock)

   _____

### *Relevant Information:* A(n) *and* The *with Singular Count Nouns*

*Common focus* can be established through the use of *zero (or no) article* with (1) a *plural noun* or (2) a *noncount noun*. However, the purpose of this discussion is to clarify article usage with *singular count nouns*. The following chart can guide you in determining whether to use *a(n)* or *the* with *singular count nouns*.

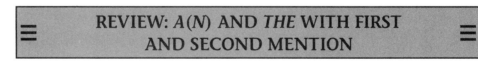

A(n) or *the* with singular count nouns:

**First mention of an idea** ⟶ A(n)

**Second mention** {
1. The same noun
2. A synonym ⟶ The
3. A part or other closely related idea
}

## REVIEW: A(N) AND *THE* WITH FIRST AND SECOND MENTION

 **Exercise A**   Selecting *A(n)* or *The*—The Right Attitude

Write the appropriate articles *a*, *an*, or *the* in the blanks.

### The Right Attitude

Whenever I think about the importance of attitude, I remember _____ old
                                                                   1

story. Eleven men were living in one room. They were not getting along very

well. They called _____ rabbi to settle their problem.
                    2

_____ rabbi told them, "I can help you, but you must do whatever I say."
  3

The men agreed, and _____ rabbi continued.
                     4

"You must get _____ donkey to live here with you for exactly one month.
              5

After that, _____ problem you're having will disappear."
            6

Adding another living body to _____ already crowded conditions wasn't
                              7

_____ solution the men wanted to hear. But a promise was a promise.
  8

Several weeks later, _____ rabbi saw one of the men.
                     9

"Well, how are you, and how's _____ donkey?
                              10

"Everything's wonderful now," replied _____ man. "We got rid of _____
                                       11                         12

donkey and got _____ cat instead!"
               13

## Writing Assignment: *Summary and Reaction—"The Right Attitude"*

Write a summary and reaction paragraph based on the story "The Right Attitude." In the first sentence, identify the story. Next, write a short summary. After the summary, write a reaction to the story. Your reaction may address one of the following questions: (1) Was the rabbi wise? (2) What does the title of the story mean? Support your reaction with an example from your personal experience or from another source.

**Exercise B**   Editing for the Articles *A* and *The*—A Lie and a Half

Edit the following story.

### A Lie and a Half

A man returned to his hometown after a long trip.

He told his neighbor, "On my trip I saw huge ship with gigantic sails. Ship   2
was bigger than anything anyone could ever imagine. Young boy walked from
one end of ship to other end. But his hair and beard turned white before he got   4
to other end!"

Man's neighbor replied, "That's not so remarkable! I once passed through   6
tremendous forest. Forest had the tallest trees in world. In fact, bird tried to fly
to top, but bird flew for ten years and only made it to halfway point!"   8

"That's dirty lie!" shouted first man. "That simply can't be possible!"

"Why not?" asked his neighbor. "Where do you think ship you described 10

°**mast:** a long pole to hold   got the wood for mast°?"
a sail

# ▬▬▬ ESTABLISHING COMMON FOCUS WITH A MODIFIER

 **Essential Information: ESTABLISHING COMMON FOCUS WITH A MODIFIER THAT LIMITS THE MEANING OF THE NOUN**

Look at the following phrases from the reading at the beginning of this section (page 126).

the smell of dust

the side of the desk

the phone number that went with it

Why is *the* used in the above phrases?

_____

Don't worry if you can't explain it. Read the following explanation.

*The* can be used with the first mention of a noun when the writer immediately follows the noun with a phrase or clause that makes the noun specific.

Read two more examples from material that appeared in previous chapters.

*The birth of a lamb* is a remarkable event. (Ch. 1)

*The person who caused the first major incident* of the civil rights movement was Rosa Parks. (Ch. 3)

 **Exercise**   Establishing Common Focus with a Modifier That Limits the Meaning of the Noun

Write complete sentences using the ideas given below.

### My Dream Life

**Example**

. . . house that I live in . . .

The house that I live in will have seven bathrooms, one for each day of the week.

1. . . . car of my dreams . . .

   *The car of my dreams costs fifty thousand dollars.*

2.   . . . vacation spot where I have a second home . . .

   _____

3.   . . . store where I shop for most of my clothes . . .

   _____

4.   . . . restaurant where I have a table permanently reserved for me . . .

   _____

5.   . . . kind of watch I wear . . .

   _____

6.   . . . brand of stereo equipment I buy . . .

   _____

7.   . . . vacation of my choice . . .

   _____

# NATURAL COMMON FOCUS

 ## Essential Information: NATURAL COMMON FOCUS

Answer these questions. You do not have to write a complete sentence.

1.   Where do you brush your teeth?        *in the bathroom*

2.   Where do you cook dinner?        _____

3.   Where do you entertain guests?        _____

4.   Where do you park your car overnight?        _____

5.   Where do you park your car when you wash it?        _____

6.   Where do you watch TV?        _____

7.   Where do you cash your checks?        _____

8.   Where do you go to get your teeth cleaned?        _____

9.   What provides warmth and energy for plants
     to grow?        _____

10.  What controls the tides of the oceans?        _____

11.  Where do you read about news?        _____

Why did you use the word *the* in your answers?

_____

Read the following sentence from the Chandler selection "The Office in the Cahuenga Building."

"Not beautiful, not gay, but better than a tent on the beach."

Why is *the* used with *beach* when this noun has not been mentioned before?

---

In many contexts in English, common focus preexists even when the noun appears for the first time. This is called *natural common focus*, and the definite article *the* can be used on first mention. See parts A through C below for more examples.

### Part A: Items Unique in Nature

Many items in nature are unique; that is, only one exists. Consequently, *the* is used with nouns that represent these unique items:

the sun

the moon

the sky

### Part B: Items in a Person's Everyday Environment

The article *the* is used with common nouns used in a person's everyday environment, even though others exist.

Inside the house

the kitchen
the bathroom (even though there might be more than one)
the wall
the garage
the corner

Outside the house

the garden
the driveway

Moving away from the house

the street
the sidewalk
the curb
the corner

Moving farther away from the house

the freeway
the beach
the park
the library
the desert

Frequent destinations

the doctor
the dentist

the bank
the store
the mall

### Part C: Regional/Local

People live and work in groups. Within the groups, they have shared knowledge, and therefore may have natural common focus with other members of the group.

### Example from "Going to My Son's Swim Lesson"

Then we got in *the* car and drove to *the* pool.

 **Exercise**  Editing for *The* for Natural Common Focus—Love

The following sentences are based on Jesse Stuart's short story "Love." In this story, a boy, his father, and his dog "Bob" are returning home after a walk on their farm. Bob has just killed a snake, and the boy feels sad about the snake's death.

Edit for the article *the*.

### Love

°**panting:** taking quick, short breaths
°**shaggy:** covered with long, rough hair
°**flecks:** small amounts
°**foam:** whitish mass of bubbles
°**chestnut:** tree that produces reddish nuts
°**ridge:** long, narrow top of a hill
°**lark:** bird

°**sinking:** going down below a surface

Bob was panting°. He was walking ahead of us back to ^*the* house. His tongue

was out of his mouth. He was tired. He was hot under his shaggy° coat of hair. His    2

tongue nearly touched the dry dirt. White flecks° of foam° dripped from it. We

walked toward house. I said nothing. My father said nothing. I still thought about    4

the dead snake. Sun was going down over chestnut° ridge°. A lark° was singing. It

was late for a lark to sing. The red evening clouds floated above the pine trees on    6

our pasture hill. My father stood beside path. His black hair moved in the wind.

His face was red in the blue wind of day. His eyes looked toward sinking° sun.    8

## ▬▬▬ *THE* WITH SUPERLATIVES AND RANK ORDER

 **Essential Information: SUPERLATIVES**

Read the following sentences from "An Irish Legend" on page 81.

A long time ago, an aging king ruled a large kingdom in Ireland. He had three sons and wanted to leave his kingdom to *the* most intelligent of the three.

Why is *the* used before *most intelligent*?

Read the following examples also based on "An Irish Legend."

*The* eldest son, *his* eldest son

*The* youngest son, *his* youngest son

In addition to the definite article *the*, what else can appear before a superlative?

_____

Read a few more sentences from "An Irish Legend."

*The* next day the king left with *his* next son on the same trip, and the same thing happened.

On *the* third day, the king took his youngest son, and after a few hours said to his son, "Son, shorten the road for me."

Why is *the* used before *next* and *third*?

_____

In addition to the definite article *the*, what else can appear before a word that indicates rank order?

_____

Why is *the* not used in the following italicized expressions?

*First of all*, I like living in California because of the warm weather.

*Second*, by listening to a parent read to them, children can learn the rhythm of the language.

_____

*First of all* and *Second* are transitions. They do not require the use of *the*.

 **Exercise**   Editing for Articles before Superlatives and Rank Order

Edit the following sentences from readings from Chapters 3–7.

1. Pele is one of <sub> the </sub> most famous soccer stars in history. (Ch. 3)

2. Pele soon became best player on the team. (Ch. 3)

3. The mother and daughters, eldest of whom is ten, bewitch me. (Ch. 4)

4. By the time Hiroki gets home, he is tired and ready to go to sleep. He needs his rest for next busy workday. (Ch. 5)

5. It (going to school for first time) was first experience to interfere with my freedom. (Ch. 5)

6. First smell of the sea was heaven to our nostrils. (Ch. 5)

7. There has been only one inmate death in last ten years at the hands of another. There have been only thirty-five escapes from Japanese prisons in last seven years. (Ch. 6)

8.   Right now business is booming for Asian food in the United States. Immigrants are providing biggest boost for authentic Asian food. (Ch. 6)

9.   First of all, the instructor gives a lot of homework. This leads to third and most important reason the class has been so helpful. (Ch. 7)

10.  I once passed through a tremendous forest. The forest had tallest trees in the world. (Ch. 7)

11.  At next corner I bumped over disused interurban tracks and on into a block of junk yards. (Ch. 7)

# ☰  REVIEW: *A(N)* AND *THE*  ☰

*Reminder: When you proofread your writing for articles and other determiners, the most helpful rule to remember is the following.*

> A singular count noun almost always has a determiner before it.

## CHART: THE USES OF *THE* WITH SINGULAR COUNT NOUNS

| *THE* IS USED IN THE FOLLOWING CASES: |
| --- |
| **I.   AFTER THE FIRST MENTION OF A NOUN OR IDEA**<br><br>**Repeating the same noun**<br>I saw a teenage boy and a woman robbing a store.<br>**The teenage boy** got away.<br><br>**Giving a synonym**<br>A teenage boy and a woman robbed a store.<br>**The youth** got away.<br><br>**Using a part or other closely related idea**<br>I saw a robbery. **The thief** got away. |
| **II.  WHEN THE NOUN HAS A MODIFIER THAT LIMITS THE MEANING OF THE NOUN**<br><br>**The house of my dreams** is in the country.<br>**The car that I want** has leather upholstery. |
| **III. WHEN THERE IS NATURAL COMMON FOCUS**<br><br>**Nature**<br>**The sun** shone brightly in **the sky**. |

**Everyday environment**
I found a ten dollar bill on **the sidewalk** near **the corner.**
I went to **the post office** before I went to **the doctor's.**

**Regional/Local common focus**
**The wastebasket** is in **the corner** of **the classroom.**
**The baby** and **the dog** are in **the car.**

**IV. WHEN THE NOUN IS UNIQUE BECAUSE OF SUPERLATIVE OR RANK ORDER**

**The best city** for going to the theater is New York. **The first time** I went there I saw *A Chorus Line.* **The next time** I saw *Man of La Mancha.*

 **Exercise A**    Editing for *A* and *The*—The Memory of an Unforgettable Trip

Edit the following.

### The Memory of an Unforgettable Trip

I'll never forget my trip to see my father at concentration camp seven years ago. After two days on train, my mother and I got off at Vinh, small city ten    2
kilometers from A10 concentration camp. At sunrise we walked on trail through virgin forest. Along trail, atmosphere of war still remained, even after ten years.    4
There were many ponds created by the heavy bombs, now homes for frogs. Some unidentified tombs, covered by elephant grass, were scattered along the    6
sides of trail. We were alone, and I was scared to death. But I kept walking forward because I wanted very badly to see my dear father after ten years of    8
being separated.

Finally, we reached A10 concentration camp, which consisted of several    10
rows of thatched huts in jungle. My mother submitted visitors' permit to guard at entrance, and then we waited. Shortly afterward, I heard someone calling my    12
name. I turned around and saw old man behind me. He stared at me. I didn't recognize him. His head was bald, his cheeks were hollow, and his body was    14
very skinny. He looked like walking skeleton, rather than a live human being. Only one thing looked familiar to me—his eyes. His look made my heart jump.    16
Then he called my name again, "Huong! This is your daddy!" Oh, my God! This walking skeleton was my dear father! I fell into his arms and cried bitterly. After    18
ten long years, I was finally in my father's loving arms again.

To me, this was unforgettable trip because I was witness to the change of    20

my dear father into walking skeleton in concentration camp. When I returned to

the town, I left my heart behind me in the A10 concentration camp.          22

Adapted from a composition by Huong Nguyen

 **Exercise B**    Adding the Missing Articles—
The Detective and the Murderer

The following excerpt from Raymond Chandler's *The Lady in the Lake* appears in telegraphic style. Many articles are missing. Add the missing articles.

*Note: Telegraphic style is a conversational and note-taking style of English. In telegraphic style, articles and other words that are not essential to the central meaning are omitted.*

### The Detective and the Murderer

"I've never liked this scene," I said. "Detective confronts murderer. Mur-

derer produces gun, points same (gun) at detective. Murderer tells detective    2

the whole sad story, with the idea of shooting him at the end of it. Thus wasting

a lot of valuable time, even if in the end murderer did shoot detective. Only    4

murderer never does. Something always happens to prevent it."

 **Exercise C**    Writing about Tasks

In a small group, make a list of items you need for the following tasks. Use *a/an* before all singular count nouns.

**Example**

To hang wallpaper, we need a table, a ladder, glue, a brush, a straight
edge, a bucket, warm water, a sponge, a narrow roller, and a sharp knife.
( . . . and patience?)

1.  To wash a car, we need _____

2.  To write a paragraph, we need _____

3.  To bathe a baby, we need _____

4.  To paint a room, we need _____

5.  To take a weekend trip, we need _____

 **Writing Assignment:** *Writing about a Task*

Select one of the tasks from the previous exercise. Write a process paragraph to describe the steps necessary in performing the task. Start your paragraph with a topic sentence. Explain the process, using plenty of specific details. Write a concluding sentence that gives a feeling of finish to your paragraph.

 **Essential Information: GENERIC SINGULAR COUNT NOUNS**

Singular count nouns are often used generically—to express a total class of objects (or ideas).

### Examples

The (A) snake kills mice.

The (A) ewe is a female sheep.

> Before a generic singular count noun, use *a(n)* or *the*.

 **Exercise**   Generic Singular Count Nouns—Occupations

Complete the following sentences:

### Examples

A carpenter _____.

A carpenter *builds houses*.

_____ delivers mail.

*The mailman* delivers mail.

1. A plumber <u>*unclogs toilets.*</u>

2. _____ fixes cars.

3. _____ helps people learn a subject.

4. _____ helps sick people.

5. _____ fills prescriptions.

6. The fireman _____

7. _____ writes books.

# ═══ NONCOUNT NOUNS

 **Essential Information: NONCOUNT NOUNS**

The following sentences are taken from the sample paragraphs at the beginning of this chapter. The nouns in italics are noncount nouns.

In high school and college, he (Daniel) had competed in *swimming*, *track*, and *tennis*.

He had at once begun a strict program of *diet* and *exercise*.

He ate fresh *fruit*, vegetables, broiled *fish*, salads with a dressing of fresh lemon *juice*.

Do noncount nouns normally take a plural form?

---

**COMMON NONCOUNT NOUNS**

| | | |
|---|---|---|
| †advice | †homework | rice |
| air | †information | sand |
| beauty | jewelry | †scenery |
| clothing | †luggage | silk |
| computer science | meat | †snow |
| †equipment | music | soccer |
| freedom | nature | stationery |
| fruit | nutrition | †sunshine |
| furniture | peace | swimming |
| gold | poverty | †underwear |
| health | †research | †vocabulary |
| | | †water |
| | | weather |
| | | †work |

Noncount nouns differ from language to language. The noncount nouns listed here may or may not be noncount in your native language.

*Note: A dagger indicates that the word appears in the exercises in this section.*

**Sample Sentences**

After Gilda and Daniel's divorce, Gilda got half of the *furniture*, so Daniel had to buy a bed, a sofa, and several chairs.

Daniel kept his mountain climbing *equipment*—his ax, boots, nylon line, and rucksack.

Gilda kept all her fine *jewelry*—her wedding ring, a pearl necklace, and diamond earrings.

Daniel got the expensive leather *luggage*—two suitcases, a carry-on bag, and a briefcase.

 **Exercise A**   Editing for Correct Noncount Nouns—My English Class

Edit the following for noncount nouns.

**Paragraph A**

### My English Class

I am learning a lot in my English class this semester. First of all, the instructor gives a lot of homeworks. We have to do two writing assignments a week.    2

Also, we have learned a lot of new vocabularies. We have to make a list of all
the new words in every book or article we read for our research paper. This     4
leads into the third and most important reason the class has been so helpful.
We're doing researches for a term paper, and this assignment has helped me     6
tremendously in locating useful informations in the library. Even though the
class has given me a lot of extra works to do this semester, I'm really glad I took     8
my counselor's advices and signed up for it.

**Paragraph B**

### The Mountain Fishing Trip

Last spring my brother and I spent a memorable week on a fishing trip in
the mountains. The sceneries ~~were~~ <sup>y was</sup> absolutely gorgeous. The snows had recently     2
melted, and the waters in the streams danced and flowed with energetic joy.
Also, every day the weather blessed us with plenty of bright sunshines. Nature     4
truly showed us her best. One more memory stands out in my mind. My brother
forgot part of his fishing equipments, so we had to take turns with mine. In fact,     6
this oversight simply served to make our trip more enjoyable to look back on.
We laugh every time we reminisce about the trip. At least we remembered our     8
luggages and did not have to share underwears.

 **Exercise B**   Writing Sentences with Noncount Nouns

Write original sentences using the given topics and nouns.

School

1. vocabulary _I learned a lot of new vocabulary in my reading class._

2. advice _____

3. homework _____

Travel

4. scenery _____

5. luggage _____

6. information _____

The topic of your choice _____

7. (your choice of noncount noun = _____)

_____

8. (your choice of noncount noun = _____)

---

 **Essential Information: GENERIC NONCOUNT
NOUNS AND ZERO ARTICLE**

Noncount nouns are often used generically—to express the total class of objects or ideas included in the noun.

### Examples

*Honesty* is the best policy. (American proverb)

We wish you *health*, *wealth*, and *happiness*.

> Before a generic noncount noun, use zero article.

 **Exercise A**   Editing for Articles in Proverbs and Quotations

Edit for articles that do not belong.

1. ~~The~~ charity begins at home. (American)
2. The peace is more valuable than the gold. (Finnish)
3. The money cannot buy the happiness. (American)
4. The common sense is very uncommon. (Horace Greeley)
5. The drunkenness is temporary suicide. (Bertrand Russell)
6. The kindness gives birth to the kindness. (Sophocles)
7. The leisure is the mother of the philosophy. (Thomas Hobbes, *Leviathan*)
8. The talk is cheap. (English)
9. The time is the money. (Edward Bulwer-Lytton, *Money*)
10. The time is the wisest counselor. (Pericles)

 **Exercise B**   Writing Sentences with Generic Noncount Nouns

Write sentences giving your opinion on three of the topics given below. Follow the examples.

### Examples

love        Love makes the world go around.

literature   Good literature entertains and teaches about life.

Topics: friendship, poverty, health, happiness, wealth, money, violence, life, success, failure, war, peace, nature, sunny weather

1. _____

2. _____

3. _____


# ☰ PLURAL NOUNS

### ▶ Sample Paragraph

Read the following paragraph about a parent whose children are getting ready to start a new school year.

#### Back to School

My three *kids* are going back to school soon, so my wife and I need to make three *lists* for back-to-school *supplies* for their *classes*. Gary, my youngest, needs paper, *pencils*, *crayons*, *scissors*, a ruler, and some *folders*. Liam, my second son, needs five spiral *notebooks*, some paint *brushes*, and a thermos bottle for his *lunches*. Brendan, who is starting high school, needs a huge list of *supplies:* two three-ring *binders*, marking *pens*, a compass, a note pad to keep track of his homework *assignments*, two *boxes* of floppy *disks*, and a pair of *goggles* for his chemistry lab. Now that we have three *lists* of *things* to buy, there is only one thing we need before we can get started: a loan from the bank.

What letter do the plural nouns in the above paragraph end with? _____

###  Essential Information: SPELLING PLURAL NOUNS

Read the following and answer the questions.

#### Part I

| SINGULAR | PLURAL |
|----------|--------|
| kid | kids |
| list | lists |
| pencil | pencils |

What's the basic rule for making a noun plural?

_____

#### Part II

The following singular nouns end in a sibilant sound. The sibilant sounds are often spelled with *s*, *z*, *sh*, *ch*, and *x*.

| SINGULAR | PLURAL |
|----------|--------|
| lunch | lunch*es* |
| brush | brush*es* |
| class | clas*ses* |
| box | box*es* |
| buzz | buzz*es* |

What's the rule for adding a plural ending to a noun that ends in a sibilant sound?

___

### Part III

The following singular nouns end in a consonant plus *y*.

| SINGULAR | PLURAL |
| --- | --- |
| supply | suppl*ies* |
| family | famil*ies* |
| lady | lad*ies* |

What's the rule for adding a plural ending to a noun that ends in a consonant plus *y*?

___

If a vowel comes before the *y*, the plural form follows the basic rule.

| SINGULAR | PLURAL |
| --- | --- |
| toy | toys |
| day | days |
| holiday | holidays |

*Note: The spelling rules for plural nouns are the same as the rules for the third person singular form of the present tense of the verb.*

### ▶ Sample Paragraph

The following paragraph is from Naguib Mahfouz's *Wedding Song*. It includes several irregular plural nouns.

#### Loneliness

Loneliness and the old house were the two *companions* of my childhood. I knew it inside out: the big arched *portals*°, the door with its small hinged *panes* of red, blue, and brown stained glass, the reception-room window with its iron *bars*, the upstairs and downstairs *rooms* with their high *ceilings* and painted wooden *rafters*°, their *floors* covered with Masarany *tiles*; the old, shabby *couches*, *mattresses*, *mats*, and *carpets*, the undaunted° *tribes* of *mice*, *cockroaches*, and wall *geckos*°, the roof, crisscrossed with *clotheslines* like streetcar and trolley-bus *wires*, overlooking other *roofs* that on summer *evenings* were crowded with *women* and *children*. I roamed around the house alone, my voice echoing from its *corners* as I repeated my *lessons*, reciting a poem, did a part from some play, or sang. Looking down on the narrow street for what might have been *hours* at a time, following the flow of *people*, I'd yearn° for a friend to play with.

°**portals:** entrances

°**rafters:** roof supports
°**undaunted:** not discouraged, bold
°**geckos:** lizards

°**yearn:** wish strongly

### Writing Assignment: *A Feeling from the Past*

Recall a feeling you experienced in the past, such as loneliness, disappointment, satisfaction, or excitement. Write a paragraph describing the circumstances surrounding this feeling.

Start your paragraph with a topic sentence. Explain your feeling, using plenty of specific details. Write a concluding sentence that gives a feeling of finish to your paragraph.

 **Essential Information: IRREGULAR PLURAL NOUNS**

English has many irregular plural nouns.

**Examples**

| | |
|---|---|
| woman | women |
| child | children |
| mouse | mice |

### *Relevant Information: People*

Points to keep in mind about the noun "people":

1.  It's an irregular plural. It has no "s" ending.

2.  The singular is "person."

**Examples**

People try to avoid loneliness.

A person who is lonely yearns for a friend.

 **Exercise**  People

Edit the following sentences.

1.  The one ~~people~~ *person* I can count on is my brother.

2.  The peoples in my family all love children.

3.  The people in my neighborhood is unhappy about the local air pollution.

4.  My sister is a salesperson and loves to talk to peoples.

5.  I really enjoy people who is open and honest.

### *Relevant Information: -ives*

Some singular nouns ending in *ife* change into the plural as follows.

life    lives

Change the following nouns to the plural form:

1.  wife _____

2.  knife _____

## REVIEW: PLURAL NOUNS

 **Exercise**   Editing—Christmas for the Corona Family

Edit the following paragraph. Change singular nouns to plural nouns, as necessary.

### Christmas for the Corona Family

Christmas for my neighbors, the Coronas, might be very expensive this
year. Arturo wants art supply, and quality watercolor brush can cost up to one          2
hundred dollars each. Barbara is asking for gold jewelry. She wants a necklace
and matching earring. Carmen would like a silk outfit: a blouse and pant. David          4
wants salt water aquarium equipment. Along with a fish tank, he has his heart
set on two baby shark and an octopus. Last, Mr. and Mrs. Corona want a set of          6
steak knives with rosewood handles. They'll also need a money tree to pay for all
these costly gifts.          8

 *Writing Assignment: Gifts*

Write a paragraph about one of the following:

> What gifts you received on a special occasion
> What gifts you would like to receive on a special occasion
> What gifts you gave to people on a special occasion
> What gifts you would like to give to people on a special occasion
> Any other topic about gifts

When you finish writing, proofread your sentences carefully for articles. Make sure
that you use an article (or other determiner) with every singular count noun. Your
instructor may   ask you to underline the articles (or other determiners) plus
singular count nouns.

Next, exchange your sentences with a partner. Edit your partner's sentences,
looking for the correct use of articles (or other determiners) plus singular count nouns.

 **Essential Information: NONCOUNT NOUNS THAT END IN *S***

Read the following paragraph and answer the question below.

### THE SIX O'CLOCK *NEWS* ORAL ESSAYS

The six o'clock *News* often broadcasts "oral essays" on various topics
of general interest after the regular news report. Last night, for example, the

presentation discussed the importance of *electronics* in our daily lives. It is virtually impossible to find a home these days that does not have several electronic devices. It's no wonder that *electronics* is a leading industry in today's economy. The night before last, the presentation covered another topic of concern for all adults: *economics*. Even if people do not know a lot about *economics*, they usually agree on one point: *economics* affects the quality of our day-to-day living. A few weeks ago, the oral essay talked about the changing trends in colleges. Apparently, *mathematics* is becoming a more popular major for women in many colleges. For me, these "oral essays" make the *news* worth watching because they help me keep up on issues of current importance in everybody's lives.

Are the nouns in italic letters in the previous paragraph singular or plural?

_____

 **Exercise**   Noncount Nouns That End in *S*

Write complete sentences using the words given.

1.   The news _____
     (*Hint:* Is the news too violent? Is it interesting? Is it boring? Is it important to watch?)

2.   Electronics _____
     (*Hint:* Is electronics important in modern life? Is it boring to study or to talk about? Is it difficult?)

3.   Economics _____
     (*Hint:* Is this an easy subject? Is it interesting? Is it a difficult subject? Is it an important course to take in college?)

4.   Mathematics _____
     (*Hint:* Is this an enjoyable subject? Is it an important subject to take as a prerequisite for other courses?)

 **Essential Information: GENERIC PLURAL NOUNS AND ZERO ARTICLE**

Plural nouns are often used generically—to express the total class of objects or ideas included in the noun.

### Examples

*Cigarettes* are highly addictive.

*Computers* have changed the work environment.

> Before a generic plural noun, use zero article.

**Exercise A**   Editing for Articles in Proverbs and Quotations

Edit for articles.

1.  ~~The~~ flies don't enter a closed mouth. (Italian)

2.  The laws die; books never. (Edward Bulwer-Lytton)

3.  The misfortunes always come in by a door that has been left open for them. (Czech)

4.  The still waters run deep. (English)

5.  Death and the taxes are inevitable. (Thomas Haliburton)

6.  The words are the most powerful drug used by mankind. (Rudyard Kipling, Speech, 1923)

 **Exercise B**   Generic Plural Nouns

Write sentences—general statements—giving your opinion on three of the topics given. Follow the examples.

**Examples**

pets:       Pets can teach children responsibility.

people:   People learn while they teach.

Topics: politicians, doctors, parents, true friends, horror movies, weekends, carrots, dogs, cats, cigarettes

1.  _____

2.  _____

3.  _____

## ≡     REVIEW: GENERIC USES OF NOUNS     ≡

Generic uses of nouns include:

1.  *A(n) / the + Singular count noun*
    A/The carrot is rich in vitamin A.

2.  *Zero article + Noncount noun*
    Rice is rich in vitamin B.

3.  *Zero article + Plural noun*
    Oranges are rich in vitamin C.

# PROPER NOUNS

▶ **Sample Paragraph**

Read the following paragraph. With the exception of *They* and *Everyone*, the nouns that begin with a capital letter are proper nouns.

**Trang and Mohammed**

    Trang and Mohammed are studying English at Maricopa Community College. Trang is from Vietnam and speaks Vietnamese. Mohammed is Iranian and speaks Farsi. They are going to a Christmas party at the teacher's house on Saturday. Trang is taking paper plates, and Mohammed is taking Pepsi and Fritos. Everyone is looking forward to having a good time.

 **Essential Information: PROPER NOUNS**

Proper nouns include the following categories:

| | |
|---|---|
| Personal names: | Trang, Mohammed, Ann, Robert |
| Certain time units: | Saturday, December |
| Geographic names: | Vietnam, Iran, El Salvador, Japan |
| Languages: | Vietnamese, Farsi, Korean, Chinese |
| Nationalities: | American, Thai, Mexican, French |
| Holidays: | The Fourth of July, Labor Day, Memorial Day |
| Commercial names: | Pepsi, Chevrolet, Smuckers, Fritos |
| Course names: | Electronics II, Introduction to Psychology |

> Use a capital letter to begin a proper noun.

 **Exercise**   Editing an Interview

Edit the following.

1. I interviewed Vinh Duc Tran in beginning ESL composition today and learned several things about her.

2. First, She was born in saigon, vietnam, in October, which is the same month that I was born in.

3. She speaks vietnamese and french.

4. In addition to this course, she is taking math b this semester.

5. She drives her old pontiac firebird to School, but she hopes someday to get a new honda accord.

6. During break times, vinh duc often buys a coke from the machine, and after class, she likes to go to mcdonald's for a quick snack with Friends.

7. Vinh Duc's favorite actor is tom cruise because she really enjoyed the movie top gun.

8. Vinh Duc's favorite Day of the week is tuesday because that is her day off from work.

9. Her favorite american holiday is the fourth of july because she loves fireworks.

10. Next Summer Vinh Duc plans to visit the grand canyon.

11. I hope she has a Great Time.

 **Writing Assignment:** *Interviewing a Classmate*

Interview a classmate. Ask the following questions and write the answers in complete sentences in paragraph form. Start your paragraph with a topic sentence. Support your topic sentence with plenty of specific details. Write a concluding sentence that gives a feeling of finish to your paragraph.

1. What's your full name?

2. What city and country were you born in?

3. In what month were you born?

4. What languages do you speak?

5. What's the exact name of another course you're currently taking?

6. What kind of car do you have or would you like to have?

7. What's your favorite soft drink (soda pop)?

8. What's your favorite restaurant?

9. Which famous person do you admire the most?

10. What's your favorite day of the week? Why?

11. What are your three favorite American holidays?

12. Where would you like to go on your next vacation?

 **CHANGED:** **CHAPTER REVIEW**

 **Exercise**   The Defective Stereo

Read the paragraph and answer the following question.

### The Defective Stereo

I bought a new personal stereo, a calculator, and a package of diskettes

last week at Sears. When I got home, I discovered that the stereo didn't work.    2

The buttons were defective. I couldn't find the receipt, so the salespeople wouldn't exchange it for me. Later, I found the receipt on the dining room     4

table under the diskettes.

Why is *the* used in the following cases? Write the letter of the correct answer in the blank.

   A. The same noun appears earlier.
   B. A synonym appears earlier.
   C. A part or other closely related idea

1. _____ the stereo

2. _____ the buttons

3. _____ the salespeople

4. _____ the dining room table

5. _____ the diskettes

 ## Writing Assignment: *A Description*

Describe the food in your refrigerator, or describe the food in an imaginary refrigerator. Start your paragraph with a topic sentence. Support your topic sentence with plenty of specific details. Write a concluding sentence that gives a feeling of finish to your paragraph.

**Example**

### MY SISTER'S SWEET TOOTH

My sister's refrigerator is chock full of junk food. The top shelf is loaded with cans of Pepsi. On the next shelf, three boxes from Becker's Bakery are stacked together. They contain cake and other bakery items. Next to the boxes is a carton of milk—chocolate milk. In the vegetable bins, several cans of pudding crowd out a few old carrots way in the back. The door of the refrigerator is filled with sweets, too. Several jars of Smuckers jam and jelly sit next to a can of butterscotch syrup. At least in the freezer, I can find some real food: two Swanson TV dinners, and next to the dinners are four tubs of Baskin-Robbins ice cream. I wonder what my sister will serve for dinner this Saturday night when I visit.

##  FOOD FOR THOUGHT

1. Why is *the* used in the following sentence?

Ronald Reagan is *the* only American president who used to be a movie star.

2. A.   Can the following sentences be true? _____

Bananas are black.

The bananas are black.

B.   Explain the difference in meaning.

_____

## ☰  CLASSROOM ASSESSMENT TECHNIQUE (CAT)  ☰

### THE ONE-MINUTE PAPER

Take a minute or two to write answers to the following questions. Write your answers on a separate piece of paper without your name.

1. What are the most important points that you have learned in this chapter?

2. What questions remain in your mind at the end of this chapter?

*Note:* Use this exercise to help you get answers to any questions you still have. Ask these questions to anyone who might be able to help you, such as another student or your instructor.

# CHAPTER 8

# Modals and Phrasal Modals

Modals are auxiliary verbs. This chapter presents several informational uses rather than social uses of modals, such as requests and offers. Writing assignments generally focus on informational uses, while dialogues include both informational and social uses.

▶ **Sample Paragraph**

Read the following paragraph based on an article in the *Los Angeles Times* by Mary Yarber. The modals appear in italic letters.

## Reading Aloud to Children

A child's skill in reading *can* determine his or her success in school, and the best way to develop this skill is for parents to read aloud to their children. Reading aloud is especially important for very young children. Preschoolers *will* benefit in several ways. First, they *will* learn that reading *can* be enjoyable. They do not have to worry about recognizing letters, sounding out words, or turning pages. They *can* simply enjoy listening to the story. Second, by listening to a parent read to them, children *can* learn the rhythm of the language and the correct pronunciation of words. Third, the parent's bond with his or her children *should* increase because of the physical and emotional closeness. Also, the parent's own enjoyment of the book *will* set a powerful example. Even though reading aloud to children *may* be inconvenient, it *should* be well worth the effort. It *will* definitely help the children become skillful readers.

A verb phrase consists of an auxiliary, such as a modal, plus a main verb.

### Examples

. . . can help . . .

. . . is going to help . . .

. . . is helping . . .

# THE FORM OF MODALS

 **Essential Information: THE FORM OF
THE MODAL AND THE MAIN VERB**

### A. The Form of the Modal

Look carefully at the following sentences from the reading. Underline the subjects once and the verb phrases twice.

1. A child's <u>skill</u> in reading <u>can determine</u> his or her success in school.

2. Preschoolers will benefit in several ways.

3. They can simply enjoy listening to the story.

4. It will definitely help the children become skillful readers.

  In sentences 1 and 4, the subject is third person singular. In sentences 2 and 3, the subject is third person plural.
  Look at the modals in sentences with third person singular subjects.

1. A child's skill in reading *can* determine his or her success in school.

4. It *will* definitely help the children become skillful readers.

Does the modal have an *s* form when the subject is third person singular?

Your answer: _____

### B. The Form of the Main Verb

Read these sentences again, this time focusing on the main verbs.

1. A child's skill in reading can *determine* his or her success in school.

2. It will definitely *help* the children become skillful readers.

What form of the main verb is used after the modal?

Your answer: _____

 **Exercise**  Practicing Form

Fill in the blanks with a main verb in the following sentences. Select from the following:

take      lead      find      identify

1. Some day science will _____*find*_____ a cure for Alzheimer's disease.

2. It may _____ several years, but scientists already know a lot about the disease.

3. They can, for example, _____ several physical changes in a brain with Alzheimer's.

4. This information should _____ to more discoveries.

**Essential Information: MODALS AND PHRASAL MODALS**

Eight modals are covered in this chapter:

can/could   will/would   may/might   should and must

In addition, two common phrasal modals are examined:

have to    be going to

Look at the following modals and phrasal modals.

| MODALS | PHRASAL MODALS |
| --- | --- |
| must | have to |
| will | be going to |

Pat *must register* to vote before election day.
Pat *has to register* to vote before election day.

Pat *will register* later today.
Pat *is going to register* later today.

What differences in form do you notice between the modals and phrasal modals?
List three:

1. _____

2. _____

3. _____

**Follow-up Discussion: Modals and Phrasal Modals**

1. Modals consist of only one word, whereas phrasal modals consist of more than one word.

2. The word *to* appears in the phrasal modals. In contrast, the modals do not include the word *to*.

3. *Have* and *be* have additional forms:

    have/has    had

    am/is/are   was/were

Don and Sue *are going to* get a marriage license this afternoon.

Their wedding *is going to* be in June.

They *have to* shop for wedding rings.

Don *has to* buy them on credit.

They *had to* get their blood tests yesterday.

The choice of the form depends on the subject and on the tense.

**Exercise**  Forms of Modals and Phrasal Modals

Underline the correct verb phrases in the following excerpts from a speech Barbara Bush made to the 1990 graduating class of Wellesley College in Massachusetts. In this speech, she is telling her audience about important life choices she made.

And early on, I made another choice, which I hope you (1. <u>will make</u>, will to make) as well. Whether you are talking about education, career or service,    2 you are talking about life, and life really (2. must have, must to have) joy.

It (3. should be, should to be) fun. One of the reasons I made the most    4 important decision of my life—to marry George Bush—is because he made me laugh. It's true. Sometimes we laugh through our tears, but that shared laugh-    6 ter has been one of our strongest bonds.

. . . I remember what a friend said on hearing her husband complain to    8 his buddies that he (4. had babysit, had to babysit). Quickly setting him straight, my friend told her husband that when it's your kids, it's not called babysitting.    10

# MODAL USAGE: ABILITY

 **Essential Information: *CAN***

*Can* is used to express ability in the present/future. As you read the following example paragraphs from M. Scott Peck's *The Road Less Traveled*, decide if you agree or disagree with the author's main idea.

### PROBLEMS AND PAIN

Life is a series of problems. Do we want to moan about them or solve them? Do we want to teach our children to solve them?

Discipline is the basic set of tools we require to solve life's problems. Without discipline, we *can* solve nothing. With only some discipline we *can* solve only some problems. With total discipline, we *can* solve all problems.

 **Exercise**  *Can*—Solving Problems with Discipline

The author in the previous sample paragraphs claims that with total discipline, a person can solve all problems.

### Part A

Write three sentences about the kinds of problems people can solve with discipline and how they can solve them.

**Example**

People can stop smoking if they make a decision to do so and they stick to that decision.

1. _____
2. _____
3. _____

## Part B

Write three sentences about the kinds of problems people cannot solve, no matter how much discipline they use.

**Example**

People cannot cure themselves of the HIV virus.

1. _____
2. _____
3. _____

 **Writing Assignment:** *A Problem You Solved with Discipline*

Write a paragraph about a problem you solved using discipline in some way. Start your paragraph with a topic sentence that identifies the problem. Support your topic sentence with plenty of specific details that describe how you solved the problem and how discipline played a part in solving the problem. Write a concluding sentence that gives a feeling of finish to your paragraph.

 **Essential Information:** *COULD*

*Could* is used to express ability in the past. The following paragraph from E. B. White's *Charlotte's Web* describes the arrival of the Arable family members at the County Fair. It explains what they could see, smell, and hear.

### THE COUNTY FAIR

When they pulled into the Fair Grounds°, they *could hear* music and *see* the Ferris wheel° turning in the sky. They *could smell* the dust of the race track where the sprinkling cart° had moistened it, and they *could smell* hamburgers frying and *see* balloons. They *could hear* sheep blatting° in their pens.

°**Fair Grounds:** where a fair (a show of animals, handicrafts, and rides) is held
°**Ferris wheel:** a ride in an amusement park or fair
°**sprinkling cart:** vehicle that sprays water to keep down dust
°**blatting:** sound made by sheep

 **Exercise** *Can* and *Could*

Write three to five sentences about what you *couldn't* do several years ago, but *can* do now.

**Example**

Ten years ago I couldn't drive (a car), but I can now.

1. _____
2. _____
3. _____
4. _____
5. _____

# ≡ FUTURE: *WILL* AND *BE GOING TO*

*Will* and *am/is/are going to* are two of several ways to refer to the future.

 **Essential Information: *WILL* IN PREDICTIONS**

*Will* is often used for predictions. A prediction is a statement we make about the future when we are fairly certain about our statement. For example, when the weatherman gives the weather report, he is predicting the weather. Either *will* or *be going to* can be used when we are predicting; however, in writing, *will* is more common.

Read these examples from "Reading Aloud to Your Children."

Preschoolers will benefit in several ways.

First, they will learn that reading can be enjoyable.

It will definitely help the children become more skillful readers.

 **Exercise**   *Will*—Your Future

Write three to five sentences about what you predict for your future or for the future of your family.

1. _____
2. _____
3. _____
4. _____
5. _____

 **Essential Information: *BE GOING TO***

*Be going to* is used for plans or intentions.

My brother *is going to get* married next month.

Shortly afterward, he and his wife *are going to move* to Calgary.

They *are going to start* a computer software business there.

 **Exercise** *Be Going To*—Plans

## Part A

Write three sentences about what you are going to do by the end of the week (or this weekend, or on your next vacation).

1. _____
2. _____
3. _____

## Part B

In a small group, find out what everyone's plans are for the next weekend (or holiday or vacation). Write a sentence about each person in the group.

### Examples

Thanh is going to visit his brother next month. Berta and her husband are going to drive to Acapulco.

1. _____
2. _____
3. _____
4. _____
5. _____

 **Essential Information: *WILL* VERSUS *BE GOING TO***

We often express our plans with *be going to* and then predict the logical outcome of these plans with *will*.

### Examples

Sergio is going to apply to Stanford University because he thinks that he will get a scholarship.

He is going to live on campus because it will be very convenient.

He is going to minor in computer science because it will help him when he starts looking for a job.

 **Exercise** Planning and Predicting—Carmen's Vacation

Read what Carmen plans to do before her month's vacation, and then predict what the consequences of her planning will be.

**Example**

Cancel the newspaper

Carmen is going to cancel the newspaper so that people won't know her family is away.

1.  Hire a gardener

    *She's going to hire a gardener so that the garden will look neat.*

2.  Return her books to the library

    _____

3.  Delay the mail delivery

    _____

4.  Leave the cat with the neighbor

    _____

5.  Pay all her major bills

    _____

6.  Ask her neighbor to put out and take in the trash cans

    _____

7.  Throw away any perishable items in the refrigerator

    _____

 **Essential Information: THE FUTURE IN THE PAST**

*Will* and *am/is/are going to* are used to write about the future. However, when these verbs appear in a sentence after a past tense verb, the following changes occur:

*will* becomes         ⟶ *would*

*am/is/are going to* becomes   ⟶ *was/were going to*

**Examples**

I am definitely going to read to my child more often because she will (is going to) benefit in several ways.

> I *knew* my child *would benefit* in several ways.
> I *knew* my child *was going to benefit* in several ways.

First, she will (is going to) learn that reading can be enjoyable.

> I *thought* that she *would enjoy* reading, and she did.
> I *thought* that she *was going to enjoy* reading, and she did.

Reading aloud to my child will (is going to) help her become a more skillful reader.

I *believed* that she *would become* a more skillful reader.

I *believed* that she *was going to become* a more skillful reader.

 **Exercise A**   The Future in the Past

Read "The Right Attitude" on page 131 and do the exercise below. Answer the following questions about the story. Use *would + verb* or *was/were + going to + verb*.

1. Why did the men call the rabbi?

   They thought *he would help them.* _____

2. Why did the rabbi tell the men to keep a donkey in their room for a month?

   He knew _____

3. Why did the men not really want to add a donkey to their already crowded conditions?

   They believed _____

4. When the rabbi saw one of the men several weeks later, what did he expect?

   He thought _____

5. When you read the story, what did you think was going to happen at the end of the story?

   I thought _____

 **Exercise B**   The Future in the Past—This Country (or City)

Before you moved to this country (or this city), what did you think life would be like? Write three sentences using the future in the past. Start each sentence with "I thought that . . .," "I believed that . . .," "I knew that . . .," or other similar subject plus verb.

**Examples**

I thought that I would have no money problems.

I believed that it was going to be easy to talk to people in English.

1. _____

   _____

2. _____

   _____

3. _____

   _____

Your instructor may ask you to exchange your sentences with a partner. Do you and your partner have any similar sentences? If you find any errors in your partner's sentences, discuss them with your partner.

# ≡ SUGGESTION—ADVICE—NECESSITY

## CHART 1: FORMS, MEANINGS, AND EXAMPLES

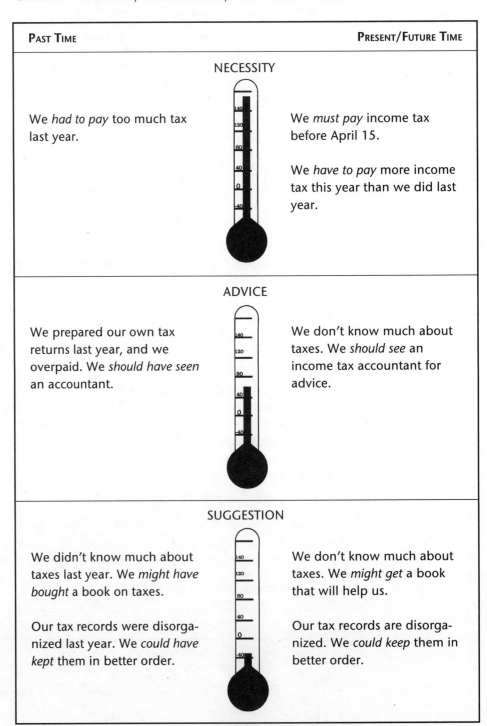

| PAST TIME | PRESENT/FUTURE TIME |
|---|---|
| **NECESSITY** | |
| We *had to pay* too much tax last year. | We *must pay* income tax before April 15.<br><br>We *have to pay* more income tax this year than we did last year. |
| **ADVICE** | |
| We prepared our own tax returns last year, and we overpaid. We *should have seen* an accountant. | We don't know much about taxes. We *should see* an income tax accountant for advice. |
| **SUGGESTION** | |
| We didn't know much about taxes last year. We *might have bought* a book on taxes.<br><br>Our tax records were disorganized last year. We *could have kept* them in better order. | We don't know much about taxes. We *might get* a book that will help us.<br><br>Our tax records are disorganized. We *could keep* them in better order. |

**Essential Information:** *MIGHT* **AND** *COULD*
**FOR PRESENT/FUTURE TIME**

*Might* and *could* indicate suggestion.

 **Exercise A**   *Might, Could*—On a Tight Budget

Pretend you are writing a magazine article on how to save money on a tight budget.
Write three to five sentences with your suggestions on what a person might/could
do to save money. Use a variety of modals.

**Example**

   You could rent videos instead of going to movies.

1. _____

2. _____

3. _____

4. _____

5. _____

 **Exercise B**   Must—Some Guidelines for Karate

Read the following paragraph about karate.

### Some Guidelines for Karate

   When you are studying karate, everything must be fair. Both you and your
opponent have empty hands. Your only weapons are your fists and feet. Because
you have nothing else, you must learn to see trouble coming and to avoid it. To
use your feet as weapons, you must kick your opponent. Balance and timing are
important. Also, you must be fast enough to keep your opponent from grabbing
your foot.

   Write about a sport you are familiar with. Explain what the players must do.

**Example**

   In soccer, the goalkeeper must wear a different jersey.

1. _____

2. _____

3. _____

 **Exercise C**   *Have/Has to*—Getting a Driver's License

Pretend you are getting ready to write a paragraph on how to get a driver's license
(in this country or another country). Write three to five sentences about what the
reader has to do.

**Example**

You have to have your picture taken.

1. _____

2. _____

3. _____

4. _____

5. _____

 **Exercise D**   *Should, Have to, Must*—Your Opinion

Fill in the blanks with *should*, *have to*, or *must*, according to your opinion.

In college, students . . .

1. . . . ___*have to*___ take a placement test.

2. . . . _____ pay tuition (or similar fees).

3. . . . _____ buy health insurance.

4. . . . _____ attend the first class meeting.

5. . . . _____ do homework every night.

6. . . . _____ review class notes after every meeting.

7. . . . _____ take the final exam.

 **Essential Information: PAST TIME**

To express past time, most modals combine with *have* + past participle.

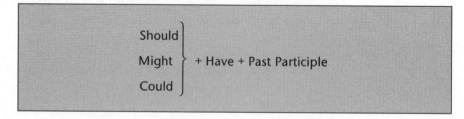

Last year . . .

. . . we *should have seen* an accountant.

. . . we *might have bought* a book on taxes.

. . . we *could have kept* our tax records in better order.

### *Relevant Information:* Must

An exception to the above is the past of *must* when it means necessity. When *must* means necessity, the phrasal modal *had to* is used.

We *must mail* our income tax forms before April 15.

We *had to mail* our income tax forms before April 16 last year because the fifteenth was a Sunday.

 **Exercise A**    *Might Have* + Past Participle and *Could Have* + Past Participle— The Cockroach

The following paragraph tells about a delicate situation. After you read the paragraph, you will make suggestions about what Amy and Chuck might have done or could have done in this case.

### The Cockroach

Amy and Chuck Henderson attended a formal business dinner at an expensive restaurant, hosted by Chuck's boss. Amy and Chuck were nervous because several important people were present, and Chuck wanted to make a good impression. Right after the waiter placed the breadbasket on the table, a huge cockroach° appeared next to the basket. Right after it appeared, it disappeared again. Amy and Chuck were the only two people who saw it. They did not know how to react because they no longer wanted to eat, but they did not want to embarrass their host.

°**cockroach:** large hard-backed household insect

Pretend it's the next day and you are one of Chuck's co-workers who didn't attend the dinner. Give Chuck suggestions. Write three to five sentences, using *might have* + past participle or *could have* + past participle.

### Example

You could have said you weren't feeling well.

1. _____
2. _____
3. _____
4. _____
5. _____

 **Exercise B**    *Had to*—Getting a Passport

Write three sentences about what you had to do to get a passport.

### Example

I had to visit the embassy in Guadalajara.

1. _____
2. _____
3. _____

**Exercise C**   Writing Sentences about a Mistake

Write about three mistakes you made in the past and what you should have done to avoid them. In the first sentence, identify what the problem was. In the second sentence, explain what you should have done.

Follow the example:

My van rolled out of the driveway.

I should have checked the handbrake.

1. _____

_____

2. _____

_____

3. _____

_____

When you finish your sentences, your instructor may ask you to do one of the following:

1.   Exchange sentences with a partner and edit each other's sentences.

2.   Select one of the three pairs of sentences and write them on the chalkboard.

# POSSIBILITY—PROBABILITY—LOGICAL CONCLUSION

## CHART 2: FORMS, MEANINGS, AND EXAMPLES

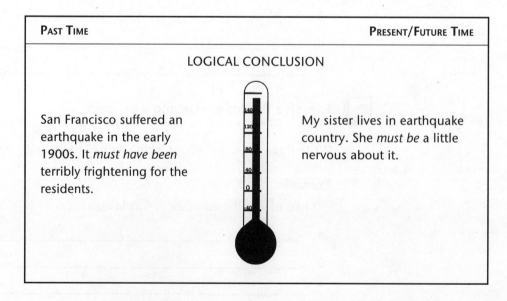

| Past Time | Present/Future Time |
|---|---|
| **LOGICAL CONCLUSION** ||
| San Francisco suffered an earthquake in the early 1900s. It *must have been* terribly frightening for the residents. | My sister lives in earthquake country. She *must be* a little nervous about it. |

PROBABILITY

Some people believe that "the big one" *should have hit* by now.

California *should have* a few more earthquakes in the next ten years.

POSSIBILITY

My grandparents lived through the last San Francisco earthquake. They *could have died.*

My uncle died in the last San Francisco earthquake. He *may have had* a heart attack.

My aunt's wedding ring disappeared in the last San Francisco earthquake. It *might have been buried* in rubble.

The next major earthquake *could cause* damage to old buildings.

People *may be* better prepared for the next earthquake.

Another large earthquake *might hit* in California at any time.

 **Essential Information: *COULD, MAY,* AND *MIGHT* FOR PRESENT/FUTURE TIME**

*Could, may,* and *might* indicate possibility in present/future time.

 **Exercise A**   Could, May, Might—Possibility: "Japanese Prisons"

In Chapter Six on page 106, you read the paragraph "Japanese Prisons." Reread the paragraph and answer the following question.

How do you explain these unusual facts about Japanese prisons? Write three possibilities, using *could, may,* and *might.*

1. _____

2. _____

3. _____

**Exercise B**   *Could, May, Might*—Possibility: *Fountain and Tomb*

*Fountain and Tomb* by Naguib Mahfouz was originally written in Arabic. In the English translation, Arabic words are sprinkled throughout the text. Write what the italicized words may/might/could mean.

1.  Seeds of hate between Shuldoom and Qormah were planted in the flowerbeds of childhood: in the middle of a festival celebration, Shuldoom ripped Qormah's brand new *gallabiya* and started a fight. Qormah belted Shuldoom with a wooden shoe, scarring his forehead forever.

    *It could be a jacket.* _____

2.  At school we all sit cross-legged for lunch, faces to the wall; each unknots his bundle and spreads it out. Everybody has a flat round bread and some *helwa.*

    _____

3.  Auntie Umzaki is really very ill, and she loses weight with incredible speed. Her son is finally forced to send her to a government hospital in a jolting donkey cart. She waves to me saying, "Pray for me. Allah listens to children." But it was as if the donkey cart had taken her to the land of *Waka-Waka.*

    _____

4.  My memory always links Ibraham Tawfeek with clowning. During the short recess, he squashes his *tarboosh* down till it looks like a skullcap, turns his jacket backwards, and imitates Charlie Chaplin.

    _____

 **Exercise C**   *Should*—Probability: "The Wind and the Sun"

Write answers to the following questions.

1.  In a fistfight between an adult and a child, who should win? _____

    Why? _____

2.  In a fight between the wind and the sun, who should win? _____

    Why? _____

Now, read the story "The Wind and the Sun" and find out who really won.

### The Wind and the Sun

One day the wind and the sun had an argument over who was stronger. They decided to test their strength by seeing which one could get a man to remove his jacket. The wind then blew very hard, but it couldn't blow the jacket off the man. Next, the sun began to shine brightly on the man, and the man took off his coat. The sun, then, won the argument.

**Exercise D**  *Must—Logical Conclusion*

Write the missing verb phrases. Use *must.*

1.  My study partner is Noriko Martinez. She _____*must be*_____ married to a
    Spanish-speaker.

2.  Noriko has lived in an English-speaking country for ten years. She

    _____ English fairly well.

3.  I saw Noriko conversing with my friend Antonio. Antonio just arrived from
    South America recently, and he doesn't speak any English.

    Noriko_____ Spanish fairly well.

4.  Antonio showed Noriko some photographs of his children, and Noriko

    showed Antonio some photographs. Noriko_____ children, too.

5.  Noriko has several travel brochures for South America. She _____
    planning a vacation.

 **Exercise E**  *May, Might, Could, Should, Must*—Food Clues

Read the following clues describing types of food. Write sentences guessing what
the food is. Use the modals *may, might, could, should,* or *must.*

**Part A**

1.  It has bread on the top and bottom, and meat in the middle.

    *It might be a sandwich.*

2.  It has bread on the top and bottom, and ground beef in the middle.

    _____

3.  It has bread on the top and bottom, and ground beef with melted cheese
    in the middle.

    _____

**Part B**

1.  They are made with butter, sugar, eggs, and milk.

    _____

2.  They are usually round.

    _____

3.  They have little bits of chocolate inside.

    _____

**Essential Information: PAST TIME**

To express past time, most modals combine with *have* + past participle.

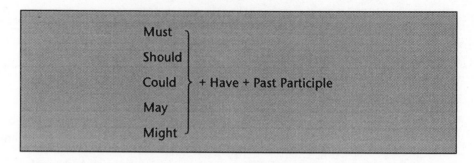

The San Francisco earthquake *must have been* terribly frightening for the residents.

My grandfather *could have died* in the earthquake.

My uncle *may have had* a heart attack.

 **Exercise A** *May Have, Might Have, Could Have*—The Absent Student

Pretend that your friend George, a classmate, called you last night and told you that he would be in class this morning for sure. Now you are in class, and George is absent. Write several sentences about what may/might/could have happened to George.

**Example**

George could have overslept.

1. _____

2. _____

3. _____

Exchange sentences with a partner. Check your partner's sentences for correct form.

 **Writing Assignment:** *Conflict Resolution*

Read the following story by Alfie Kohn from *The Brighter Side of Human Nature*.

### Pretty Smart!

°taunted: angered by mistreatment; ridiculed

There was once an old man who was taunted° by the neighborhood school children. After they came out of school they would walk onto his lawn and yell, "Hey, you stupid, old bald-headed . . ." and so on.

He got tired of this pretty fast, so he came up with a plan. He said, "If you kids come back tomorrow and yell those things at me, I'll pay each of you a dollar." Well, they thought that was pretty good. So they came back the next day and yelled even louder about how ugly and stupid he was. And he said, "Thank you, here's your dollar, here's your dollar, here's your dollar. If you come back tomorrow, I'll pay each of you a quarter."

Well, they thought that was still pretty good, so they came back the next day and yelled about how stupid and ugly he was, and he paid each of them a quarter, and he said, "Thank you. If you come back tomorrow, I can only pay each of you a penny." They said, "A penny? Forget it." And they never came back again.

The old man used his intelligence to solve the problem. He might have screamed at the kids, threatened them, or chased them. He might even have moved from the neighborhood. Instead of fighting or running away, he used his head.

Think of a conflict that you solved unsatisfactorily. Write a paragraph about what you might have or could have done. Start with a topic sentence that identifies the conflict and your feelings about it. Describe the conflict, and then explain what you might have or could have done. Write a concluding sentence that gives a feeling of finish to your paragraph.

 **Exercise B**   *Should Have* + Past Participle

Pretend you and your spouse are out for the evening, and you have left your two young children with a babysitter. It's 10:00, and you're thinking about the children and imagining what they should have done by now.

*Note: Keep in mind that this use refers to probability.*

Write the missing verb phrases in the following sentences. Use *should have* + past participle.

1. The children ____*should have had*____ dinner by now.

2. They _____ already _____ their baths.

3. They _____ already _____ their toys away.

4. They _____ their teeth by now.

5. They _____ already _____ their favorite TV program.

 **Exercise C**   *Must Have* + Past Participle—Life in the Past

Pretend you are writing some ideas for a composition on what life must have been like for your parents (or grandparents). Write three to five sentences, using *must have* + past participle.

**Examples**

It must have been boring in the evenings without television.

The air must have been cleaner.

1. _____

2. _____

3. _____

4. _____

5. _____

# REVIEW: POSSIBILITY—PROBABILITY—LOGICAL CONCLUSION

 **Exercise**   *May (Have), Might (Have), Could (Have), Should (Have), Must (Have)*—Situations to Consider

Imagine the following situations and guess what *may/might/could/must* be true for each of them. On a separate piece of paper, write at least three sentences for each situation.

**Example**

Situation: Class has started, and the student who always sits in the front is not in class.

He may be late.

He could be sick.

He might have dropped the class.

He must be on his way.

He must have had trouble finding parking.

1. Your best friend has a worried expression on his face.

2. The instructor looks tired.

3. You hear a siren outside.

4. There's a traffic jam on the freeway.

5. You can't find your wallet.

6. Your friend promised to call, but she didn't.

7. Your TV doesn't work.

8. Your car won't start.

9. You look at the clock, and you're surprised. It says 4:11 P.M., but it's already dark outside.

10. Your checkbook balance and your bank statement don't agree.

11. Your favorite neighborhood restaurant suddenly closed.

12. Your car has a piece of paper under the windshield wiper.

## CHAPTER REVIEW

 **Exercise A**  All Modals—How to Write a Good Paragraph

Write the missing modals. Answers may vary.

1. A paragraph _____ have a topic sentence.

2. The topic sentence _____ include a controlling idea.

3. Sentences _____ start with a capital letter.

4. The paragraph _____ have a logical system of organization.

5. Run-on sentences and sentence fragments _____ be avoided.

6. Transitions _____ help give coherence to a paragraph.

7. Beginning writers _____ make some mistakes in sentence structure.

8. If you need help, you _____ ask someone to read your paper.

9. A good paragraph _____ have an appropriate conclusion.

 **Exercise B**  All Modals—The Stolen Camera

Pretend that your friend has come home to an open bedroom window and finds that his $600 camera is gone. On a separate piece of paper, write several sentences about what could have happened or what might have happened. Include what your friend should have done or could have done before he left his house. In addition, include what he might or should do about it now.

 **Exercise C**  All Modals

Use your skill at making logical guesses based on your observations of people in various situations. Read the following situations, and on a separate piece of paper write sentences based on what you guess about the people. Include sentences with examples of modal + *have* + past participle.

Your instructor may ask you to work in small groups. If so, each group may be asked to write the answers for one situation on the chalkboard.

**Example**

Two small children are standing at the edge of a busy street. They are looking out into the traffic. One child is holding a baseball bat.

They may want to cross the street.

Their ball could have bounced into the street.

They should ask an adult for help.

They must be careful.

Their mother shouldn't have let them play near a busy street.

1.  A middle-aged man and a woman in her twenties are having dinner at a nice restaurant. The woman is holding a photo album, and they're both smiling.

2.  Two adults are sitting on a bench in the park. One person is crying, and the other is talking softly to the other person and checking the time frequently. (You decide if these people are men, women, or a man and a woman.)

3.  A policeman is talking to a young man at the edge of the road. There's a motorcycle nearby. The young man is showing the policeman something.

4.  It's 1:00 A.M. A young man is driving home alone from a wedding reception. He's having trouble staying in his own lane.

5.  A student is sneezing repeatedly and coughing loudly in class. The other students nearby look annoyed and nervous.

 **Writing Assignment A:** *A Good Instructor (or Person)*

In a small group, select one of the following people to write a paragraph about:

An instructor, a student, a parent, a child, a boyfriend or a girlfriend, a boss, a neighbor

Tell what this person might/could/should/has to/must do in order to be a good (ideal, excellent) instructor, student, etc. Your paragraph should be a report of the group's opinion.

Start your paragraph with a topic sentence.

### Examples

A good instructor should have a sense of humor.

An ideal boyfriend should have several desirable qualities.

A good instructor has many of the following qualities.

Support your topic sentence with plenty of specific details.

### Examples

A good instructor should have a sense of humor.

An excellent student might form a study group.

A good parent must serve as a good example for his or her children.

An ideal boyfriend has to remember special occasions, such as birthdays and Valentine's Day.

Write a concluding sentence that gives a feeling of finish to your paragraph.

 **Writing Assignment B:** *Expectations for the Future*

Write about your expectations for your future after you finish your education. Include thoughts about your family, your career, or any other aspect of your life. Use a variety of modals, as appropriate. Start with a topic sentence such as the following:

I have several expectations for my future.

Support your topic sentence with plenty of specific details. Write a concluding sentence that gives a feeling of finish to your paragraph.

## ≡    FOOD FOR THOUGHT    ≡

My wife said the following to me when I got home:

"You might check on the boys. They may be awake."

1.  What is the function of *might*? _____

        *may*? _____

2.  Can *might* and *may* be interchanged? _____

## ≡  CLASSROOM ASSESSMENT TECHNIQUE (CAT)  ≡

### THE ONE-MINUTE PAPER

Take a minute or two to write answers to the following questions. Write your answers on a separate piece of paper without your name.

1. What are the most important points that you have learned in this chapter?

2. What questions remain in your mind at the end of this chapter?

*Note: Use this exercise to help you get answers to any questions you still have. Ask these questions to anyone who might be able to help you, such as another student or your instructor.*

# Conditional Sentences and *Hope* versus *Wish*

Read the cartoon and answer the following questions.

(*The Wizard of Id* by Brant Parker and Johnny Hart. Reprinted by permission of Johnny Hart and Creators Syndicate)

1.  What time is the cartoon referring to?

    Circle one:    past time    present/future time

2.  What tense of the verb is used after *wish*?

    Circle one:    past tense    present tense

3.  What tense of the verb is used after *if*?

    Circle one:    past tense    present tense

## ═══ CONDITIONAL SENTENCES

▶ **Sample Paragraph**

The following paragraph is based on information from *Almanac for Kids*. The dependent *if* clauses appear in italics. Answer the questions that follow.

## The Stock Market

°**stock market:** where stock is bought and sold

°**stock:** part ownership of a company

°**profit:** money left after paying expenses

°**stockbroker:** one who buys and sells stock for customers

Understanding the stock market° does not have to be difficult *if you focus on a few basic ideas.* To begin, when you buy stock°, you are buying a part of a company. Your money goes to pay the workers and to buy materials and equipment. Next, *if the company makes a profit°,* you usually get part of it. *If the price of your stock goes up,* you can sell it and make money. Of course, it can work the other way, too. The company may lose money. *If it loses money,* the price of your stock may go down. Also, *if you are under twenty-one,* you may need your parents to help you buy stock through a stockbroker°. Finally, *if you make more than $1,000 from stocks,* you will have to file a federal tax form. *If you want to learn more about the stock market,* you can find many excellent books on the topic in your local library.

1.  Look at the sentences containing *if.* How many clauses do they have?

    Circle one:   A.  one     B.  two (or more)

2.  Is the *if* clause the first or the second clause in its sentence?

    Circle one:   A.  the first     B.  the second     C.  either the first or the second

 ### Essential Information: CONDITIONAL SENTENCES

A conditional sentence contains a condition and a result. The condition appears in an *if* clause. The result appears in the main clause. The result depends on the completion of the condition.

> A Conditional Sentence = (1) Condition—*If* Clause
> (2) Result—Main Clause

### Example

If you want to learn more about the stock market, you can find many excellent books on the topic in your library.

| | |
|---|---|
| If you want to learn more about the stock market, . . . | *Condition* |
| . . . you can find many excellent books on the topic in your library. | *Result* |

Often, the *if* clause appears first, but the order may be reversed. When the *if* clause is first, a comma is usually used after the *if* clause.

> ### If Clause, + Main Clause

If the company loses money, the price of your stock may go down.

OR

> ### Main Clause + If Clause

The price of your stock may go down if the company loses money.

## THE MEANINGS OF CONDITIONAL SENTENCES: REAL CONDITIONS

 **Essential Information: HABITUAL ACTION**

Real conditions express either (1) truth or (2) possibility. One of the most common types of truth refers to what the subject does habitually. In this case, *if* is equivalent to *when*.

> If the company makes a profit, you usually receive a part of it.

> If I have a few extra dollars on payday, I buy some lottery tickets.

These conditions express habitual experience. The verb in each clause is in the present tense.

> ### For a condition of habitual action:
> *If* Clause: Present Tense      Main Clause: Present Tense

In an interview with Robert Jacobs in *Writer's Digest*, Ray Bradbury recalls his lack of ability in sports as a teenager. Because he was not good in sports, the other boys treated him cruelly. As a result, Bradbury criticizes the way boys treat other boys who do not behave in certain ways. In the following, Bradbury expresses his dislike for the "male animal."

### BOYS

°**gang:** group of friends (often violent)
°**diversify:** be different
°**I.Q.:** measure of intelligence (intelligence quotient)
°**slaughter:** kill in a violent manner

We are not a very nice sex. If you don't join the gang°, if you don't play baseball or football, if you don't run fast enough, if you think too much, you are in big trouble. Boys are dreadful. If you diversify° in any direction, if you let them see that you have an I.Q.°, if you are dumb enough to let your brightness out, they *kill* you! They slaughter° you! They pull your skin off! . . . So I went off and hid and became a writer.

**Exercise** "Problems"

Finish the following sentences by telling what you habitually do if you have these problems. For numbers 7 and 8, write your own original sentences.

1.  If I have a car problem, *I take my car to a mechanic.* _____

2.  If I need cash, _____

3.  If I'm sick, _____

4.  If I have plumbing problems, _____

5.  If I have trouble spelling a word, _____

6.  If I'm homesick, _____

7.  _____

8.  _____

**Essential Information: PREDICTION**

In a prediction, the writer is making a guess about the future based on a condition that may or may not be satisfied.

$$\text{If Terry passes Physics 1A, she} \begin{cases} \text{can} \\ \text{will} \\ \text{may} \\ \text{could} \\ \text{might} \\ \text{should} \end{cases} \text{take Physics 1B.}$$

Assume that Terry passes the course. In this case, she satisfies the condition in the *if* clause, and the prediction in the main clause becomes possible.

> In the *if* clause of prediction, use the present tense.

If I *buy* some stock, . . .

If I *subscribe* to *Business Week*, . . .

If I *read* the business section of the newspaper, . . .

> In the main clause, use a modal.

If I buy some stock, I *might make* a lot of money.

If I subscribe to *Business Week*, I *should stay* up to date.

If I read the business section of the newspaper, I *can check* my stocks.

> For a condition of prediction
>
> *If* Clause: Present    Main Clause: Modal

 **Exercise A**  Identifying Conditions of Prediction

Read the following paragraph from Roald Dahl's *Danny*. In each conditional sentence, underline . . .

1. the verb in the *if* clause and

2. the verb in the main clause.

*Note: In the following, you will find several clauses in one of the sentences.*

### A Fine Mechanic

My father was a fine mechanic. People who lived miles away used to

bring their automobiles to him for repair rather than take them to their nearest   2

garage. He loved engines. "A gasoline engine is sheer° magic," he said to me

once. "Just imagine being able to take a thousand different bits of metal—and if   4

you <u>fit</u> them all together in a certain way—and then if you feed them a little oil

and gasoline—and if you press a little switch°—suddenly these bits of metal will   6

all come to life—and they will purr° and hum° and roar°—they will make the

wheels of a motor car go whizzing° around at fantastic speeds . . ."   8

°**sheer:** total
°**switch:** what turns something on or off
°**purr:** make a soft, pleasing sound
°**hum:** make a soft, murmuring sound
°**roar:** make a loud, deep sound
°**whizzing:** making a buzzing sound while moving quickly

 **Exercise B**  Conditions of Prediction—Parents and Children

Parents usually know what is best for their young children. Children often make demands or requests that their parents have to refuse, and often the children want to know the reason. Take the part of a parent and respond to the child's demand or request.

**Example**

    *Child:*  Drive the car faster!
    *Parent:*  If I drive faster, we might get into an accident.

1.  Child: I want to watch the late Sunday night movie.

    Parent: *If you stay up late, you'll be tired at school.*

2.  Child: Let me play baseball in the street.

    Parent: _____

3.  Child: Can I eat an ice cream sundae before dinner?

    Parent: _____

4.  Child: I don't want to wear a sweater to the football game tonight.

    Parent: _____

5.  Child: Let's park the car in the handicapped parking space.

    Parent: _____

**Exercise C**   Writing Conditions of Prediction—Common Signs
                 Found in the Community

Look at the following signs found in many communities. Write conditions of prediction based on the information given in the signs.

**Example**

NO PARKING MONDAYS 10–12

If you park here on Monday between ten and twelve, you will get a ticket.

1.  DO NOT ENTER

    *If you go beyond this sign, you could get in trouble.*

2.  HARD HAT AREA

    _____

3.  KEEP OFF THE GRASS

    _____

4.  NO SMOKING

    _____

5.  USE QUARTERS ONLY

    _____

6.  STAFF PARKING ONLY

    _____

7.  HANDICAPPED PARKING ONLY

    _____

8.  EMPLOYEES ONLY

    _____

## REVIEW: REAL CONDITIONS

 **Exercise**    Identifying Conditions of Habitual Action
and Prediction—The Job Interview

In "How to Take a Job Interview," Kirby Stanat writes about what happens when job recruiters visit college campuses to interview students. The following selection describes what is going on in the mind of the recruiter.

Read the selection and decide if each real conditional sentence is *habitual* or *prediction*. Write H or P on the line following each conditional sentence.

**The Job Interview**

°**recruiter:** one who
searches for employees

After introducing himself, the recruiter° will probably say, "Okay, please

follow me," and he'll lead you into his interviewing room.

When you get to the room, you may find that the recruiter will open the

°**gesture:** motion with a
hand

door and gesture° you in—with him blocking part of the doorway. There's

enough room for you to get past him, but it's a near thing.

°**scrape:** rub against

As you scrape° past, he gives you a closeup inspection. He looks at your

°**greasy:** oily

hair; if it's greasy°, that will bother him. _____ He looks at your collar; if it's dirty,
\
1

that will bother him. _____ He looks at your shoulders; if they're covered with
\
2

°**dandruff:** bits of dead
skin in the hair

dandruff°, that will bother him. _____ If you're a man, he looks at your chin.
\
3

_____ If you didn't get a close shave, that will irritate him. _____ If you're a
\
4                                                                                    5

woman, he checks your makeup. _____ If it's too heavy, he won't like it. _____
\
6                                                                         7

## ═══ THE MEANINGS OF CONDITIONAL SENTENCES: UNREAL CONDITIONS

 **Essential Information: PRESENT/FUTURE TIME**

Unreal conditions express ideas that are untrue, imaginary, or unlikely to occur.

**Examples**

If I *had* a million dollars, I *would buy* a lot of shares in the stock market.

If I *could buy* shares in only one company, I *might buy* shares in Microsoft.

If the stock market *crashed* tomorrow, many people *could lose* their life's savings.

If my brother *were* a stockbroker, I *would do* business with him.

The key to understanding unreal conditions is in the *tense* of the verbs in all the above examples.

In unreal conditions for the *present/future time*, use the *past tense* form of the verb—*had, would, could, might, crashed, were*. The *past tense* is not the same as *past time*.

The *past tense* main verbs in the examples above are *had, crashed,* and *were*. The *past tense* modals are listed below in the right-hand column.

| PRESENT TENSE | PAST TENSE |
|---|---|
| can | could |
| will | would |
| may | might |

Historically, the modals in the second column are considered *past tense* (not to be confused with *past time*). These *past tense* modals are used in unreal conditional sentences.

The following chart shows the verb tenses in unreal conditions for present/future time.

| *IF* CLAUSE | MAIN CLAUSE |
|---|---|
| PAST TENSE<br>or<br>could | PAST MODAL:<br>{ would<br>could<br>might |

*Note: In standard written English, use* were *for all the past tense forms of* be.

If I *were a* millionaire, I would buy a huge house.

 **Exercise A**  Writing Correct Verbs in Unreal *If* Clauses—Cuba

What would your life be like if you lived in Cuba right now? Write the missing verbs in these sentences.

1.  If you _____*lived*_____ in Cuba, you wouldn't need winter clothes.

2.  If you _____ to school there, you would learn about Communist doctrine.

3.  If you _____ a car, it would probably be an old American one.

4.  If you _____ another language, it would probably be Russian.

5.  If you _____ to visit friends in the United States, it would probably be impossible.

**Exercise B**   Unreal Conditions—Tic Tac Toe

Imagine that two of your friends are playing Tic Tac Toe and you are watching. Answer the questions based on the illustrations. Tell what move you *would make* if you *were playing.* Answer in complete sentences.

1.  Player *O* has just put his second *O* in square 2. If you were player *X*, where would you put your next *X*?

    *If I were "X," I'd put it in square 8.*

    _____

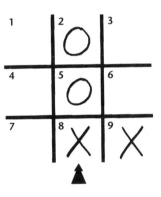

2.  Player *X* has just put his next *X* in square 8. If you were *O*, where would you put your next *O*?

    _____

    _____

3.  If you were *X*, where would you put your next *X*?

    _____

    _____

 **Exercise C**   Unreal Conditions—Special Resource Center

Read the following paragraph and write answers to the questions that follow it.

### Special Resource Center

In 1972 El Camino College established a special program to assist students with disabilities. The staff is specially trained to help disabled students, especially those with physical and learning disabilities, the deaf and hard of hearing, and the visually impaired. The center houses special equipment, such as large-print typewriters, talking calculators, and reading machines. The center's high-tech lab makes computers accessible to disabled students through specially designed equipment that helps students input, process, and output information. The curriculum includes special classes in English, math, and career preparation. Especially useful are the adaptive physical education classes, specially created for disabled persons needing an individualized exercise program. All of these services are offered on a relatively small, flat campus that has been specially constructed to meet the needs of students with physical disabilities.

1.  If you were disabled, would you like to study at El Camino College? Why?

    _____

2.  If you were visually impaired, what kind of typewriter would you use?

    _____

3.  Could you take physical education classes if you had a physical disability?

    _____

4.  If you used a wheelchair, what feature of the campus itself would be helpful to you?

    _____

*Note: The paragraph "Special Resource Center" appears again in Chapter Twelve under a discussion of* special, specially, *and* especially.

## Writing Assignment A: *Unreal Conditions—What If?*

Answer the following questions. Use complete sentences.

1.  If you had thirty-hour days, how would you spend the extra six hours a day?

    _____

2.  If you won ten million dollars in the lottery, would you still want to work? Why?

    _____

3.  If you could travel to any three countries, which countries would you choose? Why?

    _____

Select one of the previous questions, and write a paragraph to explain your answer. Start your paragraph with a topic sentence such as the following:

> If I had thirty-hour days, I would spend the extra six hours a day learning how to play the piano.

Support your topic sentence with plenty of specific details. Write a concluding sentence that gives a feeling of finish to your paragraph.

## Writing Assignment B: *Unreal Conditions—Imaginary Situations*

In "Little Things Are Big," Jesús Colón, a black Puerto Rican from New York, has written a powerful essay about seeing a white woman with two children and a lot of luggage in a subway station at midnight. He wants to help her, but he is undecided. He writes the following.

> What would she say? What would be the first reaction of this white American woman with two children on her arm? Would she say: Yes, of course, you may help me. Or would she think that I was just trying to get too familiar? Or would she think worse than that perhaps? What would I do if she let out a scream as I went toward her to offer my help?

Read the following imaginary situations, and explain what you would do in these cases.

1. What would you do if you wanted to help someone, and the person screamed?

   *I would try to explain that I wanted to help.*

2. What would you do if you lost your wallet?

   _____

3. What would you do if you lost your job?

   _____

4. What would you do if your car caught on fire?

   _____

5. What would you do if you witnessed a murder?

   _____

Write a paragraph about any one of these situations. Start with a topic sentence that identifies the situation. Write specific supporting details to explain what you would do. Finish with a concluding idea that gives a feeling of finish to your paragraph.

## Writing Assignment C: *Unreal Conditions—Prisons in Japan*

Read this paragraph from James Webb's "What We Can Learn from Japan's Prisons."

American jails are filled with hate. If their walls fell down today . . . an American prisoner might kill you, just because you're the first person he sees. If the walls of the Japanese prisons fell down, the Japanese prisoners would just go on home.

*Note: This American writer is presenting an imaginary situation. However, something like this did actually happen. Toyofumi Yoshimasa reports what happened. "During the great Kunto earthquake of 1923, the walls of one of our prisons* did *fall down. No one escaped."*

Write about how your life would be different if you were in prison. Start your paragraph with a topic sentence. Support your topic sentence with plenty of specific details. Write a concluding sentence that gives a feeling of finish to your paragraph.

## REVIEW: CONDITIONS

## CHART: CONDITIONAL SENTENCES

| REAL CONDITIONS | | | |
|---|---|---|---|
| HABITUAL ACTION | | PREDICTION | |
| IF CLAUSE | MAIN CLAUSE | IF CLAUSE | MAIN CLAUSE |
| present tense | present tense | present tense | modal |

| UNREAL CONDITIONS | |
|---|---|
| PRESENT/FUTURE TIME | |
| IF CLAUSE | MAIN CLAUSE |
| past tense or could | past modal: would could might |

**Exercise**  Real or Unreal?

What kind of conditions are the following? Write R for real or U for unreal.

1. _____ If I have a writing assignment to do, I use my computer.

2. _____ If I had a hard disk, I would have more storage for data.

3. _____ If I get a hard disk drive for my birthday, I'll sell my old disk drives.

4. _____ If I got a $1,000 hard disk drive, I could store a lot of data.

5. _____ If Computerworld has a sale, I'll buy the hard disk before my birthday.

6. _____ If Computerworld could sell hard disks at wholesale prices, I'd get the hard disk today.

# ≡ *HOPE* AND *WISH*

### *Relevant Information: Dependent Clauses*

A clause has its own subject and verb. This section focuses on the verbs in dependent clauses that appear after the verbs *hope* and *wish* in main clauses.

### Examples

I hope (that) my stocks *make* a lot of money.
I wish (that) I *had* more shares than I do.

Anita hopes (that) she *gets* good grades this semester.
Barbara wishes (that) she *had* better grades this semester.

In these examples, the meanings of the main verbs *hope* and *wish* are different. Also, the form of the verbs in the dependent clauses is different.

*Note: Many instructors prefer to use the word* that *in these sentences.*

▶ **Sample Paragraph**

Read the following paragraph and underline the verb phrases in the clauses that appear after the verbs *hope* and *wish*.

### Anita and Barbara

My sisters Anita and Barbara differ a lot in their college plans and career goals. Both Anita and Barbara are taking classes at Polk Community College. 2 Anita hopes she can finish her coursework in a few semesters and transfer to a university as an accounting major. On the other hand, Barbara is not sure yet 4 what she wants to do. She wishes she could transfer to a university soon, but she keeps changing her major and can't decide on a goal. Next, when I ask 6 Anita and Barbara how important a career is to them, they give me different answers. Anita tells me that she hopes she gets a position in an accounting 8 company right after she graduates. She also hopes she will have her own accounting business two years later. She has confidence in her plans for the 10 future. But Barbara worries about making the wrong decision. She wishes she

°**optimist:** one who looks
  at life positively
°**pessimist:** one who looks
  at life negatively

knew what to do with her life. Some people say that Anita is an optimist° and          12
Barbara is a pessimist°, but I think that they are both simply realistic about the
future.                                                                                  14

List the verbs used in the clauses after *hope(s)*: _____

_____

List the verbs used in the clauses after *wish(es)*: _____

_____

# *HOPE*

 **Essential Information: THE MEANING OF *HOPE***

**Examples of *Hope***

> I hope (that) my daughter graduates from college in four years.
>> Meaning: It's possible.
>
> I hope (that) she gets good grades in her last two years.
>> Meaning: It's possible.
>
> I hope (that) she can find a good job after she finishes school.
>> Meaning: It's possible.

> *Hope* indicates possibility.

 **Essential Information: THE VERB IN THE
DEPENDENT CLAUSE AFTER *HOPE***

Read the following example sentence and the list of verbs that follows. All of the
verb tenses in the list can be used after *hope*.

> I hope that Anita . . . *verb* . . . hard for her next test.

(TENSES)

| |
|---|
| studies |
| is studying |
| can study |
| will study |

(present/future time)

| |
|---|
| studied |
| was studying |
| has studied |

(past time)

> The verb tenses after *hope* can belong to either group: present/future time or past time.

 **Exercise A**   Your Hopes

You probably have certain hopes about events in your life. Write five sentences that express that hope.

    The following example expresses the hope of the writers of this text.

**Examples**

    We hope that you *are enjoying* this text.

    We hope that you *have understood* most of the material so far.

1. _____

2. _____

3. _____

4. _____

5. _____

After you write your sentences, your instructor may ask you to exchange sentences with a partner. Do you and your partner have any similar hopes?

 **Exercise B**   *No One Writes to the Colonel*

In Gabriel García Márquez's book *No One Writes to the Colonel and Other Stories,* the author describes the unfortunate lives of a colonel and his wife. Even though they are poor, the colonel performs certain actions in the hope that their lives will get better. Some of these actions are listed below. Finish the sentences showing what the colonel hopes for.

1. The colonel scrapes the inside of the can with a knife until the last scrapings of the ground coffee, mixed with bits of rust, fall into the pot.

   He hopes *he can make a cup of coffee.* _____

2. The colonel enters his rooster in a cockfight.

   He hopes _____

3. He shaves by touch because he doesn't have a mirror.

   He hopes _____

4. To get money to buy food, the colonel takes an old clock to Alvaro's tailor shop to sell it.

   He hopes _____

5.  The colonel waits every Friday for the mailboat to arrive.

He hopes _____

## WISH

*Note: Limitations on the Discussion*

The following uses of *wish* are not included in this discussion:

1.  *Wish* as a formal way of saying *want*
    She didn't wish to see her husband.

2.  *Wish* followed by an indirect plus direct object
    I wish you good luck. I wish you a Happy Birthday.

3.  *Wish* as a weak command, when *wish* means *want*
    I wish you would stop snoring.

Read the following cartoon. Notice what tense of the verb appears in the dependent clause after the word *wish*.

(Reprinted with special permission of North American Syndicate)

1.  What time is the cartoon referring to?

Circle one:   past time . . . present/future time

2.  What tense of the verb is used after *wish*?

Circle one:   past . . . present

**Essential Information: THE MEANING OF *WISH***

Read the following examples from the cartoon.

> I wish we didn't have to work on Sundays.
> > (The truth is that they have to work on Sundays.)

> I wish it was cooler today.
> > (It's not cool! They're living in a desert.)

> I wish we didn't have to do this lousy job.
> > (The truth is that they have to do it.)

> I wish I knew (the answer to your question).
> > (He really doesn't know the answer.)

---

> The idea expressed in the clause after *wish* is unreal or unlikely.

---

*Note: As shown in this cartoon, the use of* was *is common in conversational English. Standard formal written English, however, requires* were *for all forms of* be *after* wish.

 **Essential Information: THE VERB IN THE DEPENDENT CLAUSE AFTER *WISH***

Read the following example sentences. What is the tense of the verbs in the dependent clause after *wish*? _____

> I wish I *had* a bigger vocabulary.
> I wish I *could read* faster.
> I wish the instructor *would assign* less homework.

---

| Main Clause | Dependent Clause |
|---|---|
| Wish | Past Tense (Be = Were)<br>Could<br>Would |

---

 **Exercise**    Wishing—Working with a Partner

**Part A**

Write five sentences expressing your wishes.

**Examples**

> I wish I owned a Picasso painting.
> I wish I were a math genius.
> I wish noncitizens could vote in local elections.

1. _____

2. _____

3. _____

4. _____

5. _____

After you write your sentences, your instructor may ask you to exchange sentences with a partner.

### Part B

Work with a partner. Find out what your partner's wishes are. Write three sentences expressing your partner's wishes.

1. _____

2. _____

3. _____

## *DIFFERENT POINTS OF VIEW*

 **Essential Information: *HOPE* VERSUS *WISH*— DIFFERENT POINTS OF VIEW**

Sometimes one person uses *hope*, and another uses *wish*.

### Examples

I hope I have time to go to a movie. (It's possible that I will.)

I wish I had time to go to a movie. (I don't have the time. It's "unreal" for me.)

I hope I can buy a Jaguar. (Maybe I will.)

I wish I could buy a Jaguar. (It's unlikely to occur.)

The point of view for each person in the previous pairs of sentences is different. With *hope*, there exists possibility. With *wish*, there exists little or no possibility.

 **Exercise** Hoping and Wishing—Resolutions

Resolutions are like promises we make to ourselves to make our lives more successful and satisfying. Many people have the custom of making New Year's resolutions at the end of the year.

Mahmood and Parinaz have several New Year's resolutions. They have the same resolutions but different attitudes about their resolutions. Mahmood *hopes* his resolutions *will come* true, whereas Parinaz *wishes* her resolutions *would come* true.

The following sentences express Mahmood's resolutions. Rewrite each sentence to express the same resolutions but from Parinaz's point of view. Use *wish* and the correct form of the verb in the dependent clause.

Since Parinaz is a woman, you will have to make other changes in some of the sentences to fit the change of persons.

**Examples**

Mahmood *hopes* he *can* get a better job.
Parinaz *wishes* she *could* get a better job.

Mahmood *hopes* his parents *will* help him buy a new car.
Parinaz *wishes* her parents *would* help her buy a new car.

1.  Mahmood hopes he can lose ten pounds.

    *Parinaz wishes she could lose fifteen pounds.*

2.  Mahmood hopes his girlfriend will stop smoking.

    _____

3.  Mahmood hopes he can stay in this country for a few more years.

    _____

4.  Mahmood hopes his little brother will move to this city.

    _____

5.  Mahmood hopes he can get a scholarship next semester.

    _____

6.  Mahmood hopes he can make several new English-speaking friends.

    _____

 **Writing Assignment:** Hope *and* Wish—*Your New Year's Resolutions*

Pretend it is the end of the year and you want to make some New Year's resolutions. Write about your hopes and wishes for your own life in the coming new year.

Start with a topic sentence that gives your main idea. Continue with specific hopes and/or wishes. End your paragraph with a concluding sentence that gives a feeling of finish to your paragraph.

## PAST TIME IN DEPENDENT CLAUSES AFTER WISH

 **Essential Information: WISHES REFERRING TO PAST TIME**

Read the following sentences based on the cartoon on page 194.

I wish I hadn't joined the Foreign Legion.

I wish it had been cooler yesterday.

I wish I could have slept all day Sunday.

What form of the verb is used in the clause after *wish* to express past time?

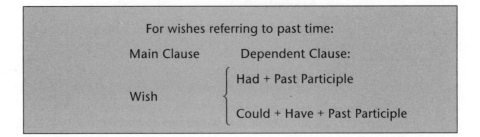

For wishes referring to past time:

Main Clause          Dependent Clause:

Wish                 ⎰ Had + Past Participle

                     ⎱ Could + Have + Past Participle

 **Exercise**   Wishing about the Past

Your answer to the following questions is probably *no*. After your *no* answer, write a sentence beginning with *I wish . . .*

**Example**

Did you learn English as a child?

No. I wish (that) I had learned it then.

1.  Did you earn $50 an hour at your first job in the United States?

    *I wish I had earned half that amount.*

2.  Did your parents send you to private schools in Switzerland when you were a child?

3.  Did you learn to play the piano before you were five years old?

4.  Did you find a good parking place near the classroom in the first few weeks of classes?

5.  Did you get a 4.0 grade point average last semester (or in your previous school year)?

6.  Did Tom Cruise call you up last night?

7.  Did Santa Claus leave a Rolls Royce in your garage last December?

## ☰ CHAPTER REVIEW: CONDITIONAL SENTENCES ☰

 **Exercise A**  Unreal Conditions—International Trivia

Answer the following questions. Ask your classmates for the information you don't know.

1. If you lived in Japan, how would you answer the phone? (In Italy? In Spain? In Mexico? In Korea? In China? In Vietnam?)

   _____

2. If you lived in Germany, what popular beverage would you drink the most?

   _____

3. If you lived in Mexico, when would your child break a piñata?

   _____

4. If you lived in China, how many children could you have?

   _____

5. If you lived in Tanzania, what would you put in stew in place of potatoes?

   _____

6. If all your neighbors spoke Urdu, where would you be living?

   _____

 **Exercise B**  Real and Unreal Conditions—Wise Peter

Read the following story that illustrates wisdom with a touch of humor. Underline the conditional sentence.

Ten-year-old Peter loved books and spent all his free time reading. His older brothers liked to laugh at him because they claimed that Peter was not very bright at all. They said that he read a lot just to appear bright.

One day Peter's brothers decided to prove their point. One of the brothers held out a nickel and a dime and asked Peter to choose a coin. He did this several times. Peter always chose the nickel. Of course, Peter's brothers loved the game.

Finally, Peter's mother happened to see the game and hear the older brothers' loud laughter. Soon afterward she asked Peter why he chose the nickel. She said that she knew that Peter was smart enough to know the difference.

"Sure, I know the difference," Peter replied. "But if I take the dime, they won't do it anymore."

Why is this story funny? _____

What wisdom does the story illustrate? _____

If Peter wanted to become a stockbroker, do you think he'd be a good one?

_____

## CHAPTER REVIEW: *HOPE* AND *WISH*

**Exercise A**    *Hope* and *Wish*—Santa Claus and "The Turtles"

Write the correct form of the verbs.

### Santa Claus and "The Turtles"

My youngest son, Aki, is crazy about the Teenage Mutant Ninja Turtles.

He has several of the toy characters, but he hopes Santa Claus (bring)

_____ him some others. It is very hard to find the most popular
        1

characters, such as Shredder. I hope I (find) _____ them. I wish the
                                                      2

stores (have) _____ a bigger selection. They seem to carry a hundred
                    3

of the less popular characters and very few of the more popular ones. Aki will be

disappointed if I do not find the right characters, so I hope I (have)

_____ success. Now I wish that I (start) _____ looking
        4                                                    5

months ago. Wish me good luck in my search for Shredder and his companions!

**Exercise B**    *Hope* and *Wish*—A Far Away Civil War

Ivan Jurjevich is from a country far away. He now lives in San Pedro, California. His home country is divided by civil war. Insert *hope* or *wish* in Ivan's following statements.

1.  I _____ the war ends soon.

2.  I _____ my family is okay.

3.  I _____ I could help them more.

4. I _____ the countries bordering my country could solve the problem.

5. I _____ the United Nations can negotiate a lasting peace.

6. I _____ I had stayed in my country to help in the fight.

## *Writing Assignment:* Homeland Hopes and Wishes

Express some of your hopes and wishes for your homeland, following Ivan's example in the previous exercise. As an option, express some of your hopes and wishes for your family.

Start your paragraph with a topic sentence. Support your topic sentence with plenty of specific details. Write a concluding sentence that gives a feeling of finish to your paragraph.

## FOOD FOR THOUGHT

**Conditional Sentences**

A. Read the following quotations and answer the question.

1. "If we have another daughter, we'll name her Danielle."

2. "If we had another daughter, we'd name her Danielle."

What is the difference in meaning in the above statements?

_____

B. Read the following sentence to yourself, and then read it again—this time aloud.

If we read to our children more often, we would form a closer bond with them.

How did you pronounce *read*? Why?

_____

*Hope* **and** *Wish*

Read the following sentences and answer the question.

1. I hope you can spend the holidays with your family.

2. I wish everyone could go home for the holidays.

3. I wish there were a Santa Claus.

Can you explain why these sentences use *hope* or *wish*?

_____

## ≡ CLASSROOM ASSESSMENT TECHNIQUE (CAT) ≡

### THE ONE-MINUTE PAPER

Take a minute or two to write answers to the following questions. Write your answers on a separate piece of paper without your name.

1. What are the most important points that you have learned in this chapter?

2. What questions remain in your mind at the end of this chapter?

*Note: Use this exercise to help you get answers to any questions you still have. Ask these questions to anyone who might be able to help you, such as another student or your instructor.*

# Prepositions—
# *In, On,* and *At*

▶ **Sample Paragraph**

Read the following paragraph. The prepositions *in, on,* and *at* appear in italics.

## The Birthday Roses

Judy totally surprised her husband Fred with one dozen gorgeous red

roses *on* his thirtieth birthday. After work, she went to a flower stand *on* the      2

corner, but she didn't like the selection there. Later she found a beautiful

selection of flowers *in* a flower shop *at* Farmers' Market. When she got home,      4

she took the roses into the kitchen and put them into a vase. Then she put

the vase *on* the coffee table *in* the living room. When Fred came into the      6

house and saw the gorgeous bouquet *on* the table, a grin appeared *on* his face.

 **Essential Information: PREPOSITIONAL PHRASES**

Prepositions have a noun or pronoun as an object. The preposition and its object
form a *prepositional phrase.*

### Examples

> in the living room
> on the corner
> at Farmers' Market

 **Exercise**   The Birthday Roses

Go back to "The Birthday Roses" and circle the prepositional phrases.

# ≡ SPACE

## *GEOGRAPHICAL LOCATIONS AND ADDRESSES*

▶ **Sample Paragraph**

### Washington

When I first lived *in the United States* as a child, I confused Washington, D.C. and the state of Washington. When I heard that the president of the United States lived *in Washington*, I thought of Washington State. The fact is that the president lives in the White House *in Washington, D.C.* Once a person is *in* the right *Washington*—Washington, D.C.—the White House is not hard to find. It's *on Pennsylvania Avenue*, not far from the Washington Monument, which is *on Fifteenth Street*. The White House is *at 1600 Pennsylvania Ave. N.W.* Next week I'm taking my kids on a trip to Washington, and I now know where I'm going.

| In + Country, State, City |
| :---: |

| On + Street |
| :---: |

| At + Address |
| :---: |

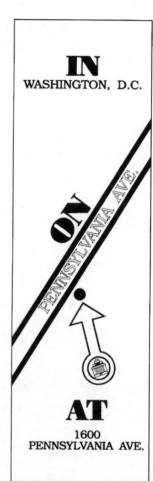

 **Essential Information: *IN, ON,* AND *AT***

Look back at the italicized information in the above paragraph and answer the following questions.

1.  What type of information follows the word *in?*

    _____

    Can you think of other similar types of information that fit into the same category?

    _____

2.  What type of information follows the word *on?*

    _____

3.  What type of information follows the word *at?*

    _____

 **Exercise** *In, On,* and *At* with Geographical Locations and Addresses

Fill in the blanks with *in, on,* or *at.*

**Paragraph One**

### My Cousin's Wedding

All is set for my cousin's wedding this weekend. The ceremony will take

place at the Starlight Wedding Chapel _____ 1383 Lankershim Boulevard. Later
                                         1

there will be a reception _____ Los Angeles. The reception hall is _____ Third
                            2                                        3

Street near the library. It's going to be a beautiful event.

**Paragraph Two**

### Plan Your Financial Future Now

The seminar titled "Plan Your Financial Future Now" is scheduled for next

Saturday at the Saratoga Bank _____ Sunset Boulevard _____ Hollywood. Inter-
                                1                      2

ested people can register at the seminar organization's main office located

nearby _____ 472 Olympic Avenue.
         3

## SPATIAL RELATIONSHIPS

▶ **Sample Paragraph**

In the following excerpt from Gabriel García Márquez's *No One Writes to the Colonel and Other Stories,* a woman and a girl are arriving at a town while all the people of the town are taking their midday nap.

### Tuesday Siesta

There was no one *at the train station*. *On the other side* of the street, *on the sidewalk* shaded by the almond trees, only the pool hall was open. The town was floating *in the heat*. The woman and the girl got off the train and crossed the abandoned station—the tiles were split apart by the grass growing up between—over to the shady side of the street.

°**drowsiness:** sleepiness

It was almost two. At that hour, weighted down by drowsiness°, the town was taking a siesta. The stores, the town offices and the public school were closed at eleven, and didn't reopen until a little before four, when the train went back. Only the hotel across from the station, with its bar and pool hall, and the telegraph office *on one side* of the plaza stayed open. The houses, most of them built on the banana company's model, had their doors locked from the inside and their blinds° drawn°. *In some of them* it was so hot that the residents ate lunch *on the patio*. Others leaned a chair against the wall, *in the shade* of the almond trees, and took their siesta right out *on the street*.

°**blinds:** window covers
°**drawn:** pulled closed

 **Essential Information: SPATIAL RELATIONSHIPS**

Look back at the italicized information in the above paragraph and answer the following questions.

1.  What spatial relationship does *in* refer to?

    _____

2.  What spatial relationship does *on* refer to?

    _____

3.  What spatial relationship does *at* refer to?

    _____

| |
|---|
| *In* = Inside, within an area |
| *On* = On top of, against a surface |
| *At* = General location—nearby or possibly in |

In some of them (the houses)
In the shade

On the sidewalk
On the patio

At the train station

 **Essential Information: *IN*—BASIC MEANINGS**

*In* refers to inside or within an area.

**Example Paragraph (from *Danny* by Roald Dahl)**

### HOME SWEET HOME

I really loved our gypsy trailer. I loved it especially in the evenings when I was tucked *in my bed* and my father was telling me stories. The kerosene lamp was turned low, and I could see lumps of wood glowing red-hot *in the old stove*. It was wonderful to be lying there snug and warm *in my bed in that little room*. Most wonderful of all was the feeling that when I went to sleep, my father would still be there, very close to me, sitting *in his chair* by the fire or lying *in the bed* above my own.

 **Exercise** *In*

Write five sentences about the classroom, the school, your home, or your workplace using *in*.

**Example**

I do my homework in the kitchen.

1. _____

2. _____

3. _____

4. _____

5. _____

 **Essential Information: *ON*—BASIC MEANINGS**

*On* refers to on top of or against a surface.

**Example paragraph**

### BERNICE'S ROOM

You can't miss it—when you walk into Bernice's room, you will know immediately that she adores birds. The first thing you will notice is a tall, wrought iron bird cage *on the floor* near the window with two pairs of chirping blue and green parakeets. *On the table* next to her bed is a smaller cage with three tiny peeping finches. Piles of stuffed animals—mostly birds, of course—lie scattered *on her bed*. She has tacked posters of various kinds of colorful birds *on the walls*, and she has even taped a large poster of the head of an Amazon parrot *on the ceiling* above her bed. Everyone says that Bernice is bird crazy.

 **Exercise** *On*

Write five sentences about the classroom, the school, your home, or your workplace using *on*.

**Example**

I have a lot of working space on the kitchen table.

1. _____

2. _____

3. _____

4. _____

5. _____

☞ **Essential Information: *IN* VERSUS *ON***

In the following examples, *in* and *on* are used with different nouns (objects of the preposition). Discuss with a partner how the meaning differs in the examples within each pair.

1. paint in a can            paint on a can

2. soup in a bowl           the design on a bowl

3. wine in a bottle         the label on a bottle

4. a letter in an envelope   an address on an envelope

✏ **Exercise**   *In* or *On*

Write the missing preposition: *in* or *on*.

1. When you buy a new can of paint, there is paint _*in*_ the can.

2. Before you start painting, you have to mix the paint _____ the can.

3. Be careful where you put the lid because there is paint _____ it.

4. As you paint, you put paint _____ your brush.

5. As you continue painting, you get paint _____ the can.

6. Soon you may have some paint _____ your hands if you carelessly hold the
   can _____ your hand. It is better to put the can _____ the ground or _____
   a ladder.

7. If you put the can _____ the ground, you should use an old newspaper or
   drop cloth in case there is some paint _____ the can and it ends up _____
   the ground.

8. If you have to take a break, you should leave the paintbrush _____ the can
   and not _____ the can or _____ the drop cloth because the paint might get
   dry and harden the brush.

9. When you are finished painting, you should put a small amount of water _____ the can. Then you should put the lid _____ the can tightly using a rubber hammer. You should store the can, upside down, _____ a cool place.

10. When you want to use the paint again, you probably won't be able to read the label _____ the can because there's paint _____ it, but the paint _____ the can lets you know the color of the paint _____ it.

## ☞ Essential Information: *AT*—BASIC MEANINGS

*At* expresses general location—nearby or possibly in.

at the window

at the bank

at the train station

## ▶ Sample Paragraph

### My Friend Yoshie

When I ran into my high school friend Yoshie *at the Galleria Center* in Houston, Texas, last month, we had a chance to catch up on news with each other. First, she is living with her sister and brother-in-law near Rice University. She is attending day classes *at the university* on Monday, Wednesday, and Friday. Most of the classes she is taking are general education requirements. She is only taking one class in her major, computer science. In the evenings and on weekends, she is working part-time *at a computer software store* in the Galleria Center. That's how we ran into each other again. I went into the software store because I was looking for a new word processing program. Shortly after we talked, she helped me get a job *at the same computer store*.

##  Exercise A   Cartoon—*At* and *In*

Read the cartoon at the top of the next page. Why does Francis use *at* in most of his statements about his location? Why does he use *in* with *kitchen*?

_____

_____

## ✎ Exercise B   *At*

Write five sentences about the classroom, the school, your home, or your workplace using *at*.

(*Momma* by Mell Lazarus. Reprinted by permission of Mell Lazarus and Creators Syndicate)

**Example**

I study at the kitchen table on weekends.

1.  _____

2.  _____

3.  _____

4.  _____

5.  _____

## REVIEW: SPATIAL RELATIONSHIPS

 **Exercise A** *In, On,* and *At*—A Whole New Roof

Write the missing prepositions.

**A Whole New Roof**

I was standing _____ the front gate talking with my neighbor Julia when I
<br>1

spotted something _____ the roof that didn't look normal. When she left, I got a
<br>2

ladder and went up _____ the roof. Unfortunately, what I saw was a hole _____
<br>3 4

the roof. The rainy season was not far away, so I immediately looked _____ the
<br>5

phone directory for a roofer. When I called, the phone number was out of

service. Then I noticed that the date _____ the phone book was very old. I looked
<br>6

_____ the bookcase for the latest directory and found it hidden under several
<br>7

books _____ the bottom shelf. The same roofer had a big ad _____ the latest
<br>8 9

directory _____ page 868. I called him and made an appointment. When he
<br>10

came out to give me an estimate, I wasn't very happy because, although I had

just one hole _____ my roof, he said I needed a whole new roof. With the rainy
<br>11

season on the way, I had no choice. Monday I'll be _____ the bank asking for a
<br>12

loan.

 **Exercise B** Pictures

The pictures on the next page differ in minor details in several ways. Write three
to four sentences that describe these differences. Include *in, on,* or *at* in your
sentences.

**Contrasts**

1. _____

2. _____

3. _____

4. _____

![icon] **Writing Assignment:** *A Description of a Scene*

Write a paragraph that describes a scene in an airport or in a bus terminal. Perhaps you might want to describe the day you left for an important trip or the day you returned. Include the prepositions *in*, *on*, and *at.*

Start your paragraph with a topic sentence that identifies the situation. Support your topic sentence with a description that includes plenty of specific details. Write a concluding sentence that gives a feeling of finish to your paragraph.

![icon] **Essential Information: EVENTS**

The following sentences are from the murder mystery novel *The Fourth Deadly Sin* by Lawrence Sanders. They explain where some of the suspects were at the time of the murder.

Why is the italicized *at* used in the following sentences?

---

1. Henry Ellerbee was *at* a charity dinner at the Plaza Hotel.

°**super:** superintendent, manager
°**pinochle:** card game

2. Dr. Samuelson was *at* the Carnegie Hall concert.

3. The super° was playing pinochle° *at* his basement social club.

4. The two ladies who run the art gallery were *at* a private dinner.

5. The movie producer was *at* a film festival in the south of France.

> *At* is used for events.

 **Exercise**  Identifying Locations and Events—An Eventful Courtship

Identify the following uses of *at* as referring either to a location or to an event. Write L (location) or E (event) over each occurrence of *at*.

### An Eventful Courtship

I met my wife *at* a party *at* a friend's house. On our first date we had fun *at* a dance the following weekend *at* El Monte Legion Stadium. However, I fell asleep *at* a concert we went to a week later. There were a lot of relatives *at* the first birthday party I went to *at* her apartment. When we got married, everyone had a great time *at* the reception, which was held *at* my in-laws' house.

# TIME

▶ **Sample Paragraph**

Read the paragraph and answer the questions that follow.

### A Friend Lost Forever

I'll never forget the sadness I felt when my grandfather passed away last year. It happened *in January*. I even remember the day. It was *on a Tuesday*. While I was at the hospital waiting for news about him, I began to recall fond memories of times we spent together. For example, *in the winter* of 1980, we went fishing together. We got up at 4:00 *in the morning* and hiked three miles down to the lake, but when we got there *at sunrise*, we discovered that we had forgotten the bait. How we laughed that day, and for years afterwards. The voice of a nurse interrupted these pleasant thoughts. She told me that my grandfather had died at 8:55. We buried him *on the fifteenth of January*. I lost one of my best friends *on that day*. Now when I can't sleep *at night*, my thoughts often turn to my wonderful friend—my grandfather.

1. What type of information follows *in*?

   _____

2. What type of information follows *on*?

   _____

3. What type of information follows *at*?

_____

 **Essential Information: *IN, ON,* AND *AT* FOR TIME**

> *In* + A PERIOD OF TIME: Year, season, month, including *morning,*
> *afternoon,* and *evening*
>
> *On* + DAY, DATE
>
> *At* + CLOCK TIME, including *sunrise, sunset,* and *night*

## IN

| in 1994 | in January |
| in the winter | in the morning |

**JANUARY 1994**

| | | | | | | 1 |
|---|---|---|---|---|---|---|
| 2 | 3 | 4 | 5 | 6 | 7 | 8 |
| 9 | 10 | 11 | 12 | 13 | 14 | 15 |
| 16 | 17 | 18 | 19 | 20 | 21 | 22 |
| 23 | 24 | 25 | 26 | 27 | 28 | 29 |
| 30 | 31 | | | | | |

## ON

on Saturday
on the fifteenth of January

**JANUARY 1994**

| | | | | | | 1 |
|---|---|---|---|---|---|---|
| 2 | 3 | 4 | 5 | 6 | 7 | 8 |
| 9 | 10 | 11 | 12 | 13 | 14 | **15** |
| 16 | 17 | 18 | 19 | 20 | 21 | 22 |
| 23 | 24 | 25 | 26 | 27 | 28 | 29 |
| 30 | 31 | | | | | |

## AT

| at 2:55 | at night |
| at sunrise | |

 **Exercise A**   *In, On,* and *At* with Time

Write six sentences about the classroom, the school, your home, or your workplace using *in, on,* and *at.*

*IN*

  1. _____

  2. _____

*ON*

  3. _____

  4. _____

*AT*

  5. _____

  6. _____

 **Writing Assignment:** *An Event with Special Meaning*

Write a paragraph that tells about an event in the past that you remember clearly because of some strong emotion you experienced at the time. Include several time expressions with the prepositions *in*, *on*, and *at*.

Start your paragraph with a topic sentence that identifies the event and your feeling about the event.

**Example**

I'll never forget the (emotion) I felt when (event).

Support your topic sentence with plenty of specific details. Write a concluding sentence that gives a feeling of finish to your paragraph.

 **Exercise B**   *In*, *On*, and *At* to Express Time

Write the missing prepositions in the blanks.

**Paragraph One**

### Election Debates

_At_ 7:30 _____ Tuesday, October 25, NBC will televise the first of three
¹      ²

election debates. _____ October 28, CBS will broadcast the second in the series.
       ³

For both of these debates, members of the audience will ask the candidates

questions. The last debates with this format took place _____ 1992.
                                                ⁴

**Paragraph Two**

### Space Travel

People have always dreamed about exploring space. _____ this century
                                                                   ¹

we have accomplished this dream. _____ 1957 Russia sent up the first satellite,
                                            ²

Sputnik I, to orbit Earth. _____ July 20, 1969, United States astronauts Neil
           <sub>3</sub>

Armstrong and Edwin Aldrin became the first people to walk on the moon.

_____ the 1970s, the United States launched spacecrafts to study the planets.
 <sub>4</sub>

These spacecrafts sent back photos of the planets along with other data. Perhaps

_____ the future, vacations on the moon will be common.
 <sub>5</sub>

 **Essential Information: *AT* VERSUS *ON*—HOLIDAYS**

Read the examples, and answer the following questions. Your instructor may
suggest that you work with a partner.

> I'll see you at Easter.
> I'll see you on Easter Sunday.

> > I hate to shop at Christmas.
> > We open our gifts on Christmas day.

> > > Airports are very busy at Thanksgiving.
> > > Airports are dead on Thanksgiving day.

What's the difference between *at* and *on* in the above examples?

_____

 **Exercise** *In*, *On*, and *At* for Time—Summer School

Write the missing words in the blanks.

1. There are several ESL classes _*in*_ the summer at our school.

2. My composition class starts _____ 8:00 A.M.

3. My ESL class doesn't meet _____ Fridays.

4. We usually take a break _____ 9:30.

5. I write my compositions in the air-conditioned library _____ the afternoon.

6. The college is closed _____ August.

7. Fall semester begins _____ September.

 **Essential Information: NO PREPOSITION**

No preposition is used with several time expressions. This often occurs when a
modifier (other than *a* or *the*) comes before the time expression.

| | |
|---|---|
| 1. I'm not going to church *this* Sunday. | 1. I usually go to church on Sunday. |
| 2. We're having a test *next* week. | 2. I'll have the results on Monday. |

3.  I got sick *last* Friday, . . .

3.  . . . so I didn't play basketball on Saturday.

4.  What are you doing *next* summer?

4.  I always have to work in the summer.

5.  I have an appointment *this* afternoon.

5.  I usually take a siesta in the afternoon.

List the time expressions that are not used with a preposition.

_____

Why are the following sentences incorrect?

*There is a company picnic on this Sunday.
*I went to the company Christmas party in last December.

_____

 **Exercise** *On* versus No Preposition

Add the prepositions to the following sentences, as necessary.

1.  We go to the library _____ every Thursday.

2.  I was sick, so I didn't go to the library _____ last Thursday.

3.  We have an exam _____ next Wednesday, so don't bring your texts.

4.  I don't think about school _____ all day Saturday.

5.  All schools are closed _____ this Thursday. It's Thanksgiving.

## CHAPTER REVIEW

 **Exercise A**   Editing—My Pain-in-the-Neck Allergies

Edit the following paragraph.

### My Pain-in-the-Neck Allergies

My allergies are a pain in the neck. To start with, I have to get shots every week. I usually go to the doctor in Tuesday afternoons, in the middle of my busy 2 day. The doctor's office is in downtown Long Beach, on the busiest part of town. It is on a tall building on Long Beach Boulevard with very little free parking 4 nearby. I usually have to park on a pay lot. After lunch, the office opens up at 2:00 P.M., and I usually have my appointment on 2:30. After I sign in on the front 6 desk, I often have to wait for almost an hour on the waiting room. After all that aggravation, I get one shot on each arm. To make things worse, I have to pay    8

for the shots once a month, and they're expensive. Not only are allergies a pain

on the neck, but they're also a pain in the wallet.    10

 **Exercise B**   *In, On,* and *At* for Time and Place—The Ellerbees

In the murder investigation of Dr. Simon Ellerbee's death in *The Fourth Deadly Sin* by Lawrence Sanders, specific facts about the time and location are important. Fill in the appropriate prepositions.

### The Ellerbees

In addition to the townhouse, the Ellerbees owned a country home near

Brewster, New York. It was the Ellerbees' custom to stay _____ the East 84th
                                                          1

Street townhouse weekdays, and on rare occasions _____ Saturday. They usually
                                                  2

left for Brewster _____ Friday evenings and returned to Manhattan _____ Sunday
                  3                                               4

night. Both spent the entire month of August _____ the country home.
                                             5

Dr. Diane said she left Manhattan _____ approximately 6:30 P.M. _____
                                  6                             7

1:15 A.M. Dr. Diane called Dr. Julius K. Samuelson. Samuelson states he arrived

_____ the East 84th Street townhouse _____ about 1:45 A.M. He tramped°
8                                    9

determinedly up the dimly lighted, carpeted staircase to the offices of Dr. Simon

_____ the third floor. Within he found the battered° body. Then, using the
10

phone _____ the receptionist's desk, he dialed 911. The call was logged in°
      11

_____ 1:54 A.M.
12

°**tramped:** walked heavily

°**battered:** beaten with heavy blows

°**logged in:** recorded in writing

 **Exercise C**   *In, On,* and *At* for Space and Time—Early Morning

The following is from Ernest Hemingway's *The Sun Also Rises.* Fill in the blanks with *in, on,* or *at.*

### Early Morning

_____ the morning it was bright, and they were sprinkling the streets of the
1

town, and we all had breakfast _____ a cafe. Bayonne is a nice town. It is like a
                               2

very clean Spanish town and it is _____ a big river. Already, so early _____ the
                                  3                                     4

morning, it was very hot _____ the bridge across the river. We walked out _____
                         5                                                6

the bridge and then took a walk through the town.

We found out _____ the tourist office what we ought to pay for a motor car
                    7

to Pamplona and hired one for four hundred francs. The car was to pick us up

_____ the hotel _____ forty minutes, and we stopped _____ the cafe _____ the
   8              9                                   10              11

square where we had eaten breakfast and had a beer. It was hot, but the town

had a cool, fresh, early-morning smell and it was pleasant sitting _____ the cafe.
                                                                    12

**Exercise D**   Space and Time—Help!

In the following story, Rita is a desperate young wife looking for her missing
husband. She secretly wants to hire a private detective. Add the missing prepositions.

### Help!

Rita decided that the only way to solve her problem was to consult with a

°**private eye:** private
detective

private eye°. Since she did not want anyone to see her, she decided to meet P.I.

Sam McSpam _____ a bar. They planned to meet _____ February 30th _____
            1                                 2                   3

10:00 P.M.

She parked her car _____ the parking lot. When she reached the entrance,
                   4

there was no one _____ the door. She could hear lots of conversation going on
                 5

_____ the bar. She opened the door. It was nice and dark.
  6

She wanted to sit alone _____ a table, but the tables were all taken, so she
                        7

sat _____ a stool _____ the bar. She put her purse _____ the bar and looked
    8             9                                 10

around. She saw someone who looked like Sam sitting _____ a corner. He was
                                                    11

°**margarita:** a tequila
cocktail
°**rim:** the outer edge

alone. There was a margarita° _____ his table with lots of salt _____ the rim°.
                              12                                13

The bartender approached Rita and put a cocktail napkin _____ the bar.
                                                        14

_____ the napkin were the words "_____ the corner, _____ the table, by the
  15                              16                17

clock." The bartender had a smile _____ his face. She smiled back. He also had
                                  18

°**Shirley Temple:** nonalco-
holic cocktail
°**purred:** made a sound
like a happy cat

an earring _____ his ear. "A Shirley Temple° _____ the rocks with a cherry _____
           19                                20                               21

it," she purred° and threw a five dollar bill _____ the bar.
                                              22

°**headed:** went toward

Soon, she had the drink _____ her hand and headed° toward the corner.
                         23

When she reached the table, she put her drink _____ it and sat down _____ the
                                              24                      25

°**sobbed:** cried

chair. She glanced around. In a low voice, she sobbed°, "I need help!" The man

°**blurted:** said suddenly

_____ the table, with surprise _____ his face, blurted°, "How did you find me,
  26                            27

Wife? I thought I'd left you forever!"

 **Writing Assignment: "Help!"**

Write a paragraph for the next scene in the story "Help!"

 **FOOD FOR THOUGHT**

Read the following sentence and answer the question.

> The Smiths bought their Christmas tree *on the corner* of Ninth and Western
> and set it up *in the corner* of their family room.

Can you explain the uses of *on* and *in* in the above sentences?

_____

**CLASSROOM ASSESSMENT TECHNIQUE (CAT)**

## THE ONE-MINUTE PAPER

Take a minute or two to write answers to the following questions. Write your answers on a separate piece of paper without your name.

1. What are the most important points that you have learned in this chapter?

2. What questions remain in your mind at the end of this chapter?

*Note: Use this exercise to help you get answers to any questions you still have. Ask these questions to anyone who might be able to help you, such as another student or your instructor.*

# Word Formation

After you read the cartoon, answer the following questions.

(*Mother Goose and Grimm* by Mike Peters. Reprinted by permission: Tribune Media Services)

According to the person who wrote the sign, what part of speech is *wet* supposed to be?

_____

What part of speech does the dog think it is? _____

## ⬛⬛⬛ PARTS OF SPEECH

 **Exercise A**   Identifying Word Forms

Identify the following words as nouns       (n.)
                                verbs       (v.)
                                adjectives  (adj.)
                                adverbs     (adv.)

1. management    _n._        6. kindness    _____

2. slowly        _____        7. friendly    _____

3. computerize   _____        8. teacher     _____

4. attendance    _____        9. rain        _____

5. plant         _____        10. creative   _____

### *Relevant Information: Identifying Word Forms*

The word endings (-ment, -ly, -ize, -ance, -ness, -er, and -ive) may have helped you identify the words. But not all of the words in the exercise have special word endings.

For those words that do not have special endings, such as *plant* and *rain*, you need to look at how the word is used in context.

### **Exercise B**   Parts of Speech

Read the following sentences and write the part of speech above each italicized word.

1. We haven't had enough *rain* this year.

2. It didn't *rain* more than a few times this winter.

3. I may not *plant* a large garden this spring.

4. I will miss having new *plants* this year.

### **Exercise C**   Nouns and Verbs That Have the Same Form—Public Speaking

Read the following paragraph and identify the italicized words as nouns (n.) or verbs (v.).

#### **Public Speaking**

             *n.*
Giving a *talk* in front of an audience can be frightening, but if you make a *plan* ahead of *time*, you will be satisfied with the *results*. Here are some *tips* to      2
help you *plan* a successful *talk*.

1. Don't let the *walk* to the front of the room frighten you. When it's your      4
   *turn* to speak, *walk* slowly and breathe deeply. *Turn* confidently toward
   the group.                                                                       6

2. Use eye *contact* with members of your audience. If, at first *try*, you
   *panic*, don't *worry*. Take a deep breath and *try* again. The *panic* will go   8
   away.

3. If your *talk* is for more than ten minutes, *request* a glass of *water*. This    10
   *request* is reasonable. And keep your *drink* within easy *reach* so you can
   *reach* for it and *drink* some *water* at any *time*. Drinking some *water* will    12
   also give you a good *reason* to pause, and *pauses* are perfectly fine.

4. *Trust* the people in your audience. They want you to succeed, so give    14
   them your *trust* from the *start*.

5. Your confidence may drop a little, but don't let your *doubts* grow.    16
   Everyone *doubts* himself or herself a little in this situation.

6. *Talk* about something you are truly interested in. Your *interest* in your    18
   topic will automatically *interest* the audience in your material.

7. If you're giving a *report*, *report* your information as clearly as possible.    20
   Organization is very important.

8. Don't *regret* any *mistakes*.  Everyone makes them. *Regrets* will only    22
   *work* against you.

It's important to plan ahead and *practice* your *plan*. This *practice* will ensure    24
your success.

# COMMON NOUN ENDINGS

 **Essential Information: CHANGING VERBS TO NOUNS**

The following word endings change verbs to nouns. If you think of other
examples, add them.

-----MENT        agree + ment = agreement

require + ment = requirement

_____

_____

-----ANCE/ENCE        accept + ance = acceptance

prefer + ence = preference

_____

_____

-----SION          comprehend + sion = comprehension

-----TION          educate + tion = education

-----ATION          inform + ation = information

_____

_____

*Note:* *Adding word endings often results in spelling changes, e.g., comprehend + sion =*
*comprehension. A good English-English dictionary gives the spelling of these combinations.*

-----ER/OR          erase + er = eraser

                    educate + or = educator

_____

_____

 **Exercise**   My Former Instructor Mrs. Albelo

Write the correct form of the words in parentheses.

### My Former Instructor Mrs. Albelo

Mrs. Albelo was one of the best (instruct) _*instructors*_ I've ever had. She

won the (admire) _____ of most of her students for several reasons. First,
                        2

her classroom (manage) _____ style was effective. She required regular
                            3

(attend) _____ . She stressed coming to class on time and handing in all
              4

our (assign) _____ on their due date. Also, she always announced (exam-
                  5

ine) _____ a week ahead of time. Second, she was an expert in (motivate)
            6

_____ . For example, she always made (discuss) _____ inter-
        7                                                              8

esting, and the (inform) _____ she presented often came within humor-
                              9

ous stories. These stories encouraged us to use our (imagine) _____ ,
                                                                          10

which added to our (enjoy) _____ of the class. Third, Mrs. Albelo made it
                                11

clear that she cared for all her students. She often stayed after class for (converse)

_____ . This attitude made a big (differ) _____ to us. I'm
        12                                                        13

really glad that my (counsel) _____ recommended Mrs. Albelo to me.
                                  14

She made getting an (educate) _____ a pleasure.
                                    15

**Writing Assignment:** *A Former Instructor*

Write a paragraph about a teacher you had in the past. Start your paragraph with a topic sentence. Support your topic sentence with plenty of specific details. Write a concluding sentence that gives a feeling of finish to your paragraph.

 **Essential Information: CHANGING ADJECTIVES TO NOUNS**

The following word endings change adjectives to nouns. If you think of other examples, add them.

-----NESS            kind + ness = kindness

                     sleepy + ness = sleepiness

                     _____

                     _____

-----TY/ITY          real + ity = reality

                     active + ity = activity

                     _____

                     _____

-----ISM             ideal + ism = idealism

                     parallel + ism = parallelism

                     _____

                     _____

 **Exercise**   The Children In the Yard Next Door

Write the correct form of the words in parentheses.

### The Children in the Yard Next Door

The kids next door inspire me when I watch them playing in their yard.

When they shout and run out onto the grass in the morning, their (loud)

_____*loudness*_____ doesn't bother me. Instead, I appreciate the sounds of joy and
  1

(happy) _____ . They ignore the (ugly) _____ in the street
             2                                          3

and focus on the beauty and (pleasant) _____ of their own world. The
                                             4

children's (playful) _____ inspires me to think about how I can become
                         5

more playful in my own life. Their (active) _____ inspires me to be-
                                                 6

come more energetic. And their (curious) _____ makes me want to
                                              7
find out more about the world around me. At the end of the day, I notice the

children's (tired) _____ , and I recognize my own need for rest. I'm
                      8
also grateful because these wonderful children have helped me remember the

(ideal) _____ I almost left behind in childhood.
            9

# COMMON ADJECTIVE ENDINGS

 ### Essential Information: CHANGING NOUNS TO ADJECTIVES

The following word endings change nouns to adjectives. If you think of other
examples, add them.

-----Y              sun + y = sunny

                    noise + y = noisy

                    _____

                    _____


----AL              nation + al = national

                    universe + al = universal

                    _____

                    _____


-----ISH            fool + ish = foolish

                    child + ish = childish

                    _____

                    _____


-----OUS            danger + ous = dangerous

                    mystery + ous = mysterious

                    _____

                    _____


-----ARY            revolution + ary = revolutionary

                    honor + ary = honorary

                    _____

                    _____

-----IC

artist + ic = artistic

base + ic = basic

_____

_____

-----LESS

use + less = useless

end + less = endless

_____

_____

-----FUL

power + ful = powerful

beauty + ful = beautiful

_____

_____

 **Exercise**   My Classmate Loc

Write the correct form of the words in the parentheses.

### My Classmate Loc

Loc Nguyen is my classmate in ESL at Rancho Santiago College. The first thing I noticed about Loc was his (boy) ___*boyish*___ smile. This made me feel
1

less (nerve) _____ about talking with him. After I found out some
2

(base) _____ background information about Loc, I asked him some
3

(person) _____ questions, such as how he likes the United States. Loc
4

said he feels (luck) _____ to be in this country. Here he can pursue his
5

(artist) _____ interests. At that point, Loc's face showed a (moment)
6

_____ frown. He then smiled again and told me (count)
7

_____ (humor) _____ stories about his first weeks in an
8                          9

American college. For example, at first he thought the word "priceless" (meaning

"without a price") meant "free." Later, of course, he learned the real meaning.

I'm sure Loc will be very (success) _____ in his future as an artist, and
10

I'm (thank) _____ I had a chance to interview him.
11

**Essential Information: CHANGING VERBS TO ADJECTIVES**

The following word endings change verbs to adjectives. If you think of other examples, add them.

-----IVE/ATIVE     effect + ive = effective

form + ative = formative

_____

_____

-----ANT/ENT     please + ant = pleasant

excel + ent = excellent

_____

_____

-----ABLE     wash + able = washable

believe + able = believable

_____

_____

 **Exercise**   Overly Talkative Salespeople

Write the correct form of the words in parentheses.

### Overly Talkative Salespeople

Salespeople aren't always helpful when a person is trying to decide on a

purchase. The other day I was shopping for a new jacket. I found an (attract)

___*attractive*___ one. I liked it because it was (conserve) _____ in color
　　　　1　　　　　　　　　　　　　　　　　　　　　　　　　　　　　2

and style. It was also (wash) _____ , and the price was (reason)
　　　　　　　　　　　　　　　　3

_____ . Furthermore, it was (return) _____ . I decided to buy
　　　　4　　　　　　　　　　　　　　　　　　　　　5

it. At that moment, a salesperson came over to me. She was very (talk)

_____ , and she talked so fast that she wasn't (understand)
　　　　6

_____ . She started to confuse me. This almost made me change my
　　　　7

mind. Then I asked her to let me think for a minute. She was (agree)

_____ . Finally, I decided for the second time to buy the jacket.
　　　　8

# PARTICIPLES USED AS ADJECTIVES

 **Essential Information: USING PARTICIPLES AS ADJECTIVES**

Read the following example sentences taken from "An Irish Legend," Chapter Five, page 81. The participles used as adjectives appear in italic letters.

> One day the king took his eldest son with him on a long trip. After several hours, he said to his son, "Son, shorten the road for me." The son had no idea how to answer, and the *disappointed* king turned around and returned home with his son.
>
> Right away the youngest son began to tell his father a long and *entertaining* story. The king became so *interested* in the story that he never noticed the length of the journey.

Present Participle:  entertain*ing*

| Present Participle = Verb + ing |
|:---:|

Past Participles:  disappoint*ed*; interest*ed*

| Past Participle = Verb + ed |
|:---:|

Describe what you see in the drawing on the previous page.

_____

_____

_____

The above drawing represents the use of participles as adjectives—the present participle *-ing* (surprising) and the past participle *-ed* (surprised). In the drawing, a man is standing on a scaffold. Then a safe falls out of a window. This event *causes* a *reaction*.

To describe what *causes* the reaction, the *-ing participle* is used. For example, in the drawing of the man on the scaffold, people watching the event might describe it as *shocking, terrifying,* or *horrifying*.

### More Examples of Adjectives Describing the *Cause* of a Reaction

1. Your twenty-two hour flight to Canada:
   The flight was tir*ing*.

2. You suffer from motion sickness, so you coudn't read:
   The flight was bor*ing*.

3. When you arrived, you saw your sister in the distance:
   The arrival was excit*ing*.

4. It took you two hours to go through immigration:
   The process was exhaust*ing*.

Now let's look at the event on the scaffold from the man's point of view. What is his *reaction* to the event? He is *shocked, terrified,* and *horrified*.

### More Examples of Adjectives Describing the *Reaction*

1. How did you react after a twenty-two hour flight?
   I felt tir*ed*.

2. How did you feel not being able to read on the flight?
   I felt bor*ed*.

3. How did you feel when you saw your sister?
   I felt excit*ed*.

4. How did you feel after spending two hours in the immigration office?
   I was exhaust*ed*.

Now describe what you see in the drawing on the previous page.

_____

_____

_____

 **Exercise A**  Culture Shock

Write the correct form of the words in parentheses.

### Culture Shock

Most foreign students experience culture shock, and I was no exception. I

was very (excite) _____*excited*_____ my first week in the United States. Everything
                        1

in the new culture was (excite) _____ , (interest) _____ , and
                                    2                          3

(entertain) _____ . For example, I was (surprise) _____ to see
                4                                                5

so many beautiful cars and large houses. Unfortunately, I wasn't (prepare)

_____ for the next stage of adjustment. After the first few months, I
        6

became (annoy) _____ at everything in America. In particular, school
                      7

bothered me. The language barrier was especially (discourage) _____ .
                                                                        8

I was too (embarrass) _____ to speak to Americans, and it was
                            9

(threaten) _____ to me when they spoke to me. As a result, life was
                10

(bore) _____ without people to talk to. After about a year, I found new
            11

friends who understood culture shock. This was (encourage) _____ to
                                                                        12

me. Once again, I became (interest) _____ in the (excite)
                                            13

_____ world around me. Finally, I became (adjust) _____ to
        14                                                            15

my new life. As I look back, it's (surprise) _____ to me that I could feel
                                                    16

so many (conflict) _____ emotions about this country in such a rela-

17

tively short period of time.

 **Exercise B**  Your Life Experience

Write six original sentences, three using *-ing* adjectives, and three using *-ed* adjectives. You may select adjectives from the following list, but you are not limited to the list.

| | |
|---|---|
| amusing | amused |
| annoying | annoyed |
| boring | bored |
| confusing | confused |
| depressing | depressed |
| disappointing | disappointed |
| disgusting | disgusted |
| embarrassing | embarrassed |
| encouraging | encouraged |
| entertaining | entertained |
| exciting | excited |
| exhausting | exhausted |
| frightening | frightened |
| frustrating | frustrated |
| inspiring | inspired |
| interesting | interested |
| puzzling | puzzled |
| relaxing | relaxed |
| satisfying | satisfied |
| shocking | shocked |
| surprising | surprised |
| tiring | tired |

**Examples**

When I arrived in Denver, I was really excited.

I saw so many interesting sights.

1. _____

2. _____

3. _____

4. _____

5. _____

6. _____

When you finish writing exchange sentences with a partner. After you read your partner's sentences, discuss any changes or suggestions.

# A COMMON ADVERB ENDING: -*LY*

 **Essential Information: CHANGING ADJECTIVES TO ADVERBS WITH -*LY***

If you think of other examples, add them.

-----LY

happy + ly = happily

private + ly = privately

_____

_____

*Note: Not all words ending in -ly are adverbs.*

**Examples**

a friendly classmate
a lovely poem

 **Exercise**   A Satisfying Lesson

Write the correct form of the words in parentheses.

**A Satisfying Lesson**

Today's ESL grammar lesson was especially satisfying for me. The instructor

explained the lesson (slow) _____*slowly*_____ . I did the exercises (careful)
                                          1

_____ and answered the questions (confident) _____ . (Final)
          2                                                      3

_____ , the instructor gave us a quiz, and I answered most of the questions
          4

(correct) _____ . I left class walking (happy) _____ to my car.
                  5                                                  6

# A COMMON VERB ENDING: -*IZE*

 **Essential Information: USING THE -*IZE* ENDING TO CHANGE NOUNS AND ADJECTIVES TO VERBS**

If you think of other examples, add them.

-----IZE

legal + ize = legalize

critic + ize = criticize

_____

_____

**Exercise**  Organization

Write the correct form of the words in parentheses.

**Organization**

When I did my last writing assignment, I (real) ___*realized*___ that
                                                        1

organizing my thoughts was extremely important. The assignment was to react

to a short magazine article. After the topic sentence, I briefly (summary)

_____ the author's main ideas. Then I (priority) _____ my
          2                                                          3

own reactions to the article and (emphasis) _____ my strongest point.
                                                      4

In the conclusion, I (final) _____ my thoughts in a few well-chosen
                                      5

words.

## CHAPTER REVIEW

 **Exercise A**  Word Form Chart

In the following chart, fill in the missing words.

|     | VERB     | NOUN        | ADJ.        | ADV.          |
|-----|----------|-------------|-------------|---------------|
| 1.  | imagine  | imagination | imaginative | imaginatively |
| 2.  |          | excellence  |             | excellently   |
| 3.  |          | comparison  |             | comparatively |
| 4.  | separate |             |             | separately    |
| 5.  | enjoy    |             |             | enjoyably     |
| 6.  |          | dependence  |             | dependently   |
| 7.  |          | playfulness |             | playfully     |
| 8.  | perfect  |             |             | perfectly     |

 **Exercise B**  Editing

Edit the following paragraph for errors in participles used as adjectives. The
paragraph contains three errors.

### The Thrill of So Many Beautiful Cars

My first reaction to Los Angeles was amazement at all the gorgeous cars. My
uncle picked me up in a huge Cadillac. The back seat was enormous, and it felt so     2
comfortable. After we left the airport, I became fascinating with the traffic. My uncle
told me to look out back, but I didn't see anything at first. Then a shiny blue Porsche     4
sped past us. When we got off the freeway, I continued to be interesting in all the
glamorous automobiles. While we were waiting at a red light, I looked out the     6
window and saw nothing but huge tires. I looked up and saw a gigantic pickup
truck. The pickup then made a right-hand turn, but I was captivating even after it     8
disappeared. Soon we drove up to my uncle's  house and parked in front. My uncle
was curious, so he asked me how I liked the United States so far. I answered, "I'm     10
already in love with this country," but my eyes weren't meeting his. My heart was
pounding, and my attention was glued to a silver gray Mercedes that was driving     12
smoothly past us.

 **Exercise C**  Editing

Edit the following paragraph for errors in word formation. The paragraph contains
six errors.

### Two Heads Are Better Than One

"Two heads are better than one." This is an English proverb about wise. It
means that working together is better than working alone so that a person can get     2
more ideas from other people. I agree with this saying. At work a few years ago, my
boss used a new network system to connection all the computers in the business.     4
After she completed the installed, only two computers worked. At first, my boss tried
to find out what was wrong by herself, but she couldn't find the problem. Then she     6
asked me to help her. When my boss explained to me how she had connected the
machines, I noticed that the order of the steps was incorrectly. When I told her     8
about my discover, we both made the necessary changes. After we finished, all the
computers in the system worked fine. This experience showed me that two people     10
working together can solve a problem better than one person working alone. It's
important to cooperation and work as a team because in this way more talents and     12
skills can be applied in any situation.

Adapted from a paragraph by Sue Sedor

## ≡ FOOD FOR THOUGHT ≡

Read the following sentence and identify the parts of speech of the words ending in *-ly*.

A friendly family kindly invited me to Thanksgiving dinner.

1. _____

2. _____

3. _____

## ≡ CLASSROOM ASSESSMENT TECHNIQUE (CAT) ≡

### THE ONE-MINUTE PAPER

Take a minute or two to write answers to the following questions. Write your answers on a separate piece of paper without your name.

1. What are the most important points that you have learned in this chapter?

2. What questions remain in your mind at the end of this chapter?

*Note: Use this exercise to help you get answers to any questions you still have. Ask these questions to anyone who might be able to help you, such as another student or your instructor.*

# CHAPTER 12

# Final Do's and Don'ts

## AFTER AND *AFTERWARDS*

 **Essential Information: *AFTER / AFTERWARDS***

Read the following.

1. I played soccer after I took a shower.

2. I played soccer. Afterwards, I took a shower.

What is the difference between 1 and 2? Number 1 is grammatically correct but not logical. Usually, we take a shower after we play soccer. Number 2 is grammatically correct and logical.

*After* in number 1 is a subordinator that introduces a clause showing a time relationship. An additional example follows.

3. I learned English after I came to this country.

*Afterwards* in number 2 is a transition word between separate sentences. An additional example follows.

4. I learned some basic English. Afterwards, I looked for a job.

Which of the following is logical?

A. I filled out a few job applications after I found a job.

B. I filled out a few job applications. Afterwards, I found a job.

 **Exercise A** Showing Time Sequence with *After/Afterwards*

Combine the information in the following sentences using *after* or *afterwards*.

**Example**

I brushed my teeth. I went to bed.

After I brushed my teeth, I went to bed.

or

I brushed my teeth. Afterwards, I went to bed.

1.  I visited my local college campus. I decided to enroll.

    *After I visited my local college campus, I decided to enroll.*

    _____

2.  I filled out an application. I took the English and math placement tests.

    _____

    _____

3.  I talked to a counselor. I applied for financial aid.

    _____

    _____

4.  I received financial aid. I paid my fees.

    _____

    _____

5.  I went to class the first day. I bought my textbooks.

    _____

    _____

 **Exercise B**   Writing Sentences with *After/Afterwards*

Write sentences about some important events in your life using *after* or *afterwards.*
Exchange sentences with a partner and check each other's sentences.

1.  _____

2.  _____

3.  _____

# ☰ *ALMOST*

☞ **Essential Information: ALL ABOUT *ALMOST***

Almost all students use *almost* correctly almost all the time. However, one common
error almost always makes instructors smile.

Error: *Almost students wear a uniform in Korea.

What are *almost students*? It's hard to imagine. Does this mean that they're *not* students yet, or that they are *partially* students? The following makes a lot more sense:

Almost all students wear a uniform in Korea.

 **Exercise A**  Using *Almost All*

Write the missing information in the following sentences. Start with *Almost all* and add a plural noun.

**Example**

*Almost all* children like ice cream.

1. ___*Almost all my friends*___ have a car.

2. _____ cause pollution.

3. _____ eat *kim chi*.

4. _____ drink milk.

5. _____ get homework.

6. _____ use a dictionary.

7. _____ have fast food restaurants.

8. _____ have fleas.

**Exercise B**  Writing Sentences with *Almost All*

Write two original sentences using the format outlined in Exercise A. When you finish, exchange sentences with a partner and check each other's work.

1. _____

2. _____

# ANOTHER AND (THE) OTHER(S)

## *ANOTHER*

(*Beetle Bailey* by Mort Walker. Reprinted with special permission of King Features Syndicate)

**Essential Information: MEANING AND USE OF *ANOTHER***

*Another* means "one additional". Therefore, it is singular.

**Examples**

1.  As an *adjective*
    Many computer owners want *another* computer—a laptop.

2.  As an *adjective + one*
    Elizabeth is selling her printer to Abdul because she bought *another one*.

3.  As a *pronoun* that replaces a singular noun
    Abdul already has a printer, but he wants to buy *another*.

 **Exercise**   *A* versus *Another*—Situations at School

Fill in the blanks with the missing information. Use *a* or *another* plus other words, as appropriate. Answers will vary.

1.  My pen just ran out of ink. I need _____*another one*_____.

2.  I need something to write with. Will you lend me _____?

3.  We had a quiz in Chemistry I last week. Next week the instructor plans to give the class _____.

4.  I got an *A* on the first quiz. I hope I get _____ on the next one.

5.  My history instructor assigned a chapter in the text last week, and next week she's going to assign _____.

6.  I've never written _____ bibliography.

7.  I wrote a term paper for Sociology I, and next semester in Sociology II, I will have to write _____.

# OTHER *AND* OTHERS

 **Essential Information: MEANING AND USE OF *OTHER* AND *OTHERS***

*Other* means "additional." It is an *adjective*. Although it can be used with noncount nouns, the most common use is as a modifier of *plural nouns*.

 *Note: English adjectives have no plural form, so as an adjective, the only form of* other *is* other.

> *Other* + Plural noun

**Example**

My word processing program has some good features, but I want *other features*, and *other features* cost more money.

*Other* is often preceded by *some*.

**Example**

The salesman at Computer World has shown me *some other word processing programs* with very advanced features.

*Others* means "additional". It is a *plural pronoun*.

 *Note:* Others *is not the plural of the adjective* other, *since English adjectives have no plural form.*

**Examples**

I priced some modems and FAX machines at Elmo Electronics. Later I looked at *other modems* at Computer World.

The salesperson at Computer World also showed me some laptop computers, but I found *others* I liked better at Elmo Electronics.

Some computers are slow, and *other computers* are fast.

Some computers are slow, and *others* are fast.

 **Exercise**   Careers in Photography

Write *other* or *others* in the blanks in the following paragraphs.

### Careers in Photography

Many people have careers in photography. Some take pictures for movies.

Some run television cameras. _____*Other*_____ people operate X-ray machines.
                                        1

Still _____ photograph weddings or _____ celebrations.
          2                                              3

There are many _____ jobs in photography besides taking pictures,
                        4

though. Some people develop film. _____ people sell cameras and
                                              5

supplies. Some people repair cameras. Many _____ people work in
                                                        6

large manufacturing plants. These companies make photo paper, film, or

_____ supplies.
      7

## THE OTHER *AND* THE OTHERS

(*Bent Offerings* by Don Addis. Reprinted by permission of
Don Addis and Creators Syndicate)

 **Essential Information: MEANING AND
USE OF *THE OTHER* AND *THE OTHERS***

*The other* means "the remaining." *The other* can be an *adjective*, an *adjective* with
*one* or *ones*, or a *pronoun*.

 *The others* also means "the remaining." It is a plural *pronoun*. *The other ones*
can be used as an equivalent pronoun.

### Examples

1. *The other* as an *adjective*

  I have two printers at home, so when one doesn't work, I use *the
other printer*.

  We have five old printers at work. With our limited budget, we can
replace three of them now, and next year we can replace *the other printers*.

**Note:** Other *has no -s ending in the previous example, even though the noun that follows
it* (printers) *is plural. Why?*

_____

2. *The other* as an *adjective* with *one* or *ones*

  I have two printers at home, so when one doesn't work, I use *the
other one*.

  We have five old printers at work. With our limited budget, we can
replace three of them now, and next year we can replace *the other ones*.

3. *The other* and *the others* as *pronouns*

> I have two printers at home, so when one doesn't work, I use *the other*.

> We have five old printers at work. With our limited budget, we can replace three of them now, and next year we can replace *the others*.

*Note:* Others *has an -s ending in the previous example. Why?*

---

 **Exercise**   Cultural Literacy—World Knowledge

Write the missing words in the following sentences. Use *the other* or *the others* as part of your answer.

1. Russia and Ukraine are the largest states in the former USSR. Can you name
   _____*the others*_____?

2. Latvia and Lithuania are two of the three Baltic republics. Can you name
   _____?

3. Lenin was the first leader of the USSR. Gorbachev was the last. Can you
   name _____?

4. St. Petersburg has had two names this century. Can you name
   _____?

5. Russian was one of the languages in the USSR. Can you name
   _____?

## ☰ REVIEW: *ANOTHER AND (THE) OTHER(S)* ☰

## CHART

|  | ANOTHER (ONE) | OTHER | OTHERS | THE OTHER (ONE) | THE OTHERS |
|---|---|---|---|---|---|
| MEANING | one additional | additional | | the remaining | |
| SINGULAR | ADJECTIVE<br>I'd like another diskette/one.<br><br>PRONOUN<br>I'd like an-other. | | | ADJECTIVE<br>I'd like the other diskette/one.<br><br>PRONOUN<br>I'd like the other. | |
| PLURAL | | ADJECTIVE<br>I'd like (some) other diskettes. | PRONOUN<br>I'd like (some) others. | ADJECTIVE<br>I'd like the other diskettes/ones. | PRONOUN<br>I'd like the others. |

**Exercise**   Editing for *Another* and *(The) Other(s)*—Daredevil Dolly

Edit the following paragraph.

### Daredevil Dolly

Dolly loves excitement and danger. She checked four books out of the

library. The first one was on how to sky dive. The second one was on how to          2

tame rattlesnakes. And the others/two books were on how to write a will.

Dolly's boyfriend Sam is asking her to look for others books. He's asking her to          4

forget about sky diving and rattlesnakes and to take another English class with

him next semester.                                                                        6

The instructor is suggesting other solution. Actually it's a compromise.

He's lending Dolly a book on other exciting subject. This book is called              8

*Dangerous English*. It's a dictionary of English words you can't find in most others

dictionaries. Dolly is interested in the book.                                          10

# ≡ *DURING AND WHILE*

 **Essential Information: THE DIFFERENCE
BETWEEN *DURING* AND *WHILE***

*During* and *while* often have the same meaning, but they are used differently in
sentences. To understand the difference, you need to look at sentence structure.
Study the following sentences. What are the differences in the groups of
words following *during* and *while*?

| CORRECT | INCORRECT |
|---|---|
| Jesse takes care of the kids *during* his wife's night class. | *Jesse takes care of the kids *during* his wife attends a night class. |
| Jesse takes care of the kids *while* his wife attends a night class. | *Jesse takes care of the kids *while* his wife's night class. |

What type of word group follows *during*?

_____

What type of word group follows *while*?

_____

*During* is a preposition. It's followed by an object of the preposition.

   *During* his wife's night class . . .
   *During* the evening news . . .
   *During* dinner . . .

*While* is a subordinator. It's followed by a clause (subject and verb).

> *While* his wife takes a night class . . .
> *While* Connie Chung reports the evening news . . .
> *While* they are having dinner . . .

 **Exercise A**  Family Habits

Add *during* or *while* to the following sentences.

1. My family watches TV _____*during*_____ dinner.

2. Before long car trips, I clean the car windows _____ my husband checks the oil.

3. _____ my grandchildren play in the park, I read.

4. My wife does crossword puzzles _____ breakfast.

5. My kids practice their times tables _____ they wash dishes after dinner.

 **Exercise B**  Writing Sentences

Think of common weekend (or occasional) activities that you and your family or friends do. On a separate piece of paper, write four sentences to describe them, two with *during* and two with *while*.

# ≡ *FOR EXAMPLE*

 **Essential Information: HOW TO USE *FOR EXAMPLE***

### Part A

*For example* is often used in writing to give a list of specific examples.

> Dr. Potter has students from the four corners of the earth, for example, Korea, Switzerland, Nigeria, and Chile.

> UCLA offers courses in many foreign languages, for example, Polish, Urdu, and Hausa.

### Part B

*For example* is also used as a transition to introduce an example expressed as a sentence.

> When there is a world problem, usually Dr. Potter finds an ESL student from the country involved who can explain the nature of the problem to him. For example, Boris has a lot of background about the upheaval in the former Soviet Union.

You must avoid writing *For example* followed by a list in a new "sentence." This produces a sentence fragment.

**Incorrect**

Life in many Communist countries has really changed. *For example,
Bulgaria, Rumania, and Poland.

**Correct**

Life in many Communist countries has really changed. For example, Bulgar-
ians can now visit Western Europe whenever they want to.

 **Exercise A**   It's a Matter of Taste

Write about foreign food or foreign restaurants. Use *for example* to introduce (1)
a list or (2) a sentence.

**Example**

We have many foreign restaurants in our town, for example, Wang's,
Marengo, Kikusui, and La Chispa.

My husband loves to cook French food. For example, at least once a month
he prepares *langue de boeuf sauce madère.*

1. _____

2. _____

3. _____

4. _____

 **Exercise B**   Writing Sentences with *For Example*

Write sentences with examples to follow the general statements given. Start your
sentences with *For example.*

**Example**

Several important changes have taken place in Europe in the last decade.
For example, the Berlin Wall has been removed.

1.  Some countries are trying to solve their overpopulation problems.

    *For example, China encourages one child per family.*

2.  Pollution is still an important problem in major cities of the world.

    _____

3.  Computers have changed modern life in several ways.

    _____

4.  Cars have caused traffic congestion in many major cities.

    _____

5. Transportation in the city where I live is inadequate.

   _____

6. On a limited budget, a person can save money in a variety of ways.

   _____

7. Meeting English-speaking people is not difficult if a person makes an effort.

   _____

# ═══ NUMERICAL NOUN ADJECTIVES

 **Essential Information: NUMERICAL NOUN ADJECTIVES**

Read the following pairs of sentences, and write a *C* for correct in the space before the correct sentences. You will check your answers at the end of this section.

_____ My wife wants a four-doors car.

_____ My wife wants a four-door car.

_____ Sam has a sixteen-years-old brother.

_____ Sam has a sixteen-year-old brother.

English count nouns have a plural form.

> George and Ginny are each taking three *classes*.

English adjectives have the *same form* when they modify singular or plural nouns.

> Ginny is taking one *difficult* class.
> George is taking two *difficult* classes.

English nouns often function as adjectives. As adjectives, they have no plural forms.

> a *paper* plate          ten *paper* plates
> an *orange* drink        five *orange* drinks
> a *milk* bottle          three *milk* bottles

> **When a noun is used as an adjective, it has no plural form.**

> George is taking two difficult *five-unit* classes.

Go back to the beginning of this section. Did you choose the correct answers?

 **Exercise A**  Roald Dahl's Career with Shell

The following sentences refer to the writer Roald Dahl's career with Shell. Write the missing numerical noun adjectives. Use the information in parentheses.

1. First he had a _____*twelve-month*_____ training period. (of twelve months)

2. The managers wanted to send him on a _____ assignment to Egypt. (for three years)

3. They eventually sent him for a _____ stay in East Africa. (for three years)

4. It was a _____ journey. (of two weeks)

5. He received a _____ salary. (of $15,000)

6. When he went to East Africa, he was a _____ businessman. (twenty years old)

**Exercise B**   Experience/Imagination

Numerical noun adjectives are often used to describe. Use your experience or imagination to answer these questions.

**Example**

Describe your house or apartment based on the number of bedrooms it has.

I live in a two-bedroom apartment.

1. Describe your garage based on the number of cars it holds.

   *I have a two-car garage.*

2. Describe your car based on the number of doors it has.

   _____

3. Describe your house or apartment based on its age.

   _____

4. Describe a family member based on age.

   _____

5. Describe this class based on the number of units.

   _____

6. Describe the break in this class based on the number of minutes.

   _____

## SAY AND TELL

▶ **Sample Paragraph**
Read the following paragraph.

## A Million Dollar Mistake

Recently I read about an unusual trial. A worker accused the boss of sexual harassment°. What was unusual in this case was that the worker was a man, and the boss was a woman. The worker *said* that his boss made his life unbearable°. He *told* the jury many specific details about her unwanted advances°. He *said* that she often embraced° him, kissed him, and *told* him that her interest in him was sexual. On the other hand, the boss *said* that she didn't do anything wrong. She *told* the jury that everything the worker *said* was false. The boss was found guilty, and the paper *said* that this was probably the first time a woman had been found guilty of sexual harassment. The court ordered her and her company to pay $1 million. After the trial, the defendant *said* to reporters, "I feel totally violated°, and I plan to appeal the case."

° **harassment:** bothering again and again

° **unbearable:** not acceptable

° **advances:** attempts to gain favorable attention

° **embraced:** hugged

° **violated:** harmed

Who do you believe? Why?

_____

_____

 ### Essential Information: *SAY* AND *TELL*

Read the following sentences and circle the correct answers to the questions.

> The worker *told* the jury many specific details about her unwanted advances.

> The boss *said* that she didn't do anything wrong.

> After the trial, the defendant *said* to reporters, "I feel totally violated, and I plan to appeal the case."

1.  Which verb can be followed immediately by *to*?    say    tell

2.  Which verb is not followed immediately by *to*?      say    tell

The following chart outlines some of the basic uses of *say* and *tell* in academic writing.

| Say | + | Something | (To someone) |
| --- | --- | --- | --- |
| | | (To someone) | Something |
| Tell | + | Someone | Something |
| | | Something | To someone |

In the above chart, notice that after *say*, only a direct object is required: *something*. (*To someone*) is optional. *Tell*, however, requires both direct and indirect objects.

### Relevant Information: Idioms

Several idiomatic expressions don't follow the above rules:

| to tell the truth | to tell a story |
|---|---|
| to tell a lie | to tell a secret |
| to tell a joke | to tell the time |
| | to tell (all) about (something) |

 **Exercise A**  Words of Wisdom

Underline the correct answers in the following.

1. My aunt told (<u>me</u>, to me) that most problems exist only in our imagination.

2. The minister told (the people, to the people) that storms make trees grow stronger roots.

3. The wise man said (his admirers, to his admirers) that people can alter their lives by changing their attitude toward life.

4. Our ESL instructor told (us, to us) that laughter translates into any language but that jokes do not.

5. My banker said (me, to me) the other day that a fool and his money are soon parted.

 **Exercise B**  Writing Sentences

Write four sentences, two with *say* and two with *tell*. Follow the examples given above. Do not use idiomatic expressions. When you finish, exchange sentences with a partner and check for errors. If you and your partner have any questions, check with your instructor.

1. _____

2. _____

3. _____

4. _____

# *SOMETIMES* VERSUS *SOMETIME*

 **Essential Information: *SOMETIMES***

*Sometimes* means "from time to time" and is used to express *experience*.

In a newspaper article, a Korean student in an American high school expressed her views.

1. I think sometimes Mom misses Korea.

2. Here I skip homework sometimes.

3. I sleep in class sometimes.

**Exercise**  Writing Sentences

Write three sentences about things you wish you didn't do but that you do sometimes. Use sentences 2 and 3 above as examples.

1. _____
2. _____
3. _____

 **Essential Information: *SOMETIME***

*Sometime* means at a point in time in the future and usually expresses *lack of experience*. It is equivalent to *someday*.

**Examples**

1. Sometime I'd like to take my family to Ireland.
2. Sometime I want to learn to play golf.
3. Sometime I hope the world is at complete peace.

 **Exercise**  Writing Sentences

Write three sentences with the word *sometime*. Use the examples above as models.

1. _____
2. _____
3. _____

# *SPECIAL, SPECIALLY, AND ESPECIALLY*

▶ **Sample Paragraph**

Read the following paragraph that contains examples of *special*, *specially*, and *especially*.

### *Special* Resource Center

In 1972 El Camino College established a *special* program to assist students with disabilities. The staff is *specially* trained to help disabled students, *especially* those with physical and learning disabilities, the deaf and hard of hearing, and the visually impaired. The center houses *special* equipment, such as large-print typewriters, talking calculators, and reading machines. The center's high-tech lab makes computers accessible to disabled students through *specially* designed equipment that helps students input, process, and output information. The curriculum includes *special* classes in English, math, and career preparation. *Especially* useful are the adaptive physical education classes, *specially* created for disabled persons needing an individualized exercise program. All of these services are offered on a relatively small, flat campus that has been *specially* constructed to meet the needs of students with physical disabilities.

 **Essential Information: *SPECIAL***

*Special* is an adjective.

> Your birthday is a *special* day.

> Your family may prepare a *special* dinner for you on your birthday.

> Most people like to feel *special* on their birthday.

 **Exercise**   Why So Special?

Write sentences naming some things that are special to you and explain why.

**Example**

> My camera is special to me because my husband bought it for me for my trip to Puerto Rico.

1. _____

   _____

2. _____

   _____

3. _____

   _____

 **Essential Information: *SPECIALLY***

*Specially* is the adverb form of *special*. It can modify an adjective, especially participles used as adjectives.

> This dessert was *specially* made by my grandmother.

> This gift was *specially* chosen for my grandfather.

 **Exercise**   *Special* versus *Specially*

Fill in the blanks with the following words: *special* or *specially*.

1. When I garden I need ____*special*____ tools.

2. Some potting soil I buy is _____ formulated for cactus and succulents.

3. Many of my plants were _____ selected for our dry climate.

4.  For African violets, I need a _____ fertilizer.

5.  I have a _____ rose that I got from my grandmother.

6.  Since my soil is mostly clay, it requires _____ amendments, such as sand and Gromulch.

☞ **Essential Information: ESPECIALLY**

The most common use of *especially* is to introduce an example.

I like holidays, *especially* Thanksgiving.

Foreign cars are common in the United States, *especially* Japanese cars.

The baby cries a lot, *especially* when he's hungry.

**Exercise**   My Personal Favorites

Finish the following sentences with *especially* . . .

**Example**

I like classical music, especially baroque music.

1.  I like sports, *especially basketball.* _____

2.  I like desserts, _____

3.  I like books, _____

4.  I like amusement parks, _____

5.  I like movies, _____

### *Relevant Information: Especially as Very*

*Especially* also means "very" or "extremely" when it modifies adjectives.

Driving on wet roads is *especially* dangerous.

Water is *especially* vital in the desert.

**Exercise**   *Especially* as *Very*

Finish the following sentences, using *especially*.

**Example**

In the summer, Mexico City is especially smoggy.

1.  In January, Niagara Falls is *especially cold* _____.

2.  In the winter, London is _____.

3.  In the summertime, Death Valley, California is _____.

4.  In July, Tokyo is _____.

5.  In the winter, Seattle is _____.

≡  **REVIEW:** *SPECIAL, SPECIALLY, AND ESPECIALLY*  ≡

 **Exercise A**  Special Resource Center

Fill in the correct forms of *special*, *specially*, and *especially*.

### Special Resource Center

In 1972 El Camino College established a _____ program to assist
                                              1

students with disabilities. The staff is _____ trained to help disabled
                                              2

students, _____ those with physical and learning disabilities, the deaf
              3

and hard of hearing, and the visually impaired. The center houses

_____ equipment, such as large-print typewriters, talking calculators,
      4

and reading machines. The center's high-tech lab makes computers accessible to

disabled students through _____ designed equipment that helps
                                  5

students input, process, and output information. The curriculum includes

_____ classes in English, math, and career preparation.
      6

_____ useful are the adaptive physical education classes,
      7

_____ created for disabled persons needing an individualized exercise
      8

program. All of these services are offered on a relatively small, flat campus that

has been _____ constructed to meet the needs of students with
              9

physical disabilities.

 **Exercise B**  Writing Sentences

Write three original sentences using *special*, *specially*, and *especially*.

1.  _____

2.  _____

3.  _____

# ≡ *TOO MUCH/MANY VERSUS A LOT*

 **Essential Information:** *TOO MUCH/MANY AND A LOT*

Are both of these sentences logical?

1. I'm happy my son makes too much money.

2. I'm taking twenty units, and I have too much homework, so I'm going to drop a class.

Both sentences are grammatically correct, but number 1 is not logical. *Too much* means beyond some acceptable standard, and since most people love to earn money, how could the writer's son earn *too much* money? What the writer means is *a lot of money.*

In number 2, the amount of homework is beyond an acceptable standard, at least according to the writer of the sentence, so *too much* is logical.

The use of *a lot* and *too much/many* is often subjective. Each person has his or her own acceptable standard. As another example, one person might say that it costs *a lot* to go to Disneyland. But another person might say that it costs *too much* to go to Disneyland.

 **Exercise** *Too Much/Many* versus *A Lot*

Write *too much/many* or *a lot* depending on your personal standard. *Too much* is used with noncount nouns. *Too many* is used with count nouns.

1. The rent of the vacant one-bedroom apartment near the school is $975.

   That's ___*too much*___.

2. My neighbor drinks a six-pack of beer every day. That's _____.

3. My cousin is taking 18 units. That's _____.

4. Ed's physics text cost him $55. That's _____.

5. My son wants a $200 high school ring. That's _____.

6. The cheapest ticket for the play is $25. That's _____.

7. My friend Sharon has 125 rose bushes. That's _____.

8. It costs about $10 to see a movie in a nice theater these days. That's

   _____.

## ≡ CHAPTER REVIEW ≡

 **Exercise** Editing

Edit the following sentences.

1. Harold studied after he went to sleep.

2. Almost children like to watch TV.

3. First, Mary Ann went to Sears. After that, she went to two others stores.

4. I hate getting up early in the morning, especially in the winter.

5. Jessica likes to go to a movie with a friend during her husband works overtime.

6. There are several sources of air pollution. For example, industrial waste and car exhaust.

7. Hank plans to attend a four-years college next semester.

8. I'd like to visit Asia sometime.

9. Jerry told to me that he is planning to enlist in the army.

10. Sometime I go to movies on Saturday night.

11. My aunt is a very especial person to me.

12. I love my parents too much.

## FOOD FOR THOUGHT

Is the following a correct sentence?

The construction of the Wilshire Boulevard Metro addition is a years-long project.

Your answer: _____

## CLASSROOM ASSESSMENT TECHNIQUE (CAT)

### THE ONE-MINUTE PAPER

Take a minute or two to write answers to the following questions. Write your answers on a separate piece of paper without your name.

1. What are the most important points that you have learned in this chapter?

2. What questions remain in your mind at the end of this chapter?

*Note: Use this exercise to help you get answers to any questions you still have. Ask these questions to anyone who might be able to help you, such as another student or your instructor.*

# APPENDIX: COMMONLY CONFUSED WORDS

1. *an*   article (Ch. 7)
   *and*   coordinator (Ch. 2)

   I wrote *an* essay *and* a poem in my English class.

2. *accept*   verb
   *except*   preposition

   The teacher will *accept* a paper written in any color ink *except* red.

3. *advice*   noncount noun (Think of the noun *vice*. [Ch. 7])
   *advise*   verb

   I *advise* you to get some *advice* before you choose a chemistry class.

4. *buy*   verb
   *by*   preposition

   When you *buy* your textbooks, you can pay *by* credit card.

5. *breath*   noun
   *breathe*   verb

   When I saw the price of my chemistry book, I almost lost my *breath*. I could *breathe* more easily when I found a used copy.

6. *fell*   verb, past of *fall* (Ch. 5)
   *felt*   verb, past of *feel* (Ch. 5)

   I *felt* like a fool when I *fell* walking into the lab.

7. *\*firstable*   (not English)
   *first of all*

   *First of all*, we need a new rubber tube to solve the problem.

8. *for*   preposition
   *four*   number

   I paid $106 *for four* textbooks.

9. *he's*   he is (Ch. 1)
   *his*   possessive (Ch. 7)

   Where's the chemistry teacher? *He's* in *his* office.

10. *hear*   verb (Think of *ear*.)
    *here*   adverb (Think of *there*.)

    Listen! You can *hear* the air escaping *here*.

11. *hole*   noun
    *whole*   adjective

    Go get the teacher. A *hole* in a rubber tube has ruined the *whole* chemistry experiment.

12. *is*  third person singular of *be*
    *it's*  it is  (Ch. 4)
    *its*  possessive (Ch. 7)

    > Good equipment *is* necessary in a chemistry lab. If the equipment is poor, *it's* hard to do an accurate experiment, and *its* results are unreliable.

13. *know*  verb
    *now*  adverb

    > *Now* I *know* how to organize a lab report.

14. *loose*  adjective; not tight
    *lose*  verb (Think of the past — lost.)

    > If a tube is *loose*, it will *lose* pressure.

15. *nobody*  pronoun
    *no body*  *no* + noun

    > *Nobody* can work on a cadaver today because we have *no body*.

16. *quiet*  adjective; not noisy
    *quite*  adverb; very

    > When I write, I'm *quite* happy if the classroom is *quiet*.

17. *than*  comparative conjunction
    *then*  adverb
    *that*  subordinator

    > I know *that* I should write my papers at home early in the morning because *then* it is quieter *than* in the evening.

18. *there*  adverb; opposite of *here*
    *there*  filler subject (ch. 1)
    *their*  possessive (Ch. 7)
    *they're*  they are (Ch. 4)

    > I like to study in the library because *there* are a lot of reference books *there*, *they're* easy to consult, and *their* information is up to date.

19. *thorough*  adjective; complete
    *though*  subordinator; although (Ch. 2)
    *thought*  verb; past of *think* (ch. 5)
    *threw*  verb; past of *throw* (Ch. 5)
    *through*  preposition
    *thru*  preposition; through (not used in formal writing)

    > *Though* I *thought* I had made a *thorough* search *through* all my National Geographic magazines, it turned out that my roommate *threw* out the one I was looking for.

20. *to*  preposition
    *to*  part of an infinitive
    *too*  adverb
    *two*  number

    > I try *to* go *to* the library, *too*, *to* spend *two* hours on my homework.

21. *were*   verb; past of *be* (Ch. 5)
    *where*   adverb

    > *Where were* you during lab time?

22. *who's*   who is
    *whose*   possessive

    > *Who's* the student *whose* poem was published in the school paper?

23. *worse*   comparative
    *worst*   superlative

    > A "C" is *worse* than a "B," but an "F" is the *worst* grade.

24. *you're*   you are   (Ch. 4)
    *your*   possessive (Ch. 7)

    > *You're* going to have *your* last chemistry quiz on Friday.

## Acknowledgments *(continued from copyright page)*

Naguib Mahfouz, *Fountain and Tomb*, Reprinted by kind permission of Three Continents Press, Washington, D.C., and © Naguib Mahfouz.

George White, "A Spicy Market." Copyright 1991, Los Angeles Times. Reprinted by permission.

Mary Yarber, "Reading Aloud." Copyright 1993, Mary Laine Yarber.

Excerpt from *Brighter Side of Human Nature* by Alfie Kohn. Copyright © 1990 by Alfie Kohn. Reprinted by permission of HarperCollins Publishers, Inc.

Excerpts from *Wedding Song* by Naguib Mahfouz. Reprinted by permission of Doubleday, a division of Bantam, Doubleday, Dell Publishing Group, Inc.

"Cecilia Rosas" by Amado Muro. From *The New Mexico Quarterly*, Winter 1964–1965 issue, Volume XXXIV:4. Reprinted by permission of Mrs. Chester Seltzer.

Banesh Hoffman, "Unforgettable Albert Einstein," excerpted with permission from *Reader's Digest*, January 1968. Copyright © 1967 by The Reader's Digest Assn., Inc.

Mario Puzo, "Italians in Hell's Kitchen" from *The Immigrant Experience* © 1971. Reprinted with permission by Doubleday, a division of Bantam, Doubleday, Dell Publishing Group, Inc.

Excerpt from *James and the Giant Peach* by Roald Dahl. Copyright 1961 and renewed 1989 by Roald Dahl. Reprinted by permission of Alfred A. Knopf, Inc.

Raymond Chandler, *Lady in the Lake*. Copyright 1943 by Raymond Chandler and renewed 1971 by Helga Green. Reprinted by permission of Alfred A. Knopf, Inc.

James Webb, "What We Can Learn from Japan's Prisons." Published in *Parade Magazine*, January 15, 1984. Reprinted by permission of Sterling Lord Literistic, Inc. First appeared in *Parade Magazine*. Copyright © 1984 by James Webb.

"Why We Throw Food Away," by William Rathje. *The Atlantic Monthly*, April, 1986. Reprinted with permission by William Rathje.

Excerpts from *The Fourth Deadly Sin* by Lawrence Sanders. Reprinted by permission of the Putnam Publishing Group from *The Fourth Deadly Sin* by Lawrence Sanders. Copyright © 1973 by Lawrence Sanders.

Excerpts from *The Fourth Deadly Sin* copyright 1985 by Lawrence Sanders, reprinted by permission of the author.

Excerpt from *The High Window* by Raymond Chandler. Copyright 1942 by Raymond Chandler and renewed 1970 by Helga Greene, Executrix of the Estate of Raymond Chandler. Reprinted by permission of Alfred A. Knopf, Inc.

Sandra Picklesimer Aldrich, "The Right Attitude," *Focus on the Family* magazine, March 1990. Sandra Picklesimer Aldrich, *Living Through the Loss of Someone You Love*, Regal Books, copyright 1990. Used by permission of the author.

Excerpts from *The Road Less Traveled* by M. Scott Peck. Copyright © 1978 by M. Scott Peck, M.D. Reprinted by permission of Simon & Schuster, Inc..

Text excerpt from *Charlotte's Web*, by E. B. White. Copyright © 1952 by E. B. White. Renewed © 1980 by E. B. White. Reprinted by permission of HarperCollins Publishers.

Fern Sanders, "Smart Way to Buy a New Car." Reprinted with permission by Trend Publications.

"The Stock Market," from *Macmillan Illustrated Almanac for Kids*, by Ann Elwood, Carol Orsag, and Sidney Solomon. Reprinted with the permission of Macmillan Publishing Company. Copyright © 1981 by Ann Elwood, Carol Orsag, and Sidney Solomon.

Kirby Stanat, "How to Take a Job Interview." Used by permission of Raintree/Steck-Vaughn Publishers, as printed in *Models for Writers*, copyright 1977.

Jesus Colon, "Little Things Are Big." From *A Puerto Rican in New York* © 1961 by Masses and Mainstreams, © 1982 by International Publishers, New York. Reprinted by permission of International Publishers.

Excerpt from "Tuesday Siesta" from *No One Writes to the Colonel* by Gabriel García Márquez. Copyright © 1968 in the English translation by Harper & Row, Publishers, Inc. Reprinted by permission of HarperCollins Publishers Inc.

Excerpt from *The Sun Also Rises* by Ernest Hemingway. Reprinted with permission of Charles Scribner's Sons, an imprint of Macmillan Publishing Company. Copyright 1926 by Charles Scribner's Sons; renewal copyright 1954 by Ernest Hemingway.

"Pockety Women Unite," by Jane Myers, published by Ann Arbor News. Reprinted with permission by Ann Arbor News.

Ray Bradbury, interview by Robert Jacobs in *Writers Digest Magazine*, May, 1977. Copyright 1977 by Robert Jacobs.

Judith E. Brady, "I Want a Wife," *Ms. Magazine*, Volume I, No. 1, December 31, 1971. Reprinted by permission of *Ms. Magazine*, © 1971.

# INDEX